# Miss of an Accidental Activist

## Rachel Mathews

### Book 3

Spain, Italy, Portugal, France & England

2nd Edition Published by Rachel Mathews
First published by Successful Design Ltd. 2025

Copyright © 2025 Rachel Mathews

All rights reserved. No part of this book may be used, reproduced or transmitted in any form or by any means, electronic or mechanical including photocopying, recording, or by any information storage retrieval system, without prior permission in writing of the author, except where permitted by law, or in the case of brief quotations embodied in critical articles and reviews.

Cover design Rachel Mathews, artwork: Luke William

A BIG thank you to everyone involved in helping bring this book to fruition.
And thank you to all the amazing, helpful people I've met on this crazy journey!

# Misadventures Series Book 1 Spain

## Misadventures of a Digital Nomad
One woman. One journey. Many mishaps.

Available from www.rachelmathews.uk/digital-nomad

# Book 2
## More Misadventures of a Digital Nomad
Spain, Hungary, Croatia, South Africa, USA, Mallorca & Sicily

(Coming 2026 - yes, they have been written out of sequence!)

# Book 3
## Misadventures of an Accidental Activist
Spain, Italy, Portugal, France & England

Audiobook available exclusively from
www.rachelmathews.uk/accidental

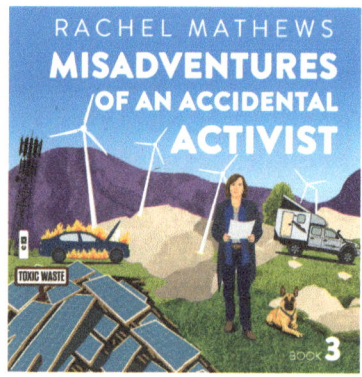

## NEW BOOK SERIES FOR TEENAGERS
## COMING 2026

The antidote to woke!

An unusual coming of age story set in Somerset, England. A book which challenges the mainstream narrative in an entertaining and magical way. Critical thinking and many other important life skills are also taught in this fabulous fictional adventure.

Acknowledging the courageous, willing to speak uncomfortable truths

"All truth passes through three stages. First, it is ridiculed. Second, it is violently opposed. Third, it is accepted as being self-evident."
Arthur Schopenhauer (allegedly)

# 1

# 1st Lockdown, Spain

Considering, I was about to do something many people fear almost as much as death, I was feeling fairly calm. Yes, there was slight anxiety, accompanied by the familiar little voice in my head asking why I insist on putting myself through these things. But other than that, I was OK.

Being OK ended abruptly when I heard the voice booming through the speaker. The words "...we're all going to die because of fossil fuel and flatulent farm animals..." echoed down the corridor in my own familiar voice. It took a moment to register why I was hearing my voice.

Carinna and I looked at each other, facial expressions mirrored. A split-second of puzzlement followed by a wide-eyed "Oh shit!" as realisation dawned. We both immediately broke into a breakneck speed sprint.

My introduction video clip was playing. The part I had just heard meant I'd got about 10 seconds to get 50 meters and onto the stage to give a talk to 300 expectant people. Technically, I wasn't due on for another ten minutes which is why I'd been in a relatively calm state. The MC had forgotten the planned interval between speakers, and had been busy introducing me, while I was blissfully unaware in the bathroom at the far end of the venue.

Thank goodness I'd given them a video or my blissful unawareness would have continued long past my introduction. I could have done with the ten minutes I thought I had, which would have given me plenty of time to get my notes in the right order, get a glass of water, brush my hair and get everything set up on stage.

5 seconds...

The middle section of the corridor I was frantically trying to run down had an area laid out for tea & coffee, which was littered with people chatting whilst they prepared and drank their beverages. I whizzed and weaved past people as fast as I could, looking like a sheepdog going through poles on an agility course, thankfully, without knocking anyone over, leaving a flurry of "sorry!" in my wake, with Carinna a few steps behind me.

2 seconds...

## Life Before the Madness

Prior to the world being turned upside down in 2020, on the surface, I had been living my perfect life. A life I had worked exceptionally hard to create. 2019 was the year I finally received the fruits of my endless labour and my business reached my desired income goals. It had taken me ten, long, hard years to achieve what I considered to be success.

I'd started teaching garden design online to homeowners in 2009 whilst simultaneously running my garden design and construction company in Cambridge. I had to work sixty hour weeks in order to do everything but in 2011 I shut down my construction company and became a full-time Digital Nomad. I ran my business from my laptop, mostly, from the warmer parts of Europe as well as further afield in South Africa and the US.

The turning point had come in 2016 when I started working with a business mentor, he connected the dots for me in a way no one else had. His guidance enabled me to make my business successful. I achieved my four hour work week dream alongside my income goals.

There was just one rather large fly in my otherwise perfect life ointment, which I will get to in due course. In retrospect it was a good job things weren't as good as they appeared on the surface or the events of 2020 would have been even more devastating.

## Something is Definitely Not Right

You're likely feeling it too. Even if not consciously, I'd put money on somewhere inside you there's a nagging feeling of discomfort that all is not well in the world.

Bizarre decisions from the government, appearing hell bent on destroying life as we know it. Everything from farming and education, to business and many more seemingly insane actions… and it is all insane, but then at the same time, if you dig deep enough, it does all make complete sense.

I drew the conclusion that something definitely wasn't right about three weeks into the first lockdown, though with little clue as to just how much. At the time I had stranded myself in Southern Spain. I'd sent my passport back to the UK in February with friends to be renewed. In March, another friend was due to bring it back after she visited family in England. You can probably guess how well that idea panned out.

With her trip cancelled and my new passport now posted, but marooned in Madrid airport for six weeks, I couldn't go anywhere. By the time I did get my hands on my passport, there were no flights. I was stuck in Spain whether I liked it or not.

They didn't mess about with lockdown in Spain. No one was allowed out to even exercise for nearly three months, let alone live any sort of remotely normal life. Armed police and the army were on the streets, with police patrols around urbanisations every fifteen minutes to make sure no one was leaving their homes. In addition, there were patrol boats, drones and helicopters making sure no one was on the beaches.

People seen out were stopped and bags were searched to make sure they were only out for essentials, like a full food shop or a doctor visit. Masses of fines were issued and millions of euros made in a matter of days. Foreigners appeared to be a particular target for the authorities. A great way to find out who had overstayed their welcome, of which, I was one.

People reported their neighbours to the police if they saw anyone doing anything or going anywhere which was not allowed. The carefree and rebellious Spanish spirit I'd warmed to so much, vanished overnight.

I diligently complied with all the rules and regulations for the first three weeks, all the while the feeling that something wasn't right gnawed away at me. It didn't make sense to stay inside when fresh air, exercise and sunshine are so vital for health. I'd already spent a fair chunk of February inside as I'd come down with something nasty just before the lockdown started.

Having got out of the habit of watching the TV for over ten years due to my Digital Nomad lifestyle, I'd not seen all the stories about the 'China virus' so I wasn't overly bothered when I got ill at the end of January. There were a couple of evenings my breathing was laboured and my lungs were congested to the point it felt like only the top half were working. I'd told myself to stop being such a drama queen and that it was just nasty flu. It's unusual for me to get chest infections and I'm normally the last person to get coughs. At the time I remember thinking you wouldn't want to get 'this' if you were an asthmatic.

I spent about five days in bed, hardly eating. My normally ravenous appetite was completely non-existent. I've always said to friends, "If I'm ever not eating, call an ambulance!" This illness totally wiped me out and it took about three weeks to fully recover. So I knew whatever I'd had was bad, but even during the worst of it, not lethal. Perhaps it made sense for the elderly and anyone vulnerable to stay inside, but everyone, no, that didn't feel right.

The rules in Spain were insane. If two people took a car journey, one had to sit in the back, and both had to wear masks, even if they were married and slept in the same bed! When they finally did let us out to exercise after ten weeks of confinement, we had an hour slot allocated dependent on age. This also changed every couple of weeks, really messing with our heads and ability to keep track of the new rules. Dogs could only ever be walked 100 meters or a 600€ fine was given. They handed those out like candy.

Once we were allowed out, we could stand on the beach for a short period but could not sit or a 150 euro fine! The police used to sit in their cars looking at their watches as I ran up the hill trying desperately to get back to the house before my allotted time was up or face a 600€ fine. Shopping was only allowed in the nearest shop to your location and you weren't allowed to go more than 5 km from your home. I never did find out if the 5 km was as the crow flies or 5 km on the zigzagging mountain roads, which meant you'd hardly get anywhere.

After three weeks of solitary confinement I started muttering on Facebook. Two things happened as a result. A barrage of abuse from the hardliners and some private messages telling me to ditch Facebook and to come over to Telegram or Signal. I'd not heard of either of them and didn't particularly want to be on different platforms. But the more I muttered, the more abuse I received.

Two of the three people who reached out to me had grown up in Eastern Bloc countries, and immediately knew government propaganda when they saw it. The third person had been at ground zero during 9/11 supporting the firefighters and other emergency services as they dug through the rubble and had been very aware all was not well in the world for quite some time. When she'd been down in the rubble helping, the FBI turned up and told all the volunteer civilians that they had one hour to get out or they'd all be arrested. No explanation was ever given.

## Research, Research, Research

My move over to the new social media platforms instigated an intense amount of research for sixteen hours a day, seven days a week. I was reading things on the new platforms that under normal circumstances I would have rolled my eyes at and moved on. But nothing that was going on was normal, and I had that prickle at the back of my neck telling me to investigate.

My internal response at that time, to the articles I was reading was, "that can't possibly be true" and I'd do all I could to prove the article wrong. I went on to government websites to read original documents to see if the authors of the articles had put their own spin on things. I didn't take anyone's word for anything, I had to see it for myself. I dug down into the finances of the foundations mentioned, which belonged to influential billionaires, and I followed the money.

It was eye-opening stuff. Trusted organisations, universities and primary news outlets were receiving millions in donations from foundations owned by people who boasted about their 20:1 return-on-investment from investing in vaccines. Even the UK's MRHA (Medicines and Healthcare Products Regulatory Agency), who are the executive agency sponsored by the Department of Health and Social Care, and who are supposed to ensure the safety, quality, and efficacy of medicines, medical devices etc. had received several million in donations from the same foundation.

The foundation of a prominent former politician, who had surfaced during the pandemic, had received around 20 million dollars, and so it went on. Purely coincidental, no doubt, but I noted that there were a lot of coincidences with the funding of all the key pandemic players from the people who push and profit from vaccines.

I found the European Commission report written in 2018, outlining their 'Roadmap on Vaccination', which showed they were going to do a feasibility study for the development of a common EU vaccination card between 2019-21. Subsequently in 2022, they commissioned a proposal for a common vaccination card/ passport for EU citizens. The EU report noted they needed "guidance on countering vaccine hesitancy tailored to specific needs identified by the Member States and/ or vaccine specific issues" to achieve that goal. The report also recommended that they "consider investing in behavioural and social science research on the determinants of vaccine hesitancy across different subgroups of the population and healthcare workers."

I checked into the backgrounds of prominent government advisors looking into their interests to see if there were any conflicts. My research was tireless. I didn't want to believe what I was reading. It didn't align with my worldview. I was determined to prove that what I was reading was wrong. But I couldn't. The more I tried to disprove, the more I found evidence to the contrary.

The vanishing videos were the tipping point. There was an interview that a man I'd never heard of, called Brian Rose, did with David Icke, which was deleted by YouTube. I'd only watched out of curiosity because I'd seen an interview two years earlier on Gaia TV when I'd subscribed to them for yoga classes. Aside from the yoga videos I'd signed up for, I started to watch some of Regina Meredith's interviews. In one, she was talking to someone who mentioned David Icke, to whom she replied that she thought he was such a brilliant man, but much maligned in the UK.

David Icke? Wasn't he the nutter in the neon tracksuit? Last time I'd heard anyone mention him was after the fateful Wogan interview. I'd found Regina to be a very sensible and intelligent interviewer, so I was intrigued. I made a mental note that if he ever popped up anywhere I would take a look and find out what he was like now.

Fast-forward two years and when I saw mention of the Brian Rose interview pop up on my Facebook feed, it triggered my intrigue again. I had nothing else to do being in lockdown, so I watched the whole thing. The interview started out well enough but before long he was ranting about how the government did not have our best interests at heart. If I'm completely honest, I still thought he sounded nuts, only this time at least he had a nice pullover and wasn't still wearing the neon highlighted tracksuit.

At the time, I had no idea what PCR tests were and most of what he said in the video went over my head. He spoke about how the PCR tests were never meant to be used as a diagnostic tool as they gave a lot of false positives, depending on how long they ran the test for. When it was pulled hours later from YouTube, it peaked my curiosity. What was it that made them pull it? There hadn't seemed to be anything particularly controversial, other than perhaps calling Bill Gates a psychopath! And I'd no idea why he'd called him that...perhaps not a fan of Windows? Certainly nothing harmful was said. I wouldn't have given the video second thought had it not been removed.

Brian then uploaded the video to Vimeo, so I started to watch it again, paying much closer attention. Halfway through watching, it vanished. Vimeo deleted it. I was on Brian's email list, so I received an email confirming Vimeo had removed it and it could now be viewed in a Dropbox folder. This time I did get to watch it again. A short while later, Dropbox removed the video from his private folder. Brian was then banned from LinkedIn and all other major platforms. This made my blood run cold. What on earth was going on?

I knew something was very, very wrong. I'd never heard of censorship like this, let alone witnessed it real time, and over what? I was determined to find out.

At the same time I had been watching the figures of the reported deaths closely. Prior to lockdown, I'd happened upon a video clip from the BBC where they gave the figures for the average number of daily deaths from natural causes in the UK. I don't remember the exact figures now, but it was something like 800 a day, rising to around 1600 in flu season. I then approximated what Spain was likely to be from the flu figures, expecting pandemic figures to be much higher. From what I could tell, there didn't seem to be many more deaths than an average flu season, according to my rough calculations. I kept shrugging it off assuming I'd miscalculated.

I researched the PCR tests and David Icke had been correct when he said they were never designed to be used as a diagnostic tool. The inventor, Kary Mullis, developed the test to amplify small segments of DNA in order to create enough copies for analysis. He said PCR tests cannot distinguish between whole, infectious viruses and dead viral fragments, making them unreliable for diagnosing active infections.

I read relentlessly trying to make sense of it all. I'm not going to cover everything I discovered, for several reasons. It would take too long and if you haven't already been on this voyage of discovery, it's something you really need to do for yourself. But in summary, from my relentless research, what's going on in the world is far worse than my original assumptions of greedy corporations taking advantage of a crisis, but we'll get into that in due course.

Even today, it can be a challenge to know exactly what is, and isn't, true. I change my mind frequently as new information comes to light. Besides, I don't really want to get down too far into the weeds of everything that is wrong, as it's not always helpful. Some things you definitely need to know, which I'll briefly cover, others just bog us down, and the purpose of this book is to help us navigate living in very uncertain times, both individually and collectively, and to not only come out on top, but to create something far better than we have now.

Once I'd researched Covid to the nth degree, I rather fatally wondered what else in the world might not be as it appeared... and I made a further mistake by allowing my mother to persuade me to do something I'd not done in ten years.

"In times of universal deceit, telling the truth will be a revolutionary act."
-George Orwell

# 2

# Unwelcome Discoveries

Being an avid reader, and confined to the house for weeks on end during lockdown, it wasn't long before I'd read all the decent paperbacks my parents had left in the house. I'd particularly enjoyed one on Bletchley Park. I'm always fascinated by code-breaking stories, and another book set closer to modern day about wartime spies in their twilight years who had never really retired. The wartime spy book was enjoyable right up until the epilogue, where the author detailed the real-life Operation Paperclip and how it had inspired the book.

The author posed the question: what if the Nazis the Americans had rounded up and put to work for the US Government after the war had offspring who were raised with their parents' beliefs? What if those children, and their children in turn, now held the highest positions of power throughout the US?

## A Big Mistake

My mother recommended I watch something on television to take my mind off all my worldly concerns. She warned me her recommendation, Outlander, was "a bit" violent. A bit! That was an understatement. There was a stark contrast between what is considered acceptable viewing now compared to when I'd last watched television ten years ago. The plot was very intriguing, but I couldn't stomach the gratuitous violence. My mother assured me the next season wasn't quite as bad and encouraged me to stick with it.

I think I lasted halfway through series three before calling it a day. Something that disturbed me, along with the violence, was that the main characters were both very likeable and had you rooting for them. But I started to notice these supposedly upstanding characters were willing to kill at the drop of a hat. It was always justified in the plot, but it felt out of kilter with who they were portrayed as the rest of the time. It was a twisting of morality, blurring right and wrong and making the unacceptable appear acceptable.

With everything I was discovering online, it was too disturbing to carry on with, no matter how much I wanted to know what happened. I felt much better when I stopped watching. Even today, I don't watch TV, except occasionally when I'm at my parents' house. The ten-year absence of television has made me really notice that, even in fairly benign programmes, there is a darkness to the plots and a twisting of morality that doesn't sit well with me.

## Rug Pulled

The online research was making it feel like I'd had the proverbial rug pulled from under me and discovering I was standing on earthquake ground. Everything constantly shifting. I'd just about processed one ugly truth only to find an even uglier one shortly after. By the time I got to what's been happening to millions of children with worldwide trafficking networks running through the highest and lowest levels of society, I couldn't bear it any more and decided to stop researching for a while. I felt like my soul had been stained to a degree I'd never recover from.

Hearing testimonies of victims and police officers was sickening. It was unbelievable that so many high profile people knew what was going on, and either did nothing, or, worse, were involved. That knowledge destroyed the foundations of my world. Yet more of that rock I believed my world to be built on was shaken reading documents from the World Health Organisation recommending children as young as four or five were taught about masturbation and anal sex. So. Deeply. Disturbing. Everything I believed in in the world was suddenly looking very dark and untrustworthy.

I tried taking solace in some of my old haunts, watching videos from people whom I had believed to be on a spiritual path. Famous names, big followings. But now that I was tuned into a different world, I'd spot something in the comments mentioning something untoward about the person, which tied in with something I'd discovered regarding the horrific child abuse.

I'd ask in the alternative social media groups I'd joined if they knew anything about these famous gurus. The replies would come thick and fast – oh yes, they are a well known paedophile etc. Not wanting to believe it, I'd end up researching for myself, all the while with a sickening knot in my stomach, and whilst you can never fully trust things you find online, there was enough to conclude that most of what I had been told was probably, shockingly, true.

So much for taking a break from it. No matter where I turned or what I did the truth would pour out from everywhere. It was like the truth equivalent of waterboarding or having the world's most obnoxious teacher constantly yelling in your face – 'there are things you need to know and I'm going to tell you whether you want to hear them or not!'

Not everything was paedophile related, but disturbing enough, nonetheless. I felt there were few organisations who weren't marred in some way. The slightest shadow of doubt made me avoid many, eventually even cancelling my Gaia TV subscription. I didn't know who I could trust, so coming away from everything and everyone, whilst perhaps extreme, felt prudent.

I took solace each day outside in nature, even though we weren't technically allowed out for exercise, I had decided that I wasn't going to partake in that level of insanity. I knew I needed to be outside for my physical and mental health. I was lucky, however, that my parents' holiday home I was staying in had a lovely big balcony where I could sit and look out to spectacular panoramic sea and mountain views whenever I wished. I don't know how the people in the high-rise flats in places like Malaga were coping with only a non-existent, Juliet balcony. The irony was that the weather had been surprisingly bad throughout nearly the entire lockdown and it wasn't really sitting out weather, besides I needed to properly stretch my legs, so out into nature I went.

The urbanisation my parents' house was situated in was largely empty. It was mostly holiday homes owned by people from Granada, there were only about three of us living there permanently. It was a gated community and although I'd see the police driving up to the entrance every fifteen minutes, they couldn't get in to stop me wandering about.

I had such a strong craving to be in nature. Just walking around a block of empty, typically Spanish, white-walled houses with very few plants didn't do it for me. So I would go down to the gate by the beach car park, wait behind the wall until the fifteen minute police car had done its patrol and then I would walk up a very steep fifty meters or so path to an abandoned chiringuito (Spanish beach bar), climb through a hole in the chain-link wire fence and sit on a crate I'd found outside the main beach front chiringuito which had been forced to close in lockdown.

I didn't risk the actual beach walk because there were police patrol boats and helicopters around, constantly making sure everyone stayed inside. The couple of occasions I had ventured onto the beach, made me feel so anxious and uncomfortable, that it just wasn't worth the stress. The lower beach was surrounded by apartments, but my hideout at the top was tucked back so much, that as long as I kept against the stone wall, no one could see me.

The danger point was coming in and out of our urbanisation's gates at the beach car park. There was a ten meter section which was very exposed. One day as I was waiting for the police to move on so I could sneak out, I saw them start to drive off, and then as I came out the gate, I heard the car stop abruptly, turn around and come back again. I clearly hadn't waited quite long enough for them to disappear and they must have seen me emerge in their mirror.

In the heat of the moment, I decided my best option was to get up to the chiringuito where I could hide, but it meant running up a very steep concrete path. I should have just turned around and gone back into the urbanisation as the locked gate would have stopped them. But my flight or fight response had kicked in so I made a dash for it.

It's probably the fastest I've ever run in my life, but with the sheer steepness, it made for a rather comical slow motion get away. It looked like the last section of the TV series Gladiator when they had to run up a steep moving escalator going in the opposite direction. Despite the enormous effort I was putting in, I wasn't getting up the sheer slope anywhere near as quickly as I wanted.

Halfway up the fifty meter concrete path, I could hear the police car door slam, shortly followed by footsteps on the gravel which was around the corner from where I'd started to run. I gave it every last bit of pace I could muster and dived head first through the gap in the wire fence, just under the 'no entrance or you'll be prosecuted' sign!

They'd obviously seen me but would they want the steep walk up the concrete path, the top of which went to another urbanisation with a locked gate? I prayed they'd be too lazy. I thought I'd got out of sight before they'd made it around the corner but I couldn't be completely sure. If they'd seen where I'd gone, they'd definitely come looking, because not only was I outside for some illegal exercise and facing a 600 Euro fine, I was now also breaking and entering. Well, I should clarify, I didn't break in, someone else had, I was just taking advantage of the hole they'd cut in the chain-link fence.

I tried to quietly pull the wire together, so it looked too small a gap for anyone to have crawled through. Now I had the dilemma of do I stay put or do I try to make it around the back of the abandoned chiringuito? The whole place was littered with broken glass from where people had either broken in and ransacked it, or just vandalised it for fun.

In the end, I didn't dare risk moving, other than to step back a bit and hide behind some Hibiscus bushes. If I'd tried to make a dash for it, they might have seen or heard the movement.

After what seemed like an eternity, I eventually heard the car doors slam and the car drive off. Even then I didn't immediately budge in case one of them was still waiting and they were using the car driving off to lure me out. Once a suitable amount of time had passed, I continued on to my normal viewing spot and sat down on the borrowed beer crate, trying to process the situation.

Never in my life did I ever imagine I'd become the type of person who would be on the run from the police! The not breaking, but definitely entering, I did have previous experience of though. A large part of my childhood was spent exploring places I probably shouldn't have been, with the four boys who lived next-door. We never damaged anything, we just weren't bothered by the fact some of the woods we liked to hang out in were privately owned! A 'keep out or else' sign is an invitation to children of a certain age to explore, isn't it?

April in Spain is glorious. The whole side of the mountain next to my hideaway was a carpet of yellow and purple flowers. Acid yellow Oxalis, purple Morning Glories and Jacaranda trees were flowering in full glory, with a backdrop of a glistening blue sea, and as the coastline arced around, I could see tantalising glimpses of the once bustling town of Almuñecar. On a clear day you could just about see the town beyond that, Motril. My heart ached to return to the 'normal' life I once had. Although I appreciated the beauty all around me, I had such a constantly heavy heart that even magnificent flowers and sea views weren't able to fully lift me out of that feeling. But they did soothe me enough to make dodging the police worth it.

## There Was No Training For This!

Other than being a garden designer and an online educator, I'm also a trained life coach. I've always had a fascination with self-development and have many tools with which to cope with what life throws at me. Or so I thought. I did not cope with this. Nothing in my toolbox had prepared me for how to deal with this earth-shattering amount of awful in one go. Having lived a pretty sheltered life, I was stunned beyond stunned, and horrified beyond horrified, to learn about the horrors of what I was uncovering - that so many people could do such terrible things to children and, it appeared, some really famous ones at that.

People in the groups I was in were sympathetic and told me to slow down. What I'd discovered in the course of a few weeks had taken them years to uncover and process, but I couldn't stop. I had to know what kind of world I was really living in. I did pull myself back from going too far into some of what has been done to these children. Let's just say the horrors go way beyond sexual abuse. As I write this, the sexual abuse is at the forefront of the media right now with rape gangs coming into the spotlight. But will the rest come out? Time will tell.

Words cannot do justice to how destabilising it is to discover the amount of evil that has been percolating through our world, probably for centuries, largely unseen by the masses. It's surfacing now, where everyone with eyes attuned to see, can't help but see it. Many people are still in denial. Too scared to open their eyes. I don't blame them, but in this case, ignorance isn't bliss. It will be their, and our, downfall. Perhaps you are living in ignorance, puzzled by what you're reading? If you're not, are you trapped in truth hell, or have you made it out the other side?

## The 5 Stages of Truth Hell

> Shock
> Fear
> Anxiety
> Grief
> Anger

If you've not made it out yet (don't worry you definitely can), I'll share how I dragged myself out of truth hell and into a place of, for the most part, joy, something I didn't think would be possible when I was going through the depths of despair with everything I discovered. Perhaps my journey out may help you on yours.

At the beginning of my journey of unwelcome discovery, other than the shock of the world not being as I had believed it to be, the worst part was seeing how many things were wrong. I couldn't make sense of it all. I'd always believed that politicians were either greedy or stupid, sometimes both. I had realised big businesses were the ones calling the shots and politicians did their bidding, the good Old Boys Club. It's a big club and we're not in it. But it had never occurred to me there was anything more disturbing than good old-fashioned greed.

The more I looked, the more I saw. Dark forces seemingly everywhere, in the highest levels of governments, corporations, trusted organisations, media, celebrities – everywhere. If someone had tried to tell me all this, I wouldn't have believed them. It was only doing week after week of intensive research, peeling back the layers, that enabled me to see it for myself. It doesn't actually take weeks to research, a day or two would probably do it. It took me weeks because I didn't want to believe what I was discovering, plus I had to pick my way through all the false information, which was endless.

The information I dug up suggested the price of fame and success at the highest levels involved being lured at celebrity parties and photographed in compromising situations, which may then become escalated into doing awful acts with children (or their dirty secret would be exposed or their own family threatened with harm), and then those people and entities that pull the strings, own that person. It's not just celebrities but many in positions of power within government, the judiciary and other powerful governing bodies were likely compromised. Everyone would do as they were told because they couldn't risk not to. Epstein's Island is the tip of the iceberg.

This process of research and acceptance plunged me from a carefree and happy existence into a world of darkness. I felt consumed by it. Once the shock subsided, then came fear.

If it had been one bad government and a few bad people and organisations, it would have been perhaps easier to process, but the extent of the rot was overwhelming. It felt like everything in the world was bad, that I couldn't trust anything or anybody, and I felt helpless that I had no way of combatting it. The problem, too big, and I, too small. Combined with the fear, a sense of hopelessness set in.

Now, many people have woken up to the fact things aren't right, but back then, when I made these horrendous discoveries, there were only a few of us. I was lucky there were so many people around me whom I could talk to. Considering I'd stranded myself in a small fishing village in Southern Spain, it was remarkable to have such a big gang of people that I could meet up with once the lockdown rules relaxed a bit.

I was in the right place, at the right time, with the right people. If I'd been in England with their fairly relaxed rules (in comparison to Spain), I doubt I'd have even noticed there was a lockdown as, it would have hardly impacted my work-from-home lifestyle. Being essentially under house arrest, not even allowed out to exercise for months on end, with just the internet, gave me far too much time to think and more importantly, research.

The fear held strong for quite some time, in part because the vast majority of people in the world were completely oblivious to the full picture. It was like living in a bizarre parallel universe. If you tried to speak out, even gently and raise any form of concern, it was met with anger and hostility. People were impossible to reach. It was like watching them walk blindfolded across a busy motorway, screaming at them to warn them about all the oncoming traffic, but they just wouldn't listen. I managed to get my two closest friends locally to see the bigger picture, but that was all.

In the end I came away from Facebook, I couldn't read any more timeline posts from so many people oblivious to what was going on. I could see the more I tried to convince people something was amiss, the more it dug them deeper into their belief that they were doing the right thing. Worst of all, it was virtually impossible to convey the depth of what I'd learned without sounding like a complete nutter.

## Overcoming Fear

There were five things that helped me get out from the feelings of fear and hopelessness. As much as the research and discoveries were awful, a turning point happened when thanks to an eye-opening YouTube Channel called the Ice Age Farmer I came across an interview with a wonderful woman called Sandi Adams. Little did I know when I watched that video that one day I'd meet her and we'd join forces to create videos sharing the truth she'd spent years researching, to a worldwide audience.

Sandi had worked in the corporate world for companies like Google and Microsoft, even meeting Bill Gates. Working for these corporations she started to see concepts these companies were presenting, which concerned her. So concerned in fact, she left the corporate world and spent the next seventeen years investigating organisations like the UN and the World Economic Forum, and studying various NGOs (non-governmental organisations), while looking very closely at something called Agenda 21 and trying to educate others on her findings.

In the video she explained Agenda 21 (which was later renamed Agenda 2030). On the surface, the UN's 17 Sustainable Development Goals, which the Agenda sets out, sound wonderful. But like anything, the devil is in the details. In the interview, she connected all the dots, and unmasked all the details, and suddenly everything I'd researched started to make sense.

All the seemingly random things that were happening lead to a very clear destination. Once I understood what the organisations who influence the governments of the world were trying to achieve, everything that I had researched fell into place and made sense, which brought me some relief. As much as making sense of this research didn't make it any better, it did make it feel more manageable to deal with. It wasn't lots of unrelated things, it was one thing that tied everything else together.

Sandi also mentioned a report commissioned by the UK Government called Absolute Zero (which can be downloaded from https://ukfires.org/impact/publications/reports/absolute-zero/). That report sounded so unbelievable I downloaded it to read for myself and sure enough everything was all laid out exactly as she had said.

In brief, the report proposed that from 2030, in the UK, all food imports from shipping and air would be phased out and cease completely by 2049. Lamb and beef would be phased out completely. All

UK airports would close. Vehicles would all be electric and subsequently a 60% reduction in road use from 2020 levels would be sought. Gas cookers would be phased out, and fridges, freezers and washing machines would be made smaller. Fossil fuels would be phased out, along with concrete and steel. The list goes on. Even if only a portion of these proposed measures are implemented, the direction is clear - our freedom to travel, eat what we want, heat our homes and live our lives, will be severely restricted.

The Absolute Zero report was debated in the House of Lords on the 6th of February 2020 and was received positively. A bit of muttering about how the masses would manage without coffee and chocolate was heard, but other than that, the Lords seemed to be fully onboard with it. You can view the debate on https://bit.ly/lords-zero

I did tell Sandi when we met that I had hoped she was as mad as a box of frogs when I first heard her talk about Agenda 2030. She laughed and said she wished she was too, but unfortunately it's being implemented more and more every day.

Not only did Sandi's information make sense, it enabled me to see the big picture and what was coming down the pipeline. Knowing what's likely to come, enables you to prepare for it. It was the not knowing, and seeming randomness of it all, which was causing part of my fear and anxiety. When everything didn't make any sense, I'd felt lost and confused. Nothing any of the governments around the world do surprises me now I know what the end game is.

If you've read my first, more lighter-hearted book, Misadventures of a Digital Nomad, you may have laughed at how much disaster planning I did for three months in a campervan around Spain, so you can only but imagine the levels of prepping that occurred once I'd grasped the severity of where we were heading globally. It was obvious there would be food and electricity shortages and the cost of basic living was going to skyrocket to unaffordable levels. Getting prepared was another step on the path to feeling less fear.

I've been unable to find the mind-opening video I saw back in 2020 with Sandi and the Ice Age Farmer. It was eradicated from the internet. I've created a resource page on my website (RachelMathews.UK), which has another interview Sandi did, but also a very important one from Richard Jeffs of Yellow Forum. If you're not up to speed with what Stakeholder Capitalism is, and how governments everywhere are in lock-step, systematically moving us from a democratic system over to this new form of global governance, which ties in with Agenda 2030, then part one of his short documentary is essential viewing.

What I like about Richard's work, other than how succinctly he explains everything, is the fact that he's created an evidence pack to back up every word he says, which could be used in court, if he ever needed to substantiate his work. You can view the videos at: RachelMathews.UK/accidental-resources

Oracle Films have also created a documentary called The Agenda, equally essential viewing.

## No Escape

There was no escaping it. I researched other countries to live in but couldn't find anywhere I'd want to live that wasn't under the control of these unelected entities who are hell bent on Agenda 2030 and all the delights that go with it. Much of what is planned will be brought in under the guise of saving the planet, but if you examine any of the so called 'green' initiatives closely, such as electric vehicles, wind, solar etc, you will read about the devastating pollution from manufacturing these things, and how hard recycling all of these relatively short-lived technologies, and you will see that they are anything but green. And I say this with a heavy heart as someone who was a big supporter of 'green energy' for over twenty years, but whose support ended the day I researched it all properly…

One of the most healing things for getting me out of fear, was the realisation that the majority of people are honest, decent and true (which is also why we've been so blind to what's being done). We have numbers on our side. If enough people understand the full picture and where the roads lead to that we are being pushed down, and if they all just say no, this insanity would stop overnight. It's clueless people following orders and a society going along with it all that enables this global corporate takeover and allows the switch to Stakeholder Capitalism to happen.

That realisation enabled me to do the thing that really helped with conquering the fear…

## Fighting Back

The sense of hopelessness was worse than the fear. It went away the moment I started to fight back, albeit in a very small way. I gathered my aware friends together into an online group and they invited their aware friends and before we knew it there were nearly seventy of us.

We shared information and created infographics, putting the research we'd gathered into easy to understand formats. I made anonymous educational videos and we did co-ordinated releases of them on our social media platforms. Some of the things we created were picked up by influencers with big followings and were spread far and wide. I was still quite fearful, not daring to appear in the videos I was creating, but I gradually became braver as time went on.

Doing something, however small, gave me a feeling of being back in control. I wasn't going to take this lying down, and neither were any of my friends. We all did our bit and pooled our collective skills together. Even today I occasionally see some of the graphics we created being shared, which brings a nostalgic smile. I also stopped supporting the big corporations as much as I could. Whilst it will make no difference to Amazon if I shop there or not, mentally, it made a difference to me.

Another part that helped me recover my sense of self was ditching my computer for six weeks and getting out and doing something else. The 'something' I chose was a natural buildings workshop.

As soon as lockdown was over I'd purchased a comedy campervan which my friend, Tom, nicknamed 'Wacky Races' or Harriet the Chariot, as I preferred to call her. It was a UK plated, silver, Ford Ranger double-cab pickup truck with a white campervan box on the back. It had enormous pimped out tyres and a large snorkel on the side. It looked utterly ridiculous and had made me laugh so much when I laid eyes on it, I knew it was the escape vehicle for me.

This thing could not only off-road, as it was 4-wheel drive, but the snorkel meant it could go through rivers, and had accommodation on the back. What more could a girl ask for? Actually, there was one more thing. A dog.

## International Rescue

Before lockdown started I'd been volunteering at the local dog rescue centre above La Herradura. I'd been socialising the timid ones, getting them used to being with people and walking them so they got some decent exercise. I planned to eventually drive back to England so this meant I could give at least one of the dogs from the rescue centre a new life.

The campervan needed refurbishing as the interior layout was awful. I commissioned a carpenter I'd found in a nearby village who specialised in campervan interiors and at the end of August 2020, I drove from Southern Spain to Southern Italy with the dog. Thankfully the dog I'd chosen, Lena, a one year old Belgian Shepherd / Podenco mix, nicknamed,

'Small Dog' (because she is considerably smaller than the German Shepherds I'd grown up with), adored travel and adventure as much as her new human.

It's hard graft building a house with your bare hands but I was with a great group of people and being outside in the fresh air and sunshine all day for six weeks worked its magic. There wasn't time to be reading and researching every awful thing that might be coming our way. It put me back in the present moment, not to mention, if everything really does go to hell in a hand-basket I can build a house out of mud and straw if I have to – an attractive one at that! If you want to see the house I helped build just go to SuccessfulGardenDesign.com/show32 - it's 13 mins into the episode.

I still had anxiety about everything that was happening, but the worst of the fear had gone. There was a great sense of loss of the world I thought we lived in, and the grief came in waves. In time that too faded and was replaced by fascination. I started to research alternative histories and discovered all sorts of amazing things. I've no way of knowing if they are true or not, but they kept me entertained with enthralling narratives I'd never considered. It helped bring back a spark of magic and intrigue, which was just what I needed to help lift myself out of the darkness.

There was also a lot of anger to process, but the thing that helped me move through that was the realisation that I'd been part of the problem. I'd allowed this to happen by not paying attention, like so many others. Never being remotely interested in politics or local government, I'd just let them all get on with it. The price to pay for that is going to be a high one. But as I'd been part of the problem, it meant I could also be part of the solution, and that is part of what this book is about… how we can all be part of the solution.

Even though I'd acknowledged all that, I could never have anticipated I would get quite so active in local governance when I eventually returned to the UK, a year later.

## Joyful

Another thing which made me feel empowered was not allowing myself to be triggered back into fear. So much of what is on the media appears designed to make people feel as frightened and powerless as possible, so for me, the biggest act of rebellion, other than saying no to nonsense, was to find joy and happiness in whatever I could, whenever I could. Stress and negative emotions are well-known to effect health, so even in very dark times, I do everything I can to find something to be grateful and joyful over, no matter how small it may seem.

To recap what got me back on track:

1. Understanding the big picture & the 'final destination'

2. Taking steps to mitigate where possible

3. Realising there's a lot more good in the world than bad

4. Taking positive action - educating others and no longer supporting large    corporations

5. Putting a cap on reading the doom and gloom – once you've got the big picture, no need to wallow in it!
6. Find joy wherever you can.
7. Bonus tip - switch off the television.

Out of all the darkness I had discovered while researching, something else more positive was beginning to happen.

## Trust Thyself

Perhaps this comes under 'know thyself', but during the depths of despair when it felt there was no one in the world who was trustworthy, the realisation came to me that I can trust myself. Once so many famous people came to light as being involved with helping get the UN Agendas (and worse) into the mainstream, I started to acknowledge that they were people I'd never really liked! And some of them I'd tried hard to like, because they appeared to be good people, but deep down, if I was really honest with myself, I wasn't keen on them.

I always wondered why I found it impossible to pick out a famous person whenever people would say in success seminars, 'think of someone famous who inspires you and imagine you are them' - the fake it till you make it type of thing. I could never think of a single person who resonated with me. When I had ditched watching television over a decade earlier, I hadn't missed it for a second. And I could never really get enthusiasm for watching movies.

Eminent political leaders, who many people adored, left me cold, as did the Hollywood scene - a place I've even visited with a friend who loved it. The whole place made my skin crawl and I had no idea why. My intuition clearly knew something was off and when each person came to light during my research, it gave me more and more faith in my ability to trust my instincts.

With my intuition vindicated, I started to tune into it more and more. That's not to say I won't ever get fooled again, but I'm much more tuned in now than I was before. If something or someone doesn't feel right, I avoid it/them as much as I'm able.

So many people have been very annoyed with me for not backing politicians they thought would be our saviours. Once again, I tried to, but I just kept getting a bad feeling about the leadership, even though there were people involved I thought highly of.

As I write this, the honourable person I knew in one of the parties has just resigned and he's been turned on by the party leader. True colours are showing. It brings me no joy because it's demoralising for those who really believed these people would be the answer. For me, our political system is broken and needs redesigning from the ground up, but we can talk about alternatives later.

For now, the most important, first and foremost, is for us all to find our own personal power. When we come from a place of power instead of anger, fear, resentment etc. it's so much more effective in making a difference to our lives and the world at large.

Whether you were an early arrival to this unfortunate party we find ourselves in, or a late one, it matters not. One thing is very clear. There are turbulent times ahead and we all need to be equipped to not only deal with the shitstorm that's heading straight for us, but to navigate our way out and stop worse ones coming.

So how do you step into your personal power if you're stuck in fear or anger?

I'll share what worked wonders for me...

# 3

# Becoming Empowered

Even though I'd got myself out of fear and hopelessness, there was still plenty of anxiety and anger because I felt powerless to stop what I could clearly see coming. Taking some action certainly helped because I was doing 'something', but I certainly wasn't coming from a place of power. It was fear-based. I was in survival mode.

The turning point for me was coming across Common Law principles. As it turns out most of what I read back then wasn't entirely useful. I, alongside a host of others, got suckered into the 'Strawman' legal fiction argument. The more I studied, the more it became apparent that it doesn't tend to work out well for those who claim they are a Freeman of the land, living man/woman, sovereign being (take your pick). The reasoning behind the 'Strawman' argument is a claim that the government create a separate entity via birth certificates to control and tax us. Our real, flesh-and-blood self (the living man/woman) is distinct from this artificial "person", a legal fiction, usually identified when written in ALL

CAPS on documents (e.g. RACHEL MATHEWS vs. Rachel Mathews).

The claim is that we're free from statutes unless we consent, based on common-law supremacy, which is all well and good until you try it in court. People claiming they're a Sovereign being, not a legal fiction and statutes don't apply to them because they do not consent to them, tend to get laughed at and then fined or imprisoned.

I eventually came across our constitutional documents and here I found enacted documents which do hold sway, rationally. The most powerful one for me was the 1688 Bill of Rights which forms part of our codified Constitution. It clearly sets out our constitutional arrangements, which was the game changer for me.

The Bill of Rights was set up to make sure we didn't get any more dictator kings in charge. It got rid of the 'Divine Right of Kings', subjecting the previously absolute authority of Kings (little more than sword law) to Parliament. Most importantly, the Bill of Rights sets out that Parliament cannot do anything to the prejudice of the people.

Specifically, the Bill of Rights stops the Crown taxing people and going to war without Parliament's consent. It makes sure there is freedom of speech in Parliament without repercussions, the one privilege it grants parliament. It prevents cruel and unusual punishments. It makes sure individuals cannot be arrested without lawful justification, protecting us from arbitrary imprisonment. Nothing can be done to the prejudice of the people.

It enforces the law, everyone is equal and accountable. The government cannot act above the law or use its authority to oppress or discriminate against its citizens. It protects our individual rights and freedoms. All decisions should protect the welfare of the people. Does this sound like any government you know? If you go to https://www.legislation.gov.uk/aep/WillandMarSess2/1/2/introduction you can download a copy.

## The Pecking Order

There was something profound for me seeing this old but still enacted, (as it is not possible to un-enact it without undoing parliament itself) document and, understanding from it the following pecking order:

Higher Power
(We) The People
Parliament & Monarchy
Agents of Government

As long as we don't cause any harm, loss or injury to another, we are only answerable to God. That's a pretty powerful position! And even if you don't have any religious or spiritual leanings, Parliament does not have the right to take away our individual rights and freedoms. We are all equal under the law. What one can do, all may do. Which is not to say that this simple rule does not hold equally true for a collective, otherwise that would be admitting a mafia state.

If you've not come across this before, or even if you have, take a moment to let that sink in.

WE ALL ARE EQUALLY POWERFUL, NO PERSON OR GROUP OF PERSONS, HOWSOEVER COLLECTED (ie: Parliament) USUALLY REFERRED TO AS "THEM" HAVE ANY MORE POWER THAN ANYONE ELSE.

All those feelings of being small and powerless had shifted from that moment. Absent causing another harm I'm answerable only to God / Higher Power, whatever you like to call it and that's it. The government and all the unelected organisations recklessly steering us and trying to control us can whatsit off!

With the Common Law stuff I'd read, I had intellectually understood that the power is with the people, but with the Bill of Rights it became a full-body feeling of power rather than purely intellectual knowledge, it's real and written down. I felt empowered.

It was like a switch had been flicked and the power had been restored. So now it was just a matter of not allowing the State or anyone else to bully me. They are there to serve us, not the other way around which on the face of it would be nonsensical. Many appear to have forgotten this fact (or maybe like me, they never knew). It's our job to politely remind them, they have taken an oath, after all. An oath for which they are richly rewarded.

I would say it probably took me about a year, to 18 months to recover from the shock, fear, and all the rest, to a point where I had educated myself into a position of power. No doubt it can be done much faster than that. If you're at the beginning of that journey, I hope this book helps, which is why I'm writing it. There are millions of people coming to the realisation that all is not well, and if they do even a tenth of the research I've done, I know they'll get one hell of a shock (that I hope will propel them into empowerment).

## Stepping into Power

Realising our own personal power, is essential. When you have a sense of power and know you're not a small insignificant person (something social conditioning seems to prefer we believe), then life gets easier. Think of people you know who come from a place of power, versus those who operate from anger.

Anger does have its place. It's a great motivator and feels better than apathy, fear or grief, but spending too long in anger is damaging. Using anger as a stepping stone to higher emotions is helpful. Have you noticed how people who aren't good at setting boundaries and saying no to others, can only do so when they are angry?

It is possible to set boundaries and not have other people take you for granted and walk all over you, without resorting to anger. Life does tend to mirror how we feel on the inside right back to us. Life seems delighted to give us opportunity after opportunity to grow and change behaviours which don't ultimately serve us.

You must know people who are continually getting the same life lessons over and over. It is said, doing the same thing and expecting different results is the very definition of insanity... Yet, how many of us do just that? I know I've certainly been guilty of it in the past.

Do you have that friend who seems to date the same type of person each time? They just get out of one bad relationship, and then dive head first into another. You try to warn them, but they tell you, 'this one will be different', but of course it isn't. We attract the same circumstances until we learn how to do things differently.

My preference over the years has been to jump before I'm pushed, or more likely kicked hard up the backside! I know that if I don't learn from my mistakes and make the internal changes necessary, I will get one almighty universal kick up the rear.

For me, this is Earth School and we're here to learn and evolve, whether we like it or not. We can do things the easy way, or the hard way. The choice is ours. I prefer easy.

The first time I was asked to be a speaker at a public event, I could almost feel my soul wringing its hands with glee and saying 'ohh you'll find that absolutely excruciating, say yes!' I could have said no, I wanted to, but I knew I was being given an opportunity to grow, and I had a sneaking suspicion that I was being given a practice run. So despite the protestations from my default introvert, I said, yes.

My debut was at the Leicester Square Theatre in London at Clive de Carle's 'Solutions for Health, Life and Football' event alongside footballing legend, Matt Le Tissier, presenter and author, Richard Vobes and Radio 2's, Janey Lee Grace. I had been giving speeches at the local council on matters concerning the environment up to now, but those were only three minutes long with every word written out so all I had to do was read them aloud!

Fifteen minutes in front of an audience without a script was something I'd never done before, and to be alongside well known accomplished speakers was nerve-wracking, as it would be for any novice. My mouth was as dry as a desert before we'd even left Colchester train station, much to the amusement of my companions, Carinna and Sharon, who were delighted to be going for a nice day out, and not being the ones having to get on stage!

It had been a really busy week writing speeches to deliver to the council whilst making an accompanying video of the process, so I had had no time to prepare so I was scrambling to think of things to say on the train journey there.

Matt Le Tissier was the first person I bumped into on arrival. Whilst I was never a football fan, I am a big fan of Matt having been one of the few celebrities to publicly speak about his concerns over Covid and the safety of the vaccines. He was a beacon of light through all the insanity and took a lot of abuse for it, even losing his Sky Sports commentator spot. His courage to speak out when virtually no one else would was a great comfort to many.

I'd had a Zoom call earlier in the week with him and the other speakers to discuss the event so I went up and said hello. I then took the opportunity to ask him if he had any advice for someone who has never done public speaking before! He looked quite taken aback by that question and double-checked, "You've never done public speaking before?"

"No, not really, only in the local council but that's written out."

He paused thoughtfully for a moment and advised me, "Don't rush. Take your time. You'll feel like you're speaking too slowly but when you watch it back, it won't be as slow as it feels, it'll be just right." I thanked him for his advice and went in search of Clive to tell him I'd arrived.

When I came across Janey Lee Grace, I asked her the same question as I had Matt. Her advice was to make sure I know what I'm going to say at the beginning and equally important, the end. I thanked her for the great advice and then took the opportunity to walk up on the stage while the theatre was empty to get myself used to it. Or at least familiar so it wasn't quite such a shock when it was my turn to come on.

I was also hoping to ask Richard Vobes for speaking tips as he's so good. I'd gone to see him speak at an event near Southend; he was brilliant, but alas, there wasn't an opportunity by the time he arrived.

I was the last to speak. All the things I'd thought of on the train had already been said by the other speakers, so I was left with a big fat nothing to talk about, and had to wing the entire thing! It was a bit waffly at the beginning while I was trying to work out what to say, but I did it. My criteria for success that day was 'don't fall off the stage and try not to say anything stupid!' So from that relatively low bar, it had been a success!

When it came to giving a forty minute speech in Bristol for <u>UK Column</u>, at least I had some experience under my belt. Horrifyingly, the beginning of my speech ended up being a bit of a shambles... Can you imagine how much harder it would have been to cope if that had been my first time public speaking? At least at the Leicester Square Theatre it was so dark that I couldn't see anyone in the audience. In Bristol the event was held in a conference room with a clear view of the three hundred people looking back at me.

What made it even funnier, when I could eventually bring myself to watch the video of my speech to see just how much of a car crash the beginning had been, was the introduction Charles Malet had given me. He'd made me sound like some Superwoman council slayer, then immediately afterwards I came skidding in with the reality.

I was in such a fluster, that I had a complete mind blank on the name of something rather vital to the story that I had started to recount and had to ask the audience for help. I was trying to remember 'Grand Canyon' and to help the audience guess, I had wanted to say 'it's the one with the Colorado River running through it', but the only thing that came out of my mouth was the word 'Colorado'! Remarkably, someone in the audience managed to guess what I was trying to say, though goodness only knows how as Colorado is nowhere near the Grand Canyon!

I was so out of breath from all the running, my ability to speak was quite impaired, so I opted to play my second video clip earlier than I'd planned, to allow time to recover my breath and senses. I only had one button to press on the computer that UK Column's Mike Robinson had set up with everyone's material. Did I press the right button? No. No, I did not, and ended up playing someone else's clip. Mike had to come on stage and salvage the situation. The only thing that could have made the start of my UK Column speech worse would have been if I'd tripped up and fallen flat on my face, which might have been on the cards had Carinna not offered to carry the water!

Whilst one doesn't get a second chance to make a first impression, the clip I played while I recovered myself was the one which had gone viral with over six million views in the first weekend on Twitter. And goodness only knows how many views it's had now as it's still doing the rounds on social media two years later, having been shared by thousands of people across multiple platforms. In the video, I was at least functioning with a higher degree of competency than the 'all of a fluster' version on stage. If you'd like to see the talk, car-crash and all, the video is on the resources page. The camera didn't capture the skidding into the room but it certainly got everything else! RachelMathews.UK/accidental-resources

So yes, I'm glad I didn't wimp out of my first speaking invitation, or the UK Column car crash would have been a million times harder to recover from. It occurred to me afterwards, a more experienced public speaker would have told the audience what had happened and explained why they were so out of breath and made it an amusing part of their talk rather than trying to do the very English 'I'm fine! It's all fine,'! I have vowed, whatever goes wrong next time will be incorporated into what I'm saying.

Still, on the plus side, I did perfectly illustrate what I wanted to get across to people, and that is that it is us regular everyday folk who are the ones taking a stand. You don't have to be Superman or Superwoman to stand up to what's happening in the world.

I still haven't managed to fully incorporate Matt Le Tissier's advice on speaking slowly, it allows the audience time to react to what is said with laughter or applause, something which catches me by surprise, but it was a lot better than the Leicester Theatre, despite the unfortunate start. A lot of people came up afterwards and said how much they enjoyed it. One lady said she'd worked in TV and very kindly said she'd seen a lot of people speak live and mine was good. She could see by my face that I didn't believe her so later, when someone else came up and said how much they'd enjoyed it and she was in earshot, she came up again and said, "See I told you!"

The person who stood out to me and delivered a masterclass in public speaking was investigative journalist, broadcaster, and documentary filmmaker Sonia Poulton. She mentioned that she often describes herself as an "accidental troublemaker" and shared stories from her time as a music journalist, including meeting P. Diddy. Sonia also discussed her investigations into the Madeleine McCann case, explaining that she had visited the crime scene twice, interviewed locals, and does not accept the narrative presented by the mainstream media. It was a fascinating talk; despite the darkness of the topics she covered, her insights and empathetic delivery made it truly compelling listening.

I've put Sonia's insightful UK Column talk onto the resources page of my website, underneath my klutz from Colchester 'car-crash start' speech!

We had to check out of our hotel room by midday, so we dashed upstairs to grab our stuff and check out before we were charged for another day. It was then I looked at myself in the mirror and saw my hair looked like I'd been dragged through a hedge backwards. I'd forgotten to pack any conditioner and the running at breakneck speed down the corridor had done my very fine, easy tangle hair, no favours.

I had brushed my hair in the hotel room before we'd gone downstairs to the event. I thought I'd finished when Carinna shook her head and said,

"Come here." And grabbed the hairbrush out of my hand. "I'll do that bit you always miss!"

"What! What do you mean that bit I always miss?!" I'd asked.

"This bit!" She had said whilst simultaneously brushing the back left side of my head.

"How many years have you known me? And you didn't think to mention the bit I ALWAYS miss until now?!"

"Hair is not a priority in my own life, so I'm hardly going to comment on yours! Besides, Cheryl is the hair expert, she should be the one to tell you."

"Well I wish someone had!" I moaned.

Physio Carinna then helpfully informed me. "It's either because of trigger points in your pec minor restricting upward rotation of your scapula within the rhombo-serratus fascial sling, or, it could be because you've got ickle arms!"

When we returned to the room to collect our stuff, on seeing what I looked like, I exclaimed, "Oh no, the state of my hair!"

Carinna consoled me with, "Well, at least that bit you always miss was brushed!"

## Growing Uncomfortably

Doing that which makes us uncomfortable, enables us to grow the most. It's a shame sitting at home eating cake and reading books doesn't appear to be the key to growth, if it was, I'd never leave the house. And yes, every time you get comfortable, along comes another challenge that makes you uncomfortable again.

It's like a computer game where every level is harder than the level before, but more rewarding. The more you overcome the challenges, the more you come from a place of power. I've got a cheat I use which helps make the process a bit easier, which I'll tell you about later.

One of the keys to personal power is valuing yourself. Not in an arrogant way, but a healthy way, like you do for others in your life. Being kind to ourselves isn't taught, but it should be. I wrote about this a lot in my first Misadventures book, so I won't cover it again here, but the sooner you can become your own best friend, the better life will get.

Remember, we are all born equal. No one is better than you. And of course, that cuts both ways.

How does it feel reading that?

Does it feel true, or like a lie?

If it feels like a lie, you've got some work to do, honey! Later in this book I'll give you a simple tool that will help get you to a place of power.

But then what? What do you do with all that power – strutting around the house with it isn't going to change things. You need to do something constructive with it, otherwise what's the point in having it?

Researching should give you reason enough to want to take action. It certainly did with me. Up until 2020, I would have sworn blind I didn't have a maternal bone in my body, but turns out I was very wrong about that. Once I understood what was coming, my primary driver for speaking out and putting myself in the firing line was for the children. Yes, children I don't even have.

A strong and urgent sense of needing to help put this right for the future generations consumed me. I realised my own comfort is nowhere near as important as protecting the children, especially knowing the scale of what's been happening and learning too many gory details. Life is full of surprises and I certainly ended up with quite a few more on this particular journey, especially with what happened in the second lockdown.

# 4

# Crypto Crazy?

It was a busy time for me once I'd got over the shock of how I now knew the world to operate. Not only was I pushing back trying to educate people on the things the mainstream media weren't saying, I was also learning about crypto.

Being stuck out in Spain with no way of getting funds if the banks came crashing down, made me feel quite uneasy. I would need money to return to England, especially as I had decided I didn't want to fly back. At the time there was talk of needing a vaccine to be able to go on a plane once flights resumed. As it turned out the vaccine came sometime after flying started again, but having already read the EU documents about bringing in vaccine passports, I decided I was going to buy a vehicle and drive back home.

I'd done more than enough research on mRNA vaccines to know there was no way in hell I would ever have one (they'd been trying to get mRNA type vaccines to market for over 20 years but had been unsuccessful because they could never make it through the safety testing after all the test ferrets died in trials).

There were stark warnings from ex-Pfizer Drug and Discovery Research Unit VP, Mike Yeadon, who wrote an open letter to the UK Government about the safety concerns of rolling out an experimental vaccine on the population. He pleaded with them not to rush them through. In interviews, he said vaccines are normally safety tested for 10 years, and around ninety percent fail those tests. This figure was later disputed by the pharmaceutical industry.

Regardless of what percentage of vaccines fail safety tests, I found death as a possible side effect rather off-putting. There's also no liability for the vaccine manufacturers, should harm be caused from their products. My cynical side views that as a win-win for them. Any harm from the vaccines would be a fantastic increase in revenue for the industry when they supply all the medications to deal with the vaccine injuries.

I'd already been ill, so I knew I didn't need one as I would already have antibodies. So even if by some miracle these experimental vaccines weren't as potentially dangerous as the other mRNA vaccines I'd read about, there was no need for me to take the risk. This was how I was thinking at the time. It was before I'd read the book 'What Really Makes You Ill' by Dawn Lester and David Parker. I now have a different view of 'illness'.

But anyway, I was determined that I was not going to be vaccine blackmailed over a flight home. I was also wanting an alternative to traditional banking and that's when I became interested in crypto. At the time, before I realised just how manipulated it was, it seemed like a light at the end of the very dark tunnel. A way to be free of the system I could see wasn't serving us. But of course, if that were really the case, the system would never have allowed Bitcoin to get established. And no, I don't buy the story of the unknown inventor/s going by the pseudonym, Satoshi Nakamoto. To this day no one knows for sure who invented it, despite the various claims.

In my naivety, thinking crypto would be the saviour, I invested in a Crypto Vigilante membership and muddled my way through getting accounts set up to buy crypto and then to get a wallet on my computer. It wasn't difficult once I got my mind around it, but to begin with it all felt very strange. Crypto transactions aren't as instantaneous as the banking system we're all used to.

You rely on third parties to do the transaction for you. It can take minutes or hours for the crypto to turn up, depending on how busy the network is. You've got to make sure you are giving the correct address for the type of coin you are sending. For instance you cannot send Bitcoin to an Ethereum address in your wallet. It won't work and your transaction will most likely be lost.

The beauty of crypto is the ease with which you can transact, and, depending on the type, it can be completely anonymous. There are fees for every transaction, but usually a lot less than it costs to send funds internationally via a bank. Also, you are the custodian of your crypto so you don't have to worry about a bank going under. But that comes with its risks if, for instance, you lose your passcode to access your wallet. It's very easy to lose money. It's also incredibly easy to make it too, which is a big part of the lure.

Crypto is the Wild West, so the rule is, never invest more than you can afford to lose. And lose it you will. I've had coins which have changed the way they worked and then because I'd not been aware they had upgraded them in the time allowed to swap them to the new version, mine became defunct. I've accidentally sent coins to a mobile device which connects with my main wallet which doesn't support that type of coin. So I could see them on the device but couldn't get them out until that particular wallet chose to accept that coin.

If you stick to a very limited portfolio, then it's safer, but the fun, of course, is in the risky Bitcoin alternatives, known as Altcoins. These are incredibly diverse with what they can do. Crypto is a whole ecosystem. It is so much more than just digital currency. The more I got into it, the more enthralled I became. It was exciting and I was doing very well with my first investment.

I bought my first dabble when Bitcoin was under 7K dollars and carried on buying every month until it reached 26K. I did very well from it before I fell out of love with crypto and mostly, got out. Once I'd figured out how to do it, I taught several friends how to set up their wallets to make their learning curve easier than it had been for me.

My business was also doing very well during Covid. With the whole world stuck at home, doing the garden became the focus of lots of people. My online course sales were through the roof. It brought me no pleasure profiting from what was happening in the world, especially when I knew so many businesses were going bust because of it. But I was pleased I could easily afford my wacky campervan, the refurb and the natural house building course once lockdown was over.

The natural house building course had been my saviour coming out of lockdown. Time spent away from the computer, doing something so physically demanding, in a stunning location, with a great group of people was the medicine which soothed my soul and more importantly, my disturbed mind. Building a house with your bare hands is a laborious process, but it certainly puts you in the present moment.

Though I could never quite remove my landscape contracts-manager's hat. With each process I'd ask our English speaking German instructor, Robert Brendler, "can't we get some machinery in for that?!" It became the running joke on site. Digging out footings by hand and carting all the materials from the top of the site to middle terraces in wheelbarrows where we were working, was painful for me, not just physically, but mentally knowing something which would take a week by hand would only be a day with a mini digger and dumper truck and considerably less effort. I was beside myself when it came to mixing all the concrete for the building footings by hand and not hiring a cement mixer!

Everyone else seemed content to do everything by hand, doing it manually was part of the appeal. I could not get myself out of contractor mode where speed had been of the essence. I did my bit nonetheless, whilst muttering how much quicker this would be with machinery, and did as much as I was physically able to do.

Even with at least fifteen of us all working flat out, we didn't manage to complete the building in the six weeks I was there. Which was a shame, I would like to have seen it finished but it was a good way there. At least my spirit had been restored even if my satisfaction of a job completed couldn't be. The group was young and fun. They were fully aware of all the woes of the world and even though we'd discuss them at meal times, we didn't get bogged down with them. It was just what I needed to help restore me.

Robert offers his natural building courses all over Europe and sometimes further afield, if you have a project you'd like him to come and build for his training courses, or you'd like to go on one, you can contact him via his website: [https://permaskills.org/](https://permaskills.org/) I will warn you though, one thing which was not mentioned on the website course signup page is the ingredients of the final coat of cob plaster. Horse poo is a rather vital ingredient to get the clay and straw mix to stick to the walls!

We celebrated the end of the course with an evening fireside picnic on the beach. Several in the group were musicians so it was a great evening with everyone joining in with their instruments and singing. Rob presented us all with certificates that we'd successfully completed the course. On the back of mine he wrote a little thank you for the knowledge and calm energy I'd brought to the group and wished me well for the future.

When it was time to leave, I drove from the West coast of Badolato, to the East coast of Tropea. I'd been told it was lovely by the people we'd been building the earth house for. It seemed like a good place to head to. Especially as I had a few days to kill before I could get my van sorted out. I'd received a factory recall notification that the airbag in the van was unsafe and needed replacing as it could explode with shards of metal coming out! The only garage that could do it was miles away in the city of Catanzaro, the capital of the Calabria region. They'd ordered the part for me at the beginning of my six week stay in Badolato, and it was due to arrive at the end of the following week.

One of the Workaway people at the permaculture place where we'd done the natural buildings course, was a lovely half-English, half-Italian lady called Francesca; we'd got along well. She had been helping in the gardens before I arrived, and we overlapped for a week or so before she moved on to another Workaway in Sicily. Workaways, if you're unfamiliar with them, is a scheme where you can volunteer your labour in return for board and lodging. We'd kept in touch and when I told her I was going to

Tropea, she decided to meet me there and stay a few days on her way back from her Workaway in Sicily.

Tropea was stunning, with gorgeous creamy-white sandy beaches. I found what I thought was a good campsite, set back a few hundred meters from the sea. Francesca rented an apartment, and we stayed just over a week. It was lovely to spend time relaxing on the beach in sunshine, after so many weeks of exhausting physical toll. I'd never done that amount of physical work before on a continual basis and at my age, I was really feeling it.

Part of the issue I now realise was the vegetarian diet provided by our hosts on the natural building course. Whilst the food had been delicious and ample, and I certainly never went hungry, my body was crying out for meat. I'd only been able to satisfy that request one day a week, as every Saturday evening we'd eat out to give the chef a break. There I could order steak.

Now before I get inundated with emails about the benefits of plant-based diets, please don't as I've tried them and whilst they may suit you, I can categorically say, they do not suit me. I tried going vegan in 2018 for four months and it damn near killed me! OK slight exaggeration but it wrecked my health and took me over a year to fully recover from that little experiment.

I tried a vegan diet because I'd been experimenting with a Keto diet but someone I had met on a mountain hike said that her uncle had done Keto for years, and whilst he looked incredibly buff, he had ended up in hospital with a heart attack! She had converted over to vegan and extolled its virtues, so I decided to try it for myself. She told me about Dr Gregor, who had written books on how to do the diet to make sure you get all the nutrients needed. So I went about it in his scientific way, following the instructions on his app and stuck to it religiously, rather than listening to my body.

I should have just taken a good look at the photograph of Dr Gregor. Let's put it this way, not a shining example of what I consider healthy to look like. My new friend on the other hand did look excellent on it and it was she I used as a role model. But considering she had spent a lot of years living on takeouts and alcohol, quite frankly any diet change would have been better than what she had been doing. So it's not surprising that she felt incredible going vegan. And she was a lot younger than me.

Anyway, I knew vegan was a no-no, and I will never, ever try that again, but I'd never liked the thought of animals dying to provide me with sustenance, especially considering some farming practices are for low-price, not animal welfare. So I figured going semi-vegetarian and doing hard physical work would be a great test to see if vegetarianism might be an option for me.

Again, I can categorically say, it wasn't! Some people may be OK on a vegetarian diet, but I am definitely not one of them.

Now, some years later, having also experimented doing the opposite extreme of full-on carnivore, I know what suits me best, and it's definitely a high meat-based diet. Full-on carnivore was a very interesting experiment. I did this for two and a half months. The results were dramatic and unexpected.

I'd always thought the carnivore diet sounded incredibly stupid and I hadn't been drawn to trying it, until two things happened. I read a book called Toxic Superfoods by Sally K. Norton on high oxalate foods, which are in quite a lot of the nuts, fruits and vegetables many of us consume. Eating a high oxalate diet can cause havoc in the body with all sorts of symptoms.

It coincided with me watching a fascinating webinar on the Ancestral Diet. Had they called it carnivore, I wouldn't have been drawn to view it with my preconceived ideas about 'that diet' but by the time I'd got to the end of the video and realised it was carnivore, I'd already been convinced it was something worth trying.

My way of getting around the factory farming issue was to avoid buying that kind of meat, and also to buy predominantly wild meat. At least the wild had been roaming free up until the day before it ended up on my plate without the trauma of going to an abattoir with all its pals.

The results of this carnivore experiment were incredible, and fast. Within the first week I noticed the change in how my body felt and bizarrely how my teeth looked. I'm someone who has spent a good chunk of my life feeling constantly hungry. I have an absolutely ravenous appetite, despite my slim build. Within a few days of just eating only meat, I finally felt satiated for the first time in my life.

My teeth, which I'd noticed on sunny days looked semi-translucent, had whitened up dramatically. I was back in England at this point and had done a bit of gardening, and for a few days afterwards felt that my back was getting more muscly – weird sensation to describe. It wasn't in a way anyone would see, but I could feel the difference. It seemed my normal high-carb diet had not been serving me well. I didn't miss fruit or vegetables, and I had a lot more energy. I loved the simplicity of cooking as well.

As someone who does not enjoy cooking, frying venison mince, or steak, in a pan was blissfully simple. I didn't think I'd cope without carbs, but I found it incredibly easy, as long as I ate enough fat. What wasn't easy, however, was keeping electrolytes balanced. The clue is in the name, carbo-hydrate. I struggled the entire time with electrolyte balance.

No matter what I did, I could not adapt. That to me said that this wasn't the right diet. I know it can take longer than three months to adapt, but I had another problem as well. I lost too much weight. The carnivore diet is incredibly slimming, great if you've got a ton of weight to shed, lousy if you're already slim.

I'd done my carnivore experiment in the months leading up to Christmas, so I took that as an opportunity to conclude it. I have continued with the venison burger for breakfast, as I've found it sets me up for the whole day. I really notice that on the days I don't have it, I remain hungry all day. I've since come across the work of the [Glucose Goddess](#) and she says how important it is to start the day with protein and not do carbs until lunch.

I'm about sixty to seventy percent carnivore. The carbs help me maintain my weight and the veg keeps my microbiome healthy.

I will never do vegan or vegetarian again willingly! Even after a week of rest in Tropea, and despite the fact that I was eating meat again, I still didn't feel right. Other than being exhausted, a rather concerning symptom had occurred. My memory was awful. Not just bad, but very concerning levels of awful. My brain function was seriously impaired. I must have used up all the nutrients I needed physically so my brain had to go without.

I still hadn't heard back from the Ford garage regarding my driver's airbag replacement, but as it was now the end of October and coming to the end of the season, the campsite I'd been staying in was closing, so it was time to move on. There were also rumblings of another lockdown, and bit by bit the shops and restaurants had started to reduce their services. It was becoming harder and harder to find places open to eat.

Francesca left the day before me. She'd had word that her Italian father, who lived near Napoli, had been taken ill and was in hospital, so she was going to head there. On the morning of my departure there was only myself and one other campervan belonging to a lovely Canadian couple. They left unexpectedly early which left just me. I was a bit uncomfortable being the only one there, so I hurriedly packed up my stuff to leave.

Before I had the chance, the elderly father of the couple running the campsite came over to bid me farewell. He was a stout man who barely spoke a word of English. Francesca had been translating whenever he'd come over to chat, which was quite frequently. He was always lingering around the site.

Just as I was getting the last of my stuff into the van he came up behind me, almost pinning me to the open door with arms open wanting a hug goodbye. Here we go again. What is it with me and old men? I'm a bloody magnet for them.

I tried to duck out of the open-armed embrace, but couldn't, and he whispered in my ear "kissy-kissy?" Er no. Thanks. Lovely of you to offer, but I'd rather kiss my dog's arse! I didn't say that last part out loud, but I was certainly thinking it.

Talking of which, where the bloody hell was the dog? My Head of Security, it turned out, was busy trying to climb up a tree at the other end of the campsite after a cat. She'd been desperate to chase it all week, but couldn't, as I had her tied to a tree by the van. With no one about, the campsite owner said I could untie her. I'd let her loose knowing there would be no way she'd actually catch the cat, but it would keep her occupied while I packed. It kept her so occupied in fact, that she was completely oblivious to the situation her human was now in.

My unwanted suitor made a left boob lunge and grabbed it with about as much delicacy as an executive with a stress ball, and this time I shouted "No!" And very possibly something else that might have ended with 'off', very loudly at him and pushed him away, hoping to attract the attention of the people just the other side of the wire fence in the adjacent, full campsite. The combination of the fierce look in my eyes, and the close proximity of other people, made him think twice and eventually he backed off.

I got the last of my belongings hurled into the van, grabbed the dog, and tried to leave. The groper reluctantly walked over to the large main gates, taking his time to open them. I will admit there was a moment when he was taking so long, that I was rather tempted to ram him up against the gates with my front bumper. I resisted that temptation, but I did rev the engine a lot, so my intentions were clear. Get that gate open now and let me out or you're going to be decorating the front of this truck, mate. I was fuming by the time I made it out.

Revenge, as they say, is a dish best served cold. And I got mine the next day when it occurred to me that the campsite had a Facebook page. I left a one star review with the title 'Not safe for women'. I started by saying that I would have liked to have left a good review as the campsite was nice, well maintained and in a good location. I went on to describe my encounter in full glorious detail with the fatherly figure who helped run the site. I mentioned his foul breath, so his family would know I'd definitely had a closer encounter with him than customers would normally.

I was fairly sure the old boy hadn't been the one running their Facebook page, besides he could barely speak a word of English, let alone read it. I assumed it would have been his children who read it. And I suspect they would have given him absolute hell over what he'd done, at least, I hoped they would. The next day their entire Facebook page had been removed! I had expected them to delete my comment but not the entire page. Perhaps Facebook doesn't allow the removal of reviews, I don't know. I felt justice had been served.

Thinking back, he had always been right there whenever I came out of the toilets. Luckily for me, my rescue dog, Lena, has separation anxiety (except when chasing cats, obviously) and would always follow me to the toilets and sit outside the door. I did wonder afterwards if he'd have tried pushing me back into a cubicle when no one was about had the dog not been there every time.

Yuck! Doesn't bear thinking about. Another narrow escape with an elderly man to add to my list. Things like this always catch me by surprise. Whilst with enough makeup and the right clothes I can scrub up reasonably well, I tend to look like a down-and-out after a few days of camping. Any interest amazes me. Perhaps that's why it's only the old and decrepit ones that pursue me as their eyesight isn't good enough to see how I really look!

I stocked up with provisions and left Tropea in quite a foul mood. I'd been hoping to find a police officer to report him, but no sign of any. Not that I'd seen one the entire eight days I'd been there. I reminded myself that most men are nice and nothing like this guy. I just had an unfortunate knack for finding creepy ones when campervanning. The weather also didn't help my mood, it was grey and drizzly and I had a long drive ahead of me to get to Cantanzaro. Worse was to come though. It turned out my concerns about my brain function were justified, as I found out to my great detriment a week after leaving Tropea.

# 5

# Bang, Crash, Wallop

It proved a complete nightmare finding a campsite in southern Italy in November, in part because it was the end of the holiday season, but also because another lockdown was imminent. So my first night leaving Tropea was a wild one! I ended up spending the night in a beach car park just outside of Cantanzaro.

The next day, I found an all but deserted campsite in Cropani Marina a little further down the coast. The Ford garage had finally booked me in for two days later, so then I would be able to start my journey back to the UK.

Unfortunately for me, on my last night, I slipped on the tall van steps and badly hurt my left shoulder. The dog had displaced the steps earlier in the evening when she'd jumped into the campervan and when I went out to get something from the cab of the van, it had been so dark that I didn't see the black plastic steps at an angle and put my full weight on them with my left hand hanging onto the door handle. When I came crashing down with the steps, my arm twisted and my shoulder took the brunt of it.

I had hoped that it would be ok in the morning, but it wasn't, and ended up taking several months to heal.

The next day I duly turned up at the Ford garage at the appropriate time and sat with my laptop working in their waiting room with the dog. About an hour passed when the bald-headed Service Manager returned to tell me that they hadn't been able to fix the airbag. He did not have enough English to tell me why, and even with Google Translate, I couldn't find out what the issue was. I tried to ask them to just take the airbag out. It was better to have it removed than to continue to drive with something faulty that could malfunction and possibly kill me.

The man shook his head to say no. Again, without explanation and shooed me on my way. Well this was rather concerning. What was I going to do now? I'd just have to get it repaired when I got back to England and make darn sure, whatever I did between now and then, I didn't crash!

That was the plan anyway... do not crash.

I started the long drive back. I decided to head to the most touristy places in the hope that I might find a campsite open. On the way, a warning light came on, and after I'd stopped for diesel, I had trouble re-starting the van. The steering wheel had badly locked. I had quite a battle to release it. It was rather disconcerting, and of course, I blamed the garage. They must have tinkered with something, because it was fine before they'd had it.

I'd driven for nearly five hours at this point, so I wasn't going to turn around and take it back.

Besides, they hadn't been overly helpful, so I couldn't imagine they'd be any more helpful if I did go back.

On my third attempt, I found an open campsite just south of Salerno in Pontecagnano. It wasn't the nicest area, a bit rundown, but I didn't have a lot of options. The campsite itself was nice enough though. Francesca was staying not a million miles away in Sorrento, as she was still frequently visiting her father who lived on the outskirts of Napoli.

I booked in to the campsite for a few days and found a Ford garage in the vicinity. I wrote out everything that had happened using Google Translate and took it in for them to look at. The mechanic cast his eyes over it, checking all the obvious things it might be, but he said that if I wanted a full investigation, it would have to be the following week, and it would be costly. The mechanic didn't seem to think it was warranted. They hadn't been able to recreate the issue, and neither had I. So I decided to stay in the area for a week and if it played up again, I would take it back. At least they spoke a little bit of English in this one.

If I was completely honest with myself, I had no desire whatsoever to return to England for the winter. Never my favourite time of year, combined with the small issue of not having anywhere to live. I'd sold my house back in 2011, expecting the long awaited property crash, but it never came. Whilst I'd safely invested my house sale money, I didn't have as much as I would have liked for a deposit, which meant I'd end up with a larger mortgage than was comfortable. In the meantime, renting in England was going to be a minimum of a thousand pounds a month, plus the difficulty of finding a rental that allowed pets. I really did not want to go back to that, but I'd well and truly fallen out of love with Spain because of the first lockdown.

Besides, I was expecting a financial crash, so buying a house now didn't seem a good idea, and I wasn't entirely sure I wanted to live in England again after ten years of sunny weather. But my family were there, and that was the most important factor with what I knew was likely to be coming. I had still wanted to check out Portugal as a possible place to live. At the time it was one of the simpler places to get a visa. I assessed that I could easily have got the D7 Digital Nomad visa. I thought it would be worth checking out as I doubted I'd get the opportunity again the way everyone was talking about vaccine passports being required.

I decided it would be a good idea to rent an Airbnb for a week in case the van needed to be worked on and it would allow me a decent break to get my energy back. I was still exhausted from all my physical labouring. I found one that was around two hundred euros for the week, now that it was winter season, in a stunning location called Agerola, known for the breathtaking Path of the Gods walking route.

I told Francesca of my plans when she visited me at the campsite that weekend. She said Agerola was a lovely place and she'd come and see me when I moved into the Airbnb.

There had been few shops within walking distance around the campsite, and little choice of food, so I headed off to stock up in the next town for me and the dog. Having already driven on the winding Amalfi coast road on my way down through Italy, I took the motorway towards Naples and found an amazing organic shop. I bought plenty of provisions for my week's stay, knowing I'd have a fridge at long last. I had one in the van, but it wasn't working.

On my third attempt at finding a decent pet food store, I took a wrong turn and ended up on a road to nowhere that looked like it was going off into farmland. I needed to turn around, but there was an enormous concrete pole in the road. It was a bit bizarre, all the others were situated in the field except for this one. I found a part of the road that looked possible to turn around in, but it proved to be rather difficult.

Here's where my concerns about my memory became apparent. I had a complete mind blank about the pole in the middle of the road, which I now could not see in my mirror and my brain thought that turning around in the wider part of the road I'd just come from would be easier. So I started to do just that until there was an almighty bang!

For one dreadful moment I thought I'd reversed into a car I couldn't see in my mirrors but no, when I got out to look, it was the pole! I couldn't believe I'd blanked out on the reason I hadn't tried to turn around in that part of the road in the first place.

Miraculously, the crash hadn't triggered the airbag. The dog didn't look happy. Shards of glass surrounded her where the camper had been shoved into the back window of the van cab. I got her out and cleaned up the glass. Most of it was in her seat cover, so it was easy to gather up and deposit in a conveniently located skip nearby.

I pulled forward a touch and looked at the rear of the camper. The side that had hit the concrete pole was completely done in. The camper box jutted out past the end of the van so it had taken the full force of the collision, not the bumper. I debated what to do. The vehicle itself was fine, other than the rear glass panel but the camper was another matter.

I was equal distance from the campsite I'd just come from, and the Airbnb I had booked. Going to the Airbnb meant going up steep mountain roads whereas the previous campsite would be quicker, but on the motorway. I'd have to rent a cabin once there. I'd never been to Agerola and didn't know what the shop situation would be like, but I knew there was little choice to get decent food from the place I'd just come from, so I opted for the unknown and decided to at least try to get to the Airbnb.

I got the emergency tow rope I'd purchased and tied it as tight as I could around the camper box, as I had visions of the whole of the back ripping off as I drove up steep, winding mountain roads. I just hoped it would suffice, and that I wouldn't be stopped by the police.

I took it slowly, much to the annoyance of fellow road users, and miraculously managed to make it to the Airbnb about forty-five minutes later. Relieved that the back hadn't fallen off, I surveyed the damage more closely. The camper box door frame had shifted and the back area with the gas hob and storage section had completely broken and the whole of the end side had been smashed in. I prayed it was fixable.

What concerned me most of all, was the fact that my brain had completely blanked out on the pole in the middle of the road. I'd known my memory had become bad, but in the space of thirty seconds… to forget something so important! That was truly scary. I just hoped that with enough rest and the right nutrients, my brain would be restored to its previous level of function.

Remarkably, I found a campervan repair specialist called Romano Caravans, the other side of Napoli, about an hour away. I thought if anyone could fix it, they could. I sent them photos of the damage but they said they would need to see it and that it would cost a lot so it would be best if I did it through an insurance company.

I contacted my Spanish insurance company, Liberty Seguros and to their credit, they were wonderful. They allowed me to choose Romano Caravans to send it to. It was just a matter of waiting to find out if it was repairable.

Despite my concerns over my brain, and feeling like a complete muppet that I could have done something so incredibly stupid, I did also count my blessings. I didn't kill anyone and the dog was fine once I'd picked the glass lumps out of her coat. The van was drivable and I'd made it to the Airbnb and wasn't stuck in the area I hadn't liked around the last campsite. The concrete post stayed put and didn't take out anyone's power or telephone or whatever it was.

Wandering around Agerola I was very happy with my choice. It was a tiny town but vibrant. There was a small but well stocked organic food shop, a pet food shop, a nice selection of restaurants and coffee and clothes shops all within walking distance, which was just as well with how long I ended up stranded in Agerola.

And of course, there was one of the most spectacular walks right on my doorstep, the Path of the Gods. To add to my good fortune, I managed to negotiate a good monthly rate directly with my Airbnb host of €600 a month including electricity and wifi. The people who ran it for him spoke excellent English and also ran a nearby restaurant called The Crazy Burger. Hilariously, guess what the one food they didn't sell was? Burgers. Crazy as the name suggested!

I had Francesca staying just down the road. I was so incredibly grateful I'd followed my instincts and risked the mountain drive and hadn't picked the easier to drive to the campsite. So all in all, I'd really landed on my feet. I could not have picked a better place to become stranded if I'd tried!

Once again, if I'm completely truthful, I was rather pleased that I'd got a great excuse not to have to face an English winter, and I wasn't in the least bit bothered about my situation. There was no need, my mother was worrying constantly, so it didn't feel like the situation needed me to worry as well. That would have been unnecessary since I knew from our conversations she was on the job of worrying 24/7.

Every time we spoke she'd ask "What happens if they can't fix it? Then what will you do? How will you get back? It's not like you can fly with that great big dog of yours!" My response was always the same, "I'm sure it will all work out Mother, don't worry."

Getting a dog had been a bit of a bone of contention between us because she didn't want a dog in her house, and she was worried I'd return with it and there would be dog hair everywhere. As much as my parents love dogs, we've always had them, when their last one died they decided not to get another because they were travelling to Spain for long periods. Now, having got used to a nice clean house, the prospect of me returning dog in hand, had not gone down well. Not to mention the problem they were having with very inconsiderate neighbours.

My mother isn't a deep sleeper and the neighbours would let their dogs out at 6am every morning and leave them outside barking for an hour. Not ideal if you want to sleep. Despite asking them not to do it, they carried on regardless. The last thing my mother wanted was a dog in the house that might bark back. It was almost entertaining; now that I couldn't come back with the dog she didn't want in her house, she was spending so much time worrying about it.

## Sweet Time

Things in Spain always get done, but not usually with any great rush. Italy isn't far off Spain in that respect, getting things done in their own time.

The Spanish insurance company would only allow a certain agreed assessor to view the vehicle. It took a week to even get it collected. To my horror, they sent just a driver and not a flatbed vehicle to pick it up. I prayed the driver took it carefully and the back end didn't end up getting torn off on route.

It was early November 2020, I'm in Italy with a smashed up English vehicle, a Spanish insurance company, an Italian company fixing it and lockdown number two was just around the corner. Oh, and Christmas. Can you imagine the complications that caused? I'll spare you the full saga, but let's just say, it became very clear, very quickly, I wasn't going to be going anywhere any time soon...

# 6

# 2nd Lockdown, The Path Of The Gods

Francesca's father improved and was home from hospital. She would drive up to see me at weekends, and we'd do The Path of the Gods hike. It turned out she was going to need to find her father a care home to move into. She'd go everyday and cook for him and take him to medical appointments and to see his friends, but he clearly wasn't going to be able to cope on his own for the long term. She couldn't stay with him as he only had a tiny one bedroomed apartment.

It was going to take her a while to find somewhere for him, so she'd be staying on for the foreseeable. Her shared rental in Sorrento was coming to an end so I enquired with my landlord if he could do the same price for her per month, as I'd found out he owned the two apartments above the one I'd rented. He agreed and she moved in upstairs just before the second lockdown was declared.

As much as I enjoy spending time alone and even having the dog, I was forever grateful when Francesca moved in upstairs. Like me, she's a naturally cheerful person, no matter how bad things get, she always makes the best of it. That made spending time together easy. Unlike me, however, she is a bit of a fitness fanatic! Well, fanatic to someone who who hates exercise. In reality, she's just making sure she stays fit and strong.

Thirteen years older than me, her fitness levels put mine to shame. She and the dog would bounce up and down the mountains like they were nothing while I lumbered behind with heavy footsteps like someone ten times my weight. It was annoying to be lumbering quite so much because at this point, I was probably at the fittest I'd ever been since childhood. One of the reasons I got the dog was because I knew she'd keep me honest on exercise when I returned to the UK. I knew there'd be no way I'd go out regularly in UK weather unless I had to. I was definitely a fair-weather walker.

I enjoy my morning walks with my four-legged friend - it's a fantastic way to start the day. Where I'm not quite so good is the afternoon walk. Francesca was more expert at getting me out the door every afternoon than even the dog. And in all weathers. She told me on more than one occasion that there is no such thing as bad weather, only bad clothing. She went with me to the Outward Bound shop and made sure I was kitted out in the correct waterproofs after seeing my efforts one afternoon with bin bag waterproofs I'd made for myself and the dog! I'm still not convinced that there's no such thing as bad weather though.

Francesca was also keen to learn about crypto, so I got her wallet set up, and each morning we would study the markets, after having listened to Ivan on Good Morning Crypto. I didn't like not really understanding the technology, so I enrolled in his Crypto Programming Academy so I could at least understand what it was I was trading. I can't program my way out of a paper bag. I never intended to take it up. I did it purely for understanding. I am terminally curious about how things work.

At the time I did understand, though don't ask me to explain it now because I've forgotten more than I can remember. The world of crypto became more and more fascinating. I could see so much potential with it. It will revolutionise the world.

For example, imagine buying a house, and within the purchase is contained the legal agreement, the land registry, the searches etc. Every single thing you need to do is in the transaction itself. Crypto isn't just a means of exchange, it can also contain something called Smart Contracts. Just imagine how simple house buying would be. No solicitor involvement, the transaction contains everything.

If you were to sell music or art online, contained in the transaction and smart contract would be which end-user could listen to the track or use the image, thereby stopping illegal downloads and streaming.

Another example of a smart contract in action would be online betting companies doing automatic payouts to winners. The smart contract would have something called a consensus algorithm which would check five leading and trusted news outlets for the winner of a horse race and if they all agree or at least four out of five agree a certain horse won, then all the winners would be automatically paid. The possibilities are endless. It is incredible and exciting technology.

And what's more, I was doing very well out of it. Which is just as well with what happened next. After nearly two months, the loss assessor finally got to see my van, and just before Christmas wrote it off. The cost to repair it would have been at least fifteen thousand euros. Well, the camper part was written off, thankfully not the van itself. They paid me about five thousand euros and some of my accommodation costs and that was it, I was on my own.

## A Gamble Worth Taking?

The insurance company paid up quickly. I took a gamble and put 3K into crypto, Ethereum to be precise. Bitcoin had had a tremendous rally up to over twenty eight thousand dollars, but Ethereum hadn't done much yet. My studying at that time showed that Bitcoin goes first and then when it peaks, off go the Altcoins. The insurance payout timed it perfectly.

I had email exchanges with Romano Caravans to see if there was anything they could do that would cost less than fifteen thousand euros. They said I'd need to come in to speak to them. Francesca drove me there in her nippy little black Audi and did all the translating. They listed all the issues and complications of the repair and said that they guaranteed their workmanship, so it had to be done properly. I asked if they could just fix it up enough for me to make it back to England, with no guarantees?

It took Francesca a lot of persuading for them to agree. She explained that I'd no way of getting home with the dog without that campervan! Reluctantly, and to my great relief, they said they would try their best. They would be closed over Christmas and New Year and didn't know how much they'd be able to work if the threatened lockdown occurred.

## An Italian Christmas

For Christmas, Francesca had her father over for a few days. He was frail but in good spirits. He used to be the head chef at a hotel on the south coast of England, and Francesca is also a great cook, so I chipped in with supplying some of the food from the organic shop. They cooked it while I made a luxurious table centre from Abies fir and pine I'd collected on our walks, and decorated it with Christmas berries and sparkly decorations that I'd purchased with a big red candle in the town.

Every morning Francesca's father was there, I'd hear the television on the music channel, and opera would waft through the ceiling with him singing along. He had a great voice, thank goodness, because I could hear every word sung! I enjoyed it so much that once he'd gone back home, I purchased Classic FM's most popular collections.

Sure enough, after Christmas another lockdown was announced. Well, more restrictions on what we'd already got used to. With the first lockdown, the UK had got off lightly, this time it was the other way around - Christmas was cancelled. I was so grateful that I was in Italy with fairly decent weather, not as warm as Spain, but certainly a lot nicer than England.

Our days consisted of studying crypto intently in the mornings, then after lunch going for a mountain hike and then each evening we'd take it in turns cooking. The lockdown in Italy was nowhere near as savage as Spain had been. The only thing that affected us was not being able to eat out. It was takeaways only. Exercise was still permitted. And face coverings were required in public places. We chose to wear a buff instead of a mask. I had one round my neck because of the cold anyway so it wasn't a big deal to pull it up when in shops. Occasionally we got pushback for it with people demanding we wear masks but I'd just shrug and walk off.

Surgical masks tend to have a hole size of about 3 microns, the alleged virus was approximately 0.3 microns. So it would be about as effective as trying to stop a mosquito with a picket fence! It even said on the box they weren't effective against viruses.

On the natural house building course in Badolato, we had a German ex-surgical nurse with us. She quit over Covid, knowing full well it was rubbish, she was not prepared to go along with it all. She said in Germany the surgeons changed their masks every 20 minutes or so and additional oxygen was pumped into the operating theatre. Her face was a picture when she described how unhygienic and ridiculous it was for people to be wearing the same mask all day, every day.

## The White Stuff

The weather had certainly turned after Christmas, so much so, for a brief time there was snow. I was fairly certain my four legged friend had never seen snow, so we took the opportunity to take her up the highest peak above Agerola, Monte Catello. It was as high as Ben Nevis! It was an arduous trek, the dog loved it and so did we. Although there was a bit more cloud than we would have liked, by the time we made it to the peak it cleared just about enough for us to see Vesuvius in all its glory.

We had many amazing walks, especially on the Monte Tre Calli trail, and encounters with all sorts of animals. Agerola was a wonderful mix of a tourist town with its farming roots strongly evident. The hillside was littered with goats, and the clanging bells would echo through the surrounding areas.

A huge pig would wander up and down The Path of the Gods when it heard the goats returning with the farmer whistling and whooping them back to their enclosure, closely guarded and followed by large white dogs, who eyed my little one with suspicion. And so they should. My little friend is a mix of

Belgian Shepherd and Podenco, which is a Spanish hunting dog. She will chase absolutely anything that moves, given half a chance. I've even watched her chase a raindrop down a window... as a sighthound, if it moves, she's interested.

I had to keep a very close eye on her when out walking these mountain paths. They would be littered with donkeys, pigs, goats and the occasional horse. I soon knew, on the one occasion that she did manage to escape my watchful gaze. I could hear a tremendous commotion of bells all ringing and heading in the opposite direction. I knew instantly what the cause was, and prayed I could reach her before the farmer and his dogs did. She came back on my third bellow. She could tell by my tone of voice she'd better get back asap. Thankfully she's not great at hunting, trying to catch everything at once rather than moving in on one. It's the thrill of the chase she seems to enjoy. But even so, I didn't want to take risks, just in case she got lucky.

She was both, equal parts terrified and curious about the giant pig. She was chased by a donkey, who took an instant dislike to her, and she found the not-so-wild boar we encountered, equally terrifying. She was both curious and wary of the cows. Goats were by far her favourite. I suspect that this was an animal she had been used to chasing in Spain before I got her. I filmed many of her amusing encounters which can be seen on the 'Italian Job' video on the resources page of my website.

At that point, I'd only had Lena a few months, so with the restrictions and not being able to go anywhere, I decided we must concentrate on training her after the incident with the goats. My father had done a lot of dog training with a police dog handler he'd got to know, and I'd grown up with well-trained German Shepherds. However, since I'd never been the one responsible for the training, I purchased three online courses.

The first was hopeless. It was run by an irritating, soppy couple whose method revolved entirely around bribing the dog with treats. Lena has zero interest in dog biscuits when there's fresh meat running past her nose. The second course featured a trainer who used overly aggressive methods, which didn't suit Lena at all.

We began the new training every morning at the punto di vista, a large open deck viewing area at the top of Agerola. I wanted to teach Lena a command I'd seen my father use with our dogs: "DOWN." When bellowed, even if the dog was running at full pelt, they would immediately drop to the ground in the down position. Unfortunately, I made a pig's ear of it. I was too aggressive with my commands, and Lena kept thinking she'd done something wrong, becoming quite phobic about the word. Up until this point, I'd only trained her with commands like "sit," "stay," and "wait." In the end, I changed the command to "STOP" and taught her to apply the brakes whenever I yelled it.

Third time lucky, the next course I tried was from a company called Leerburg. The main trainer, Ed Frawley, had spent his life training German Shepherds for the police. His training focused on being a good pack leader and gaining the dog's complete respect. Rewards were given but not excessively, unlike the first course. It was an excellent course and made me immediately realise I'd been behaving more like Lena's servant than her master.

One key takeaway was that if you don't have good recall of your dog off-lead, they shouldn't be off the lead, as what you have is a potentially dangerous dog. Lena isn't aggressive and would never start a fight, but she also won't tolerate it if another dog starts one with her. From the training videos, I learned that as the pack leader, I had to prevent aggressive dogs from getting near her. Once I understood my role, to protect her, it made me more observant of how other dogs approached her.

One day, a large Rottweiler charged at us with its hackles up and slightly snarling. Without thinking, I immediately stepped in front of it, loudly made a "Shhst" sound, and told it to back off. Lena ducked behind me, taking herself out of the equation. The dog backed down and left us alone. For clarity, Leerburg doesn't suggest you hurl yourself in front of aggressive dogs. Their advice is more about avoiding bad situations in the first place, but in that instance, I chose to step in. If I hadn't acted immediately, Lena would have had to deal with the dog herself, and it might not have ended well given how it approached us. By stepping up as a proper pack leader, I de-escalated the situation and allowed her to hide behind me.

Knowing she's safe and that I'll always protect her changed the dynamic of our relationship dramatically. She went from being quite a little madame to being uber-respectful. Now, she always looks at me for permission before hopping on the sofa, rather than just jumping up. If, by some miracle, she catches a bunny, she brings it to me to inspect and waits for me to tell her if it's okay to eat. If I say no, she drops it and leaves it, albeit reluctantly, but she does as she's told. She's even been inches away from catching a Muntjac deer and has stopped mid-pursuit when I've yelled the "STOP" command. I was amazed, as I would have thought she was past the point of no return. I could never have achieved that level of obedience with dog biscuit bribery.

Simple things, like not allowing her to go through the door first and adhering to the pecking order where I go first as the pack leader, have made a world of difference. The "thou shall not chase cats" training was challenging, but we managed it. The only real fail is that I can't seem to stop her from snapping at bees and wasps. But for the big things, at least, she's pretty good.

Training her to this level took several months and wasn't something we mastered during our time in Italy. I never managed to get her to be completely calm around the horse in the field adjacent to our apartment, even though the horse appeared to adore her. It would come over whenever Lena was with me. Lena, however, was freaked out by the size of the horse and barked at it constantly. Thankfully, the horse was used to its owner's dogs and wasn't fazed by her barking. In fact, it would try to race her down the paddock as she ran along the footpath, emitting high-pitched, freaked-out barks. It's a shame she was so scared of it, as the horse genuinely seemed to want to be her friend.

## Basking on Beautiful Beaches

There were some intermittently warm days, so whenever one occurred, we either drove down to the beach in Francesca's car, or took a hike down. One day we walked to Positano and caught the bus back up to Agerola. As beautiful as it was, and as lucky as I felt, there was still a disconcerting edgy feeling in the background. It felt like the lull before the storm. I tried to stay present, enjoying the beautiful surroundings rather than focusing on possible negative outcomes. For now I was getting a reprieve, and I knew it was important to make the most of it.

No work had happened on my campervan with the lockdown, and nor would it until it ended. I still wasn't in any rush to get back, so again, I wasn't at all bothered by my forced incarceration. I'd been loving my time spent researching the exciting new world of crypto while I waited for the camper to be repaired, but that was about to come crashing to an end...

# 7

# End of the Love Affair?

**M**y love affair with crypto started to falter the more I understood its potential. It is all encompassing and will change the world as much as the internet did back in the day. It has enormous potential to be used for good, but equally, it could easily be used for bad.

The turning point came when I watched a webinar which focused on one of the blockchains I was most excited about. I'm not going to name it in case I've not remembered all the details correctly enough four years later.

This particular blockchain had a token which had made me feel really good about this particular crypto as their main focus was to help people in Africa, I know, I can already feel those of you who have been around the block a few times rolling your eyes, but back then I was still shedding my naivety. Anyway, this token was going to provide a form of banking to those who couldn't get a bank account and set them free to trade… or at least was my understanding at the time.

I hadn't done my due diligence on everything they had planned. The ladies, whose names I cannot remember, leading the webinar, had dug below the surface and discovered this blockchain technology was going to be tied into helping farmers, but also education.

The part I found most disturbing was the educational tools built in. They were planning on monitoring children's performance at school. That might sound innocent enough, but the webinar hosts said they'd discovered documentation that showed it was a bit more than monitoring.

Monitoring was a euphemism for deciding which children would be allowed to go into further education and employment. Basically, if the computer said no, that child would be put on the scrap heap and not allowed to go any further. A truly chilling thought. Particularly for me. As someone who was a bit of a late developer, suffering from dyslexia and finding school challenging for the early part until I adapted. If a computer had assessed my reading ability at junior school, I wouldn't have made it to senior school.

It was only when I changed schools that my dyslexia was diagnosed. My mother got me extra tuition and worked with me a lot herself, believing I was young enough to adapt and improve. The private school my parents opted for was academically a year ahead of most state schools. The school I'd just come from was a year behind most schools which meant I had to catch up two years' worth in one go.

My mother later told me that I used to come home from school each day as white as a sheet with a deer in the headlights expression on my face at the shock at what was now expected of my brain. But she knew I wasn't stupid, and she had every belief that I would be able to overcome it. Eventually, with a lot of effort, I did grow out of the worst of my dyslexia. Now it only shows up if I'm really tired. So I'm glad my mother followed her instincts and sent me to a school who pushed me hard.

The thought of a computer algorithm deciding the future of children made me feel sick to my stomach. It was doubly worse because I'd believed crypto to be the saviour, and a way out of the control of the system. And it still could be, but I'm doubtful on that.

We've been living in a debt-bubble for decades and it's getting worse by the day. It simply isn't sustainable. The bubble will have to burst one day. With fully controllable Central Bank Digital Currencies already created, which, no one in their right mind would go across to willingly. But if there's a complete financial collapse, and there's little choice, then it will be much easier to get people to accept a digital currency.

Many people mistakenly think that Central Bank Digital Currencies (CBDCs) are like Bitcoin. No, they are not. Bitcoin is decentralised, meaning no one person, or organisation, has control of it. Though there are enough wealthy people and organisations who can crash the price whenever they choose.

CBDCs are the evil brother of Bitcoin. Or perhaps I should say more evil brother of Bitcoin, as I have a sneaking suspicion Bitcoin was created to get people used to using completely digital money, not necessarily with the best intentions at heart. But anyway, CBDCs are fully controlled by the Central Bank, as the name suggests. They can stop you transacting in real-time if an algorithm decides you shouldn't be purchasing what you're trying to purchase.

CBDCs are truly Big Brother technology. Or at least they will be when tied into a digital ID and carbon credits. They can also be set to expire. So if you don't spend them within a time frame, the Government decide, then they expire, poof! They're gone. Saving money will be a thing of the past if this system is brought in.

It's unlikely to be like that at the beginning of course. No, it will be introduced as a direct replacement or perhaps alongside existing currency to make sure everyone adopts it and is comfortable with it. Then over time they will start to implement the other aspects.

As soon as Central Bank Digital Currencies are here with their full control over what you purchase, they could make it impossible to trade in crypto coins that aren't state approved. You may well have Bitcoin or privacy coins like Monero, but if no one accepts them, and you can't trade them or cash them in, what use are they?

If everyone adopts them, then fine, no problem, but will people who have just been through a financial crash be ready to adopt en masse something the government doesn't want them to have, or will they do as they are told and adopt the new CBDC coin which promises to replace what they lost in the crash?

If every person on the planet cashed in all their savings and brought Monero, or one of the other privacy coins ahead of a complete collapse, then it would be game on, but after the event, I don't think that's likely, especially if what's in the bank is of no value.

I was torn for a few months. I loved the exciting crypto world, but at the same time could see the level of control it could be used for. I dumped the token they'd talked about in the webinar immediately, but the rest took me some time and I paid for that delay. I decided I would sell most of my crypto in May because it wasn't feeling good. And if I'd learned one thing over the past year it was to listen if something doesn't feel right.

Decision made, I'd sell the bulk, middle of May and walk away That would maximise my profits and be exactly a year after I'd got into it. The week before I'd planned to sell, dear Elon Musk made an announcement that he'd changed his mind about Bitcoin and the whole market came crashing down as Bitcoin went from 56k to 36k.

I got out about halfway through the drop, hoping it would pick back up. I took my initial investment out, and then the profit, and left a bit in as a hedge. I've been very grateful for that little bit left in, as it helped me out of a financially difficult time which was to come a few years later when I took up campaigning against some of the things local councils in the UK are doing. I became so consumed by that new mission, and starting Council Watch, that I took two years away from my business doing it.

Not many businesses survive with virtually no input for two years, even automated ones. If I hadn't have had the crypto to fall back on, things would have got very difficult indeed. But anyway, I'm jumping ahead. We'll get to Council Watch and all that involved in due course.

There are a lot of good crypto projects out there. I know a developer in some of them, and if everything he's told me gets off the ground, then blockchain could be very instrumental in a pushback against the powers-that-shouldn't-be. I'm sworn to secrecy on his projects, so I won't divulge them until I have permission.

I'm glad I still have some crypto for emergencies, and that I've gained the knowledge about how to use it. I wouldn't rule out using it in the future, if the tide turns that way and cash is completely abolished and I have no choice.

So I'm not entirely against it, and I own the fact I had an emotional response to a few bad apples and have thrown the baby out with the bath water as a result. It's a bit like finding out the lead actor of your favourite film is a paedophile. It puts you off the entire movie, even if the rest of the cast and crew are fine.

There was another reason though. I'd started listening to Crrow 777 podcasts. Yes there are two r's in Crrow. And although I've lost touch with listening in the last few years - note to self, start listening again - I found the topics he covered fascinating. A wide-ranging selection of guests talking about metaphysical things and many conversations regarding real world and virtual world.

Listening to his illuminating guests made me tune into nature more consciously and I enjoyed the conversations they had over the digital, artificial world we're being sucked further and further into, taking us away from who we really are and our connectedness to all that is and from this incredible world.

Those podcasts spoke to my heart in ways I can't begin to put into words. My love of crypto was a head love, it wasn't a heart love. I feel very strongly that the more time we spend in the artificial world, and not the natural one, the more bent out of shape we become. The easier to manipulate, too. We lose touch with ourselves. Constantly bombarded with other people's views, beliefs and opinions.

The irony of me earning my living and communicating with people nearly all the time in a virtual and digital way, wasn't lost on me, or the podcast hosts. It is a convenient and effective way of reaching people. It is a tool of the age we live in.

Moving away from crypto was as much as to say no to the unnatural world and state of being that's being thrown at us, as I was feeling an intense need to be more in tune with the natural world. I had, in fact, ever since the first lockdown.

The feeling had intensified in Badolato on the weekend walks that the host organised for us. Walking through the chestnut woods (one of my favourite trees) had connected me to the natural world in a way I'd not experienced before. Quite a surprise, considering all the years I'd spent landscaping people's gardens. But woods are different. The energy is different, the air, the sensations that are difficult to put into words.

I found myself with a deep yearning to live surrounded by trees. My fantasies of building my own cob home weren't quite so strong now that I knew just how much hard work it was, but the essence of really being in nature was embedded in my consciousness now I'd realised its importance.

I do make sure I get as much balance as I can away from the artificial world. Being stranded in one of the most beautiful places I've ever been, with South Africa being my number one and Hawaii number two, The Path of the Gods with the stunning mountains behind it and azure blue sea, was a close runner up.

The people were so in touch with where their food came from. Every single garden I looked into was full of vegetables or had the ground prepared ready to plant them. When the Crazy Burger restaurant owner asked what I did for a living and I told him "teaching garden design", he replied "Ah you must know a lot about vegetables then!". I realised, probably not as much as I should, and decided I had better put that right, both for me and my customers.

I decided to create a free course which people would get with every garden design course purchased, called the Food Garden Formula. I wanted to encourage people to grow food in their gardens. What puts a lot of people off is they think it will look a mess, so the course focused on how to incorporate vegetables in an aesthetically pleasing way.

It was my gentle way of encouraging folks without yelling like a conspiracy nutter, 'I'm pretty certain there's going to be food shortages, grow some food'. Though I think I did do a few emails and videos encouraging people that it would be a good idea just in case things got worse. I made the course, and added it in to my offerings, as well as giving it to all my existing customers.

Whilst I was content with my time spent in Agerola, there was always the background discomfort of what was happening in the world. I felt like I was getting a reprieve, but I knew I couldn't stay there forever, as tempting as it was.

In February, I received an email from Romano Caravans. They said the camper had been repaired as best they could. They were just waiting for someone to come and replace the broken back windscreen of the cab. They wouldn't send photos as they said they would show me when I came to collect it. That sounded a little ominous, but I knew however bad it was, it would be better than if I'd tried to do it myself, which had been Plan C if all else failed.

It took another week for the glass to be replaced, but finally, I could go and get the van and then go, where exactly? I'd managed to fall out with my family to the degree we'd not spoken in over six weeks, something that had never happened before as we were normally a close family. And even if upset with one another we'd always talk, but not this time.

Had I lost my family? If I had, what was I going to do next, where would I go?

# 8

# End of Family?

Prior to Covid, I would not have described myself as anti-vaccine. I didn't have a particularly strong view on them other than I'd been warned by a homeopath in my early twenties not to take unnecessary vaccines, like flu shots. The homeopath said to be careful because of all the other ingredients in them like mercury, which is toxic. So I would say I was vaccine cautious and after several years of ill health with M.E., a very debilitating illness which leaves you chronically exhausted all the time. I vowed only to have necessary ones if I travelled to far flung places that required them.

By the time I'd done all the research into the mRNA vaccines, I was definitely anti that one. And by the time I'd finished reading the 'What Really Makes You Ill' book, and discovered the dubious history of their introduction by someone with a fake medical certificate, and learning that the first anti-vaxxers were the qualified doctors in the late 1600s, who were aghast at the fake doctor's quackery, I soon became very anti-vaccine.

So I was horrified when in a phone call my mother informed me that both she and my father were going to get the Covid shot. After everything I'd told her that I'd discovered, I couldn't believe my ears. My mother said she didn't want to risk getting Long Covid, and that was why. She said there was no way she'd get the mRNA as she'd read all about it and didn't like the sound of that. But she'd seen a documentary on the BBC about Astrazeneca, and what nice people they were. A wonderful team working day and night to save everyone.

I tried to dissuade her by explaining that I was sure none of them were a good idea. After all, they were missing 8 years of safety testing, but she was adamant it was better than getting Long Covid. The mainstream media had done an excellent job of terrifying them over it. I tried, over several phone calls, to get them to reconsider these experimental shots, but nothing I said got through.

I then sent a series of emails laying out things I'd read in the What Really Makes You Ill book, in the hope that reading how vaccines came about might help shift their perspective. The email conversation ended abruptly with my parents no longer replying to any of my emails. They'd made it clear on the phone they simply didn't believe anything bad would be rolled out to the public, and all would be well. They thought I'd lost my mind talking about pedophiles everywhere, and everything else I spewed out, completely unfiltered every time they dared phone me.

I can well understand why they thought I'd lost my mind. The things I was telling them were so far removed from the world we all thought we knew. I wouldn't have believed me either had I been in their shoes, and had I not spent months researching it all. My behaviour was strange and concerning for them. No longer trusting the government, or any medical organisations, I even changed my email address away from Google and removed myself from the system as much as possible. Getting involved so heavily in crypto and telling them to stock up with food and provisions, I must have seemed exceptionally paranoid. And certainly not someone to take medical advice from.

I was in such a deep state of shock with everything I'd read, I found myself blurting it all out every time we spoke, unable to put a discerning filter on it. I'd never been one for conspiracy theories. I'd never even come into contact with anyone who spouted such things… well, unless you count the mad Rastafarian.

## Traumatising Texan Taxicab

In March 2011, I went to the SXSW bloggers conference in Austin, Texas, with some of my classmates from an online Teacher Training course I'd completed the year before. I'd flown into Houston and planned to stay in a hotel next to the bus stop for Austin, where I was catching a coach the following day.

When I came out of the airport, I got into the taxi assigned to me. There was immediately something about the driver that concerned me, his body language was off. I can't quite describe how or in what way, but I just felt uncomfortable. As it turned out, my instincts were spot on. We hadn't even made it out of the airport before he started ranting about President Obama, calling him the Anti-Christ.

Back in those days, I hadn't yet learned the art of traveling light with only hand luggage. Had it not been for my suitcase in the trunk of his taxi, I would have gotten out before we pulled onto the main road. As we waited in the queue to exit Houston airport, my Rastafarian taxi driver began telling me that nearly all the Presidents of the United States, including recent ones like Bush, Clinton, and Obama, were related if you traced their family trees far enough. He claimed they were controlled by people from evil bloodlines that ran the world and viewed us "normal folk" as vermin. According to him, certain lineages were bred for the role of President and did as they were told. The entire system, he said, was rigged to give the illusion of democracy. It didn't matter which one got in; they would follow orders.

Please, someone tell me, what on earth are you meant to say in situations like these? Nothing in my very limited conversational skillset had prepared me for this, especially not after a ten-hour flight and an hour-long queue to get through customs! The best I managed was a very ill-advised, "So, you're not a fan of President Obama then! I thought everyone liked him…"

I'd had the foresight to print off a map of the route from the airport to the hotel. To my horror, I noticed he'd driven past the freeway exit we needed. I interrupted his rant about how evil he thought President Obama was to point this out. He told me not to worry and that he'd take the next exit and turn around. The next exit, however, was snarled up with traffic, and we sat there for ages.

By this time, he'd thankfully changed topics. Now he was ranting about how many people had become millionaires because of the ideas he'd given them while sitting in his cab. He even declared himself a "millionaire maker." I really didn't know what to say, especially when he moved on to how evil he thought gay people were. He claimed that, as God was his witness, if a gay person touched him, it literally burned his skin. That particular rant went on for quite some time. This guy wasn't just mad, he was completely unhinged!

I was very relieved when we eventually made it to the hotel. I had been beginning to wonder if I'd make it out of his cab alive. I knew I'd been ripped off on the cab fare, but frankly, I didn't care at that point and paid him the money. He did reduce it slightly because of his mistake, but the whole episode was completely bizarre.

I'm a big believer in things happening for a reason, but at the time, I really couldn't fathom what that one had been about. Partway through my endless research, that conversation suddenly came back to me with a shudder. It appeared that some of the things he told me may not have been quite as nuts as they sounded back then. I'll leave it to you to do your own investigations as to which bits of his crazy talk might be on the money.

But anyway, after that experience, I knew how crazy I was probably sounding to my parents, but nonetheless, I was surprised that they did not reply to my evidence-based emails. That wasn't like them at all. I'd said and done everything I could, but I'd felt like I'd been kicked in the heart when they said they were going to get the Astrazeneca jab. I knew with every fibre of my being that it wasn't a good idea. Had I been in the country I think I would have had a better chance of convincing them, but I had no way to get to them. I had a very ominous feeling and prayed they'd be OK and that they would be one of the lucky ones who received a saline placebo shot. I'd read that some of the vaccines were saline to test alongside the real ones. I prayed there was truth to that.

I presumed they were OK because I kept getting weekly updates from Dropbox that our shared spreadsheet had been updated. They knew I was alive and well because of all the mountain climbing photos I was putting on Facebook. I'd given Facebook another go hoping that if people saw I was still living life, it might make them snap out of their fear.

In hindsight, I should have just phoned, but as our last call hadn't been great, I decided to let the dust settle. And settle it did, for nearly two months, the longest amount of time we've ever not spoken. I eventually received a phone call from my father, telling me he wasn't in good shape and asking when would I be coming home?

But that's jumping ahead somewhat. I ought to finish telling you about my last couple of weeks in Italy first...

## The Wacky Wreck

The day finally came for me to go and pick up the van. Francesca drove me and the dog to Romano Caravans. I was feeling quite nervous. Would it be OK and what was the bill likely to be?

The owner met us with a warm smile and had his colleague, who spoke a little English, escort us to the van. He was also smiling and there was a glint in his eyes. When I walked around the back of the van I couldn't believe my eyes. They'd done an incredible job of fixing it! They'd managed to get all the metal shell bent back perfectly into place and only the scratch on the paintwork was a giveaway there'd ever been a collision.

But how did it look inside? Not quite as good, there was evidence of the worktop breaking and they'd replaced it with wood of a different colour, but other than that it was an amazing repair. The bill came to about €1500. A tenth of the price they'd originally quoted.

They said they had been quite surprised to be able to repair it this well. Lots of smiles all round. The dog was happy to see her van again too. I paid the bill and we left. It felt weird driving again after nearly four months of being vehicle-less. It was quite a relief when we made it back to Agerola an hour later. I was scared I'd prang it again as driving felt so strange.

The following day Francesca and I walked to the next town as they had a shop like a mini Halfords which was stocked with everything car related you could think of. I purchased some reflective vehicle tape to cover all the scratches from the accident, along with some black Hammerite paint for the van chassis, which had chipped in places. I also purchased a new tyre pump as my old one had broken in Badolato when we'd tried to use it on a deflated tractor tyre.

I gave the van a good clean. There were still shards of glass in all the nooks and crannies in the back and under the seats. I painted the parts of the chassis that showed, and managed to make Wacky Races/ Harriet the Chariot look almost as good as new. I'd emptied the contents of the van into the apartment before they took it away, so everything had to be loaded back in again. That took a surprising amount of time. It's quite an art loading it so everything fits in the tiny storage compartments.

The other thing I needed to do was really clean the apartment. I knew the owner was concerned over the state of it because he kept suggesting every month that I was extending my stay that I might want to get the cleaners in. I didn't as I knew it was pointless. Living with a dog and going on long walks in all weathers meant no sooner had I cleaned then muddy paw prints appeared again.

I thoroughly blitzed it so the cleaner wouldn't have to deal with four months of built up grime in the places where the mop didn't go. I pulled out every piece of furniture and made sure I left it spotless so all the cleaner had to do was change the sheets.

I made a video and sent it to the landlord. I didn't want him to regret allowing someone with a dog to stay or he might ban them for future guests. I also knew he'd given me a good deal on the rent. And besides, I prefer to leave things as good, if not better than I find them. I'd left him with a couple of extra Pyrex dishes for the oven, and a few other useful kitchen items. He phoned me upon seeing the video and I could tell he was relieved I'd left the apartment in good condition.

I'd decided to return to Spain for a bit. I still couldn't face the thought of England in March, as they'd had horrible weather all winter. And as things didn't feel great with my family, the next best thing was my second home in Spain, as that's where all my friends were. I knew my parents were not happy with the thought of a dog in their Spanish house, so I'd arranged to stay with my friend Suzanne. She'd returned from Sweden after she'd fled the Spanish lockdown when things had become unbearable.

I decided to take the ferry from Rome to Barcelona as it would save me a lot of driving, and it would also work out cheaper. There were still a lot of travel restrictions, so I had a friend in Portugal write a letter to say I was en route to help at her farmstead. In theory, they wouldn't stop anyone passing through with a legitimate reason.

Francesca was staying on one week longer as she had nearly sorted out her father's care home.

There was a lovely facility with beautiful grounds and his own room that was state sponsored. It was perfect for him and they'd agreed to take him.

I'd suggested she come to Spain as she had nothing else planned. I could easily find her work with everyone I knew and could give her glowing references. She is the best masseuse I've ever had work on me. She managed to sort out my badly hurt shoulder. She is also a yoga teacher, so I was fairly sure she'd find something, especially with all the walking groups I had joined. If there's ever a group of people who could do with a good massage, it's mountain walkers. I wanted to do something nice for Francesca because if it hadn't been for her help translating and driving me to Romano Caravans, I wouldn't have got the van fixed.

While queueing to get on the ferry, I decided to bite the bullet and email my parents. It had been nearly two months now and it was getting ridiculous that we had not been talking. I told them I was about to head back to Spain. There were a few bits and pieces I would be picking up from the house and was there anything they needed me to do while I was there?

I knew my mother had been worried about the house with no one living there all winter. If anything would get them communicating again, it would be that. But as it turned out I was wrong. Even that email was ignored.

Getting the dog onto the boat turned out to be a bit of a palaver. I'd discovered in Italy that she is terrified of heights. When Francesca moved from the

1st storey flat up to the 2nd storey one, upon request of the landlord, I could not get her out on the tiny balcony. As soon as she looked over the edge through the railings, her little legs started to shake and she backed away into the living room refusing to come out.

Bear in mind that this is the same dog who had no trouble whatsoever ridge walking on a mountain the same height as Ben Nevis. But when it came to man-made heights, it was a very firm, no. It was clear she'd broken her front leg quite badly before I'd got her, so I wondered if it was from coming off a man-made height of some description.

Anyway, as soon as we were on the boat I discovered that her fear of heights wasn't just balconies but see-through stairs as well. She absolutely refused to budge. Now, whilst I might have been able to carry her up one flight, there was no way I was going to manage five or six flights, especially with our overnight bags slung over my shoulder.

Some crew approached asking if they could help. I could see they thought about picking her up but decided better of it. And in truth I didn't know how she'd respond with two strangers picking her up when terrified. Thankfully there was another way to get us up to the pet deck. We walked up all of the vehicle ramps until we came to a lift. Thankfully she was fine in the lift.

I took her out on deck, but the height of the boat and the movement brought back the shaky legs. She really did not like being on a boat. I decided that as there was no one about, I would go for a walk and go up and down the stairs and see if she followed. Would her fear of heights be worse than her fear of being left?

No. The fear of being left behind won and she reluctantly followed me up and down the open tread stairs. Having been successful a few times, she stopped shaking and now became interested in all the doggy smells onboard. That was a relief, as I needed her to be OK since we were going to be on this thing for the next twenty one hours.

When it came time to go to sleep she still wasn't happy. I tried putting her bed on the floor but she wouldn't settle. I then tried putting it on the tiny bunk opposite mine as she does like her comforts. Still no. She made it very clear there was only one place she felt safe. Yes, you guessed it, in my bunk! The bunks were the width that was suitable for a ten year old child. It was not suitable for a fully grown adult and a reasonable size dog.

The reasonable sized dog however had other ideas. She was going to make herself fit, whether I liked it or not. In order to accommodate her, I ended up lying on my side in a pencil-like fashion with my back pressed up against the faux-wood panelled wall. She hopped up and wrapped herself in the tightest ball possible and went to sleep in my arms. I presumed at some point in the night she'd settle on the floor or something.

Again, no. When I woke in the morning she was still in my arms, but no longer in a tight little ball. Instead, she'd managed to stretch herself out into a long sausage and had made herself very comfortable with her head on the pillow next to mine! When I got up to go to the bathroom, on my return, I found her sprawled out taking up the entire bunk, her head still on my pillow.

Getting her off the boat was even more of a trial than getting her on it. Her fear of steps and heights issue was still there. All the training I'd done the day before getting her comfortable with the stairs was forgotten and now I couldn't get her off the boat. We were already running late as I'd missed the call to leave the boat. I couldn't find the lift, and she point blank would not do the stairs. My mistake had been training her outside. The internal fear of the steps had not been conquered.

It wasn't long before I could hear my name being called over the tannoy. Would Mathews urgently return to their vehicle as they were now boarding incoming vehicles. Yes, I'd love to return to my vehicle if I could just get the damn dog down the stairs. Eventually a member of staff found us and led us down the pedestrian gangway. It still had stairs but the first part didn't and I managed to get enough momentum to keep her moving and eventually off the boat.

The car deck crew were not happy with me. They'd started to load around where I'd parked but it was hugely inconvenient for them and causing a lot of problems. I apologised and pointed at the dog. They'd seen the trouble I'd had getting her up there, but even so they were not impressed. I just prayed the van would start and the locking steering wheel issue didn't make an unwelcome return, or I'd end up back in Rome.

Thankfully it started, and we managed to get ourselves off, much to the relief of everyone. Then came the part I was dreading, clearing customs. I knew the dog would be alright because she has a Spanish passport. I wasn't so sure I'd be welcome with the restrictions. The police didn't seem overly concerned, I think they just wanted to be finished for the evening, but there was a heart-stopping moment when they closely examined all the paperwork. I had, more or less, the correct documents, probably best not to go into the details of the part that might not have been ideal. All appeared to be in order, and they let me through.

Phew, onwards. Now just a small matter of making it out of Barcelona during late night rush-hour and to the campsite I'd chosen on the outskirts. I don't love night time driving, so I came off at the first mall I could see from the motorway to grab a bite to eat. By the time I'd finished eating, the traffic had calmed enough to make it slightly less nerve-wracking.

We arrived at the campsite so late that no one was there. Luckily for us, the main gate was open, which is unusual for campsites. We parked up and got a good night's sleep. Up bright and early I took Madame to the beach for a runaround. As soon as she was on the soft sandy beach in the early morning sunshine (something we'd not seen that much of in our last few days in Italy), she literally bounced with joy. I think she realised she was home, in Spain.

We had breakfast and I packed everything away ready to leave. It was well after 9am by now but still not a sign of any members of staff. In the end, keen to get on the road, I shoved ten euros under the reception office door and left.

Still no response to my email from my parents. I really didn't know what to make of it. It was so out of character. Even if they thought I'd lost the plot, not speaking to me for two months did feel odd. Ironically, they'd always believed in me in the times I didn't, and now I believed fully in myself, they didn't. Or at least that's the conclusion I came to, until the phone call with my father the following day.

When the phone call came, I could hear immediately something was wrong. His voice sounded frailer than I'd ever heard it. My heart sank as soon as he said he was in a bad way. My mind immediately leapt to heart issues from the jab. Reports had already started to circulate on alternative social media platforms about the number of people either dropping dead or having a heart attack.

"What's wrong?" I asked, not entirely wanting to hear the answer.

"It's my knee. I've buggered my knee falling off a scaffold plank when I was trying to load a skip with soil I'd dug out. I'm going to have to have a knee replacement."

He'd had issues with his knees for years, so it was almost a relief it was 'only' that. Little did I know how awful his knee surgery was going to be.

He continued with, "Are you still in Italy? Will they ever get your van fixed?"

"No, I've just returned to Spain. Didn't you get my email? I sent it as I boarded the boat asking if you want me to check on the house when I'm in the area?"

"No, we've not had any emails from you for months. We thought you weren't talking to us."

"What do you mean? I've sent you loads of emails! Check the junk filter, see if they are in there." I instructed. My father did so.

"Yes, I can see one from you from a couple of days ago."

"See if you can find the rest."

"I'll have a look later. When will you be coming home? Your mother is worrying about this operation."

"When is it?"

"Probably end of July."

"OK, I'll be back by then, don't worry."

"Good. I'll tell your mother when she gets back from the hairdresser."

"So do you want me to do anything at the house? I've got to go there to get some things."

"Check everything is OK, that would be good."

We finished the call shortly after. My head was spinning. Why had Apple suddenly decided an email address from someone with the same surname was junk in the middle of a conversation? An email address they'd been responding to for ten months. And of all the conversations. All my efforts to inform my parents about what I'd learned about vaccines hadn't been seen.

I immediately thought back to the London riots a few years ago. I'd been living in Cambridge at the time, and my mother had emailed me with the subject line 'London riots'. I never received the email, or her follow up, asking if I'd received her email about the riots.

She was absolutely convinced Apple had censored her emails because of the mention of the riots. At the time I told her not to be so ridiculous, of course they wouldn't censor her emails…

A short while later I received another phone call. This time from my mother. I had a feeling it might be a harder conversation than the one I'd just had with my father…

# 9

# Magical Memory Mushrooms?

"We've found all your emails. It's just like that time there were those riots in London. I told you they were censoring my emails. You never believed me did you!" my mother said.

I replied, "I'd just been thinking exactly the same thing."

"You could have phoned, you know."

"Yes, and so could you!"

"How's your van?"

"They've done an amazing job on it, apart from a few minor things, it's almost as good as new."

"Thank goodness for that. I've had sleepless nights worrying about how you'd ever get home if they couldn't fix it."

Needless to say, I hadn't had a single sleepless night over it, and I was the one who was stranded for the second lockdown on the trot. But then I had complete faith it would all work out in the end.

I told my mother of my plans to stay with Suzanne, and that Francesca was coming to Spain and we'd find somewhere to rent for a bit as more travel restrictions were coming by the sound of things.

"Well you could always stay at the house as long as that dog of yours doesn't do any damage."

"She's house trained and hasn't done any damage at all in any of the places we've lived in over the last year!"

So it was settled, we'd all have somewhere to live and we'd take care of the house and very overgrown garden so that everything was sorted for whenever they next came out.

Francesca made it over the following week by the skin of her teeth, the day before the increased travel restrictions would have made it impossible. I got Lena to a good vet to have a health check.

Staying at my parents house meant I'd got access to their little Skoda Fabia car, which meant I could get the van serviced at the local Ford Garage without it causing me difficulties. My parents place was in a marina, and there weren't many shops open at the best of times, and certainly virtually nothing in a lockdown.

The Ford garage said they wouldn't be able to repair the airbag. It had to be done at the main dealership in Granada. Travel was restricted by province, and whilst we weren't allowed to go to Nerja or Malaga, I could at least go to Granada. Nothing in Spain happens quickly, so I thought I ought to deal with it immediately, judging by how long it had taken to get the new airbag not fitted in Italy.

I wasn't overly optimistic with an English vehicle. When I'd first purchased the van, the mechanic who gave it the once over prior to purchase, discovered the air conditioning didn't work, so I was able to get the price reduced. He'd taken it to a specialist garage to fix, but they weren't able to because vehicles in Spain have bigger hose connections than in the UK, where powerful aircon is rarely needed.

So when they ordered the parts in Spain, they didn't fit on the unit. They had to order them from the UK, and it took over seven weeks, and a lot of phone calls trying to find out what the problem was, and when it would be fixed. I had been on a deadline because the house building course was starting the first week of September.

Bearing in mind I had purchased the van in June, it wasn't actually ready until the last week of August with all the coming and goings to the camper refurbisher and various mechanics. It was a complete nightmare. The friend who spoke Spanish, who was helping me with the phone calls, had been at the end of her tether by the time I finally did get on the road. Without her help, who knows if I ever would have made it to Italy in time.

She drove me to Malaga to collect it from the air conditioning garage and take it to the mechanic, who'd been sorting out the other things, like connecting the auxiliary battery and getting the sink unit working. I had to wait half a day, but eventually he more or less got everything working. Though he did manage to wreck the fridge in his tampering with the electrics. I was past caring at that point. I just needed to get it back to my parents place so I could fit it out, and then get going. So much for my gentle amble from southern Spain to southern Italy.

I emailed the main Ford dealership in Granada and they requested I bring the van in for them to look at. The documentation wasn't sufficient for them to order the part, apparently. I duly did so, and was told they'd have the part in a couple of weeks time. That sounded a bit too good to be true after Italy.

The new airbag took about three weeks, and my Spanish speaking friend came with me (she'd clearly not learnt from the previous time the van needed fixing). Heavily pregnant, she didn't do well with the bouncy suspension on the van's ridiculously 'pimped up' giant wheels, so I reduced speed to 40mph and she recovered. We more or less made it to the garage at the allotted time. They changed the airbag while we went for a coffee.

On returning they said they'd discovered something else was wrong and that it would need to be replaced. This wasn't to be covered by the recall. Ah-ha so that's what had happened the first time. I did tell them there was another issue, and gave them the details of the Italian garage to find out what it was, but they hadn't.

Because this other part was broken, they couldn't replace the airbag, but at least this time they took it out as it was very dangerous to be driving with it in place. Yes, I know! A week later I went back again, this time with Francesca and they at last repaired it, costing about 135 Euros. To this day I've no idea what the other thing was as no one had enough Spanglish to describe, or understand, what was being said about this mystery part. At least it was third time lucky with finally sorting out the airbag. Wacky Races/ Harriet the Chariot was roadworthy again. It had only taken seven months.

I took Francesca to the walking groups I'd joined, and introduced her to all my friends in the area, so she was able to get a few massage clients. When we weren't working, we were walking. April and May are my favourite months in Spain. The mountains are covered with flowers, and it's warm, but not so hot that walking is hard work.

We did two particularly spectacular walks. The first was around the Tibetan O Sel Ling Centre on the southern face of the Sierra Nevada Alpujarra mountains, near Granada. It was quite a cloudy day on the coast, but by the time we made it to the centre, which is situated at 1600m, we were above the clouds and could see them sitting like a cotton wool blanket with the Alpujarra mountains poking out at the top. It was absolutely stunning and, as you'd imagine, peaceful.

Our second spectacular walk was with my friend in Otivar. The Hidden Valley walk near Lentegi had everything. The hillsides were covered in lavenders, rock roses, and rosemary bushes. There was a waterfall and rock pools, spectacular views and wooded areas. I've put a video on the Resources page, but it doesn't do the area justice.

## Limbo Land

The world felt like it was in limbo, restrictions coming and going and then back again. With the rules constantly changing, it was hard to keep up with them. I kept busy with work and sorting out the niggles in the van. An electrician came out to the house when the washing machine plug caught fire, so I got him to check out the malfunctioning fridge in the camper. It occurred to me that it might just be a blown fuse from when the mechanic had been tinkering with the electrics. Turned out I was right. The electrician fixed it and also moved the 'on' button for the sink pump off the work top to down under the sink, which was a much better location.

I gave the pine cladding and units inside the camper a white wash using chalk paint, which made it look much more stylish and brighter than the plain pine. I varnished the worktop and table as the walnut oil wasn't doing a good enough job. I also addressed some rust under the vehicle and put Hammerite on the under parts of the chassis.

My memory still didn't feel back to where it was pre-Italy, so I started to look into what I could do to help it along.

It was around mid-April that I decided to do a microdosing experiment. I'd never normally been one for taking drugs. I'd not even had a puff on a cigarette. In Badolato on our farewell evening down at the beach, I'd had a puff on a joint, but it didn't do anything other than make me feel a touch nauseous, so I didn't do it the next time it came past. That one puff was the sum total of my drug use.

Microdosing Psilocybin was something a friend had told me about. I thought I'd give it a go as it might help my brain function. In Spain microdosing is legal. I ordered from a Dutch company called Earth Resonance, which my friend had recommended, and I ordered the micro-scale as well as it's really important to get the right dose. I'd also read that Lion's Mane is good to take with it as it is believed to work synergistically and to enhance cognitive function.

I kept a microdosing diary. I'll share some of the more interesting entries. I started out with a third of the recommended dose as I knew I'm sensitive to substances. The idea is to take fourteen doses over a thirty day period.

### Microdosing Diary Highlights

DAY 1 Sunday 18th April 2021

Dose 0.21gm in a strawberry & Nispero smoothie with a touch of ginger

After a few minutes of closing my eyes I could feel the top of my head opening up and it felt as if I was wearing a small hat.

Then my jaw felt like the muscles were moving round in circles, trying to undo the tension. Then my focus went into my upper back - it was like my awareness was going to different parts of my body.

Then my feet felt very grounded and I had very heavy ankles. I was deeply relaxed, and it was similar to alcohol, but without being drunk! Slept well.

### DOSE 3

Thursday 22nd - 0.32gm in a smoothie.

Completely zonked me out within a few minutes, I was lucid dreaming in the deckchair and felt very relaxed! I could override the sleepy feeling and go back to work, but it took some doing, so I'm going to try the next dose in the evening and see how that feels, should help with sleep!

### DOSE 9

Tuesday 4th May - 0.56 gm in ginger tea

Really lovely dose - I was feeling a bit stressed out and not really in the mood for taking any but so glad I did. Took the dog down to the beach and sat and watched the waves sitting on a large warm rock - immediately relaxed and energy centres in my hands and head opened up. Deep yawning and feeling joyful despite being a slightly challenging day!

I will up the dose to 0.60gm next time, but I think 0.56gm is a really good one for me.

## DOSE 13

Wednesday 12th May 0.70 gm in ginger tea

Forgot to take it in the day, so had it just before bed - felt nice and relaxed and the usual hand centres flowing with lots of energy. I could still feel the effects when I woke up, feeling very chilled - the higher doses just seem to last longer in my body rather than causing me to trip, may try a big dose at the weekend...!

It was a very enjoyable experience. Because I'd taken such incredibly tiny doses, I had a lot left over from my month of every other day dosing, so I thought I'd try and experiment with a bigger dose and see what happened. I was considering going on an Ayahuasca retreat in the mountains that my friend, who had told me about the microdosing, had been on. She'd not been sick, and had raved about the experience. Francesca was doing a Workaway at the retreat, and I'd gone with her to the interview to see what the place and the people were like.

I did have quite a few reservations about Ayahuasca. Firstly, not a big fan of throwing up, but then who is! I knew I'd cope with me doing it, just wasn't sure I wanted to be in a teepee jam-packed with other people doing so. Also, the ceremony goes on all night for two nights. I'm not a night person at the best of times. What had been described was my idea of absolute hell. The trouble is, I am a terminally curious person, and I'd enjoyed the microdosing. I'm also not someone who allows themselves to chicken out of doing things. Not a personality trait which necessarily serves me well.

Being a recovering control freak, I suspect is the reason why I'd never tried drugs in my youth. I thought a big dose of Psilocybin would give me a sense of how I'd fare the following weekend. I'd booked my place at the Ayahuasca centre.

It certainly did that alright…

# 10

# What a Trip!

FINAL FULL DOSE EXPERIMENT!

Sunday 16th May - 6.60 gms in ginger tea

Before I started, I set the intention to show me what I need to know...

Fairly soon after a few mouthfuls of my first full dose I noticed dark red lines appearing in the bottom of the cup. I sipped a third of the tea and laid back and felt the usual relaxation, hand energy centres and something I kept forgetting to write about was the feelings of joy.

I had chosen some specifically composed mushroom music, which apparently helps with each part of the journey. Not a lot was happening, so I drank another third of the tea, and closed my eyes. I started to see fractal patterns forming on my eyelids, which moved to the music in waves. They kept changing colour - it was like being inside a kaleidoscope!

Opening my eyes overrode the process, and not a lot happened. I drank the remaining tea and laid there for about an hour enjoying the music and the inner light show, debating if I should make another cup and use all the remaining Psilocybin. I decided to go outside to look at the flowers on the terrace as I'd heard they really come to life. They did a bit, but not as much as I'd hoped. The colours were more saturated than normal, but that was about it.

I lay in the sun for a few minutes with the dog, but then suddenly felt really nauseous. I went back inside and drank lots of water and some of the vitamin C drink I'd prepared. The fractals were still there when I closed my eyes, but the waves of nausea detracted from the experience. My liver felt heavy, so I took some high potency activated charcoal which calmed things down relatively quickly, thank goodness, as I was not feeling at all good!

I can only conclude that I didn't need 6.60gm, probably half of that would have done... Still the experience gave me a good taste of what an Ayahuasca experience would be like and as I was laying on the couch feeling yucky, I decided very definitely that I was not going through a whole weekend of it!

Opening my eyes, some of the plants and pillars on the patio were phasing in and out, and when I closed them again I could see bright greeny-yellow halos around things, but still the nausea was making things unpleasant. I drank more ginger tea and a ton of water - I was told mushroom trips make you thirsty, but this was crazy thirsty. After about an hour the worst of it had subsided.

My liver felt a bit heavy the next day, so I took things gently just eating fruit. I hadn't considered the toxin aspect to these, so will read up on it and stick to lower doses, as the microdosing is really nice. Just glad I didn't open up the final packet and glug that down too!! These plant medicines are powerful and need to be used with a bit more care, methinks…

I allowed myself to chicken out and cancelled the Ayahuasca Centre. A decision I do not regret!

Francesca found herself some more Workaway opportunities, and continued on with her travels. It was going to be strange not having her around. We'd been in each other's company for nearly eight months. It was wonderful having someone so easy-going and cheerful to spend time with, sharing day to day chores. And I certainly appreciated her wonderful cooking!

It was early June, and nearly time to start my return journey to England. Before I headed home I decided to visit a few of my favourite places to test everything in the van was working as it should. Still the threat of vaccine passports hung over us, so I was determined to see as much as possible, just in case it was my last opportunity.

I bundled the dog into the van and we set off for El Torcal, near Antequera. It had been quite a few years since I'd visited there. If you've read my first Misadventures book, you'll remember this being the place of that fateful first night of wild camping with my intrepid friend, Dee. Not a night either of us will forget in a hurry!

I certainly wasn't going to camp there again, but I did want to walk around the interesting rock structures one last time. I also wanted to go to the Dolmen Tombs. I'd become quite fascinated with the Dolmens since reading the Anastasia book series, and I'd never been to one, so it was time to visit the well-known one in Antequera.

It was wonderful seeing the Cairn-like rock structures at El Torcal again, and the dog enjoyed herself immensely. It was as beautiful as I'd remembered. Our next stop was to my favourite of El Chorro. I went to a spot I'd wild-camped before by the river, just beneath the Kings Pathway, or to give it the correct name, Caminito del Rey, which overlooks a spectacular gorge. These days you have to book tickets, which are usually booked up weeks in advance, and it's not a dog friendly route, so I made do, looking at it from afar.

It is stunning as the light changes throughout the day across the rocks above the gorge. I remembered back to all the times I'd come here, including my birthday in the early days with my partner. And the first occasion when Dee and I had scrambled up to the hillside to see it. Back then, it was known as the most dangerous pathway in the world. This was a few years before the four years of work had begun to restore the pathway. Originally, it was built for the workers of the hydroelectric plant in the early nineteen hundreds. It became known as the Kings Pathway when King Alfonso XIII crossed it to open the dam in 1921.

It is an incredible place but if you have a fear of heights, you won't enjoy the see-through metal bridge which crosses the gorge at the end of the walk. It's quite bouncy if there's several people on it!

The next day I tracked down the Dolmen. It didn't go well from the moment I arrived. We got there as early as they would allow, and I parked the van in the only place with shade as I knew I wouldn't be able to take the dog inside. No sooner had I parked, than a staff member came over waving their hands. I could not park there. I explained about the dog needing shade but they said no. There was lots of space and I wasn't blocking anything, but no, the jobsworth would not allow parking there.

I reluctantly moved, and reversed into a designated parking bay so that the camper would shade the cab. I gave Lena a drink and worked out how long I could safely leave her. It was early morning and under twenty degrees, thankfully very breezy, so with all the windows open she'd be alright for a good half an hour, but I decided to see if I could whizz round in fifteen mins to be on the safe side.

I'd wanted to take my time, so I felt stressed at the thought of leaving her and rushing. I did debate tying her up outside of the van, but if someone parked too close they might run her over, so the safest option was to leave her in the van with all the windows down.

I sped walked around the outside of the tomb, and was just about to go in when I met another jobsworth. There was no going inside without a mask.

I tried to walk past but she wasn't having it. Masks weren't a necessity at this point, but the guard would not let me in without it. This encounter did not help my mood. I complied as it was pointless arguing.

Some people believe that Dolmens weren't built for burial chambers, but instead were used for healing. They are often situated in sacred places over water veins, or ley lines. The alignment of the stone is said to enhance the natural energy of the site, which can be beneficial for the sick. I can sometimes sense earth energies, so I tried to put my intense dislike of the staff I'd encountered to one side, and tune into the site.

Nada. Nothing. I couldn't pick up anything. I wandered back and forwards a bit nearer to the centre, where there was a ridiculously deep bore hole through the rock floor. It was lit, but I couldn't see to the bottom of it, but it did look like there had been water in it. The guard immediately came over and told me off. Wandering back and forth was not allowed. They had direction arrows on the entrance. Bearing in mind there were only two of us in the megalithic structure, I couldn't see how me wandering around the centre of it, in whichever direction I chose, was problematical. I was alone in that. For this lady, it was a big problem.

After this encounter, I'd had enough. I took some photos and left. I was back in the van in less than ten minutes. I needn't have worried quite so much about leaving the dog! Whilst I didn't enjoy the visit, I couldn't help but marvel at the construction. How on earth did they get the enormous rocks in place? A modern day JCB wouldn't be able to shift them. They can only move about 20 tonnes.

The largest stone in the Menga Dolmen is estimated to weigh 180 tonnes – to put that in perspective the heaviest stone at Stonehenge is about 40 tonnes. So how the hell did they build this thing? I got a possible answer a few months later when researching some ancient alternative history…

I drove back to my parents house on the coast, just below Granada. The van had passed its 'functioning-well' test. I cleaned and packed up the house, paid the agent looking after it and on the 7th June, I started my very scenic journey back to the UK.

My first stop was heading west, back to my beloved Jimena de la Frontera, to stay with Tom (the one who had named my camper Wacky Races). En route, I had an appointment booked with my natural medicine doctor in Estepona. I wanted to pick up another prescription for some sleeping pills, and also ask him about my brain function. The magic mushrooms hadn't made any difference to my still dodgy memory.

I never got a chance to ask him for another prescription. As soon as I told him about what had happened in Italy, forgetting about the pole and reversing into it, he looked very concerned. You're too young for this to happen. He looked back over his notes from the year before and exclaimed ah!

Then he went online muttering something to himself. He then said, "Those sleeping pills you asked me for, did you take them?"

"Yes", I replied.

I'm never normally someone who takes pharmaceuticals, but I always like to have some sleeping pills for emergencies. In Spain they do one called Noctamid (Lormetazepam in the UK), which is really mild and doesn't make you feel groggy the next day. I usually only need a quarter of a pill so a packet often lasts me a year, sometimes longer, as I'm normally a good sleeper.

But over the years, I've found that when the seasons change in September, it can throw my sleep out. I'd been doing the natural house building course the whole of September and kept waking up so early, so I had taken a quarter of a pill when this happened in order to go back off to sleep again, knowing I had such a physically demanding day ahead of me.

My doctor told me, "One of the side effects of Noctamid is memory loss."

Oh. Wow! Considering I was only taking a quarter of a pill, that is quite a side effect. He agreed the diet had exacerbated the situation and gave me some suggestions for some herbal supplements that might help, along with a vitamin regime.

At least I now knew what had caused it. I just hoped I could get back to normal.

We stayed five days with Tom. I hadn't meant to stay quite that long, but Jimena is very Hotel California for me. Every time I go there, it doesn't allow me to leave when I plan. Last time I'd visited Tom, I'd been in my parents' Skoda. I'd just had it serviced for them at the Skoda garage in Motril, but unbeknownst to me, some idiot had put screenwash in the engine coolant.

I just about made it to Estepona when the warning light came on. I put some water in hoping it was just a lack of coolant, not realising the danger of what had actually happened. It wasn't a happy car by the time I reached Jimena, so we took it into Tom's local garage. They soon figured out the issue and drained the entire system, but it turned out that Skodas have to have their own special type of coolant, and it had to be ordered. It took two weeks to sort that out. Good job Tom loves house guests.

My delay this time was for the van. I'd ordered some very smart blinds for it and had decided to get them delivered to his house, instead of waiting for them at my parents' house. I got a notification that they had been delivered when we were out for a walk. The only thing is, they wouldn't have fitted through the letterbox, so where exactly had they been delivered?

It took us several days to track them down, going around asking all the neighbours, but no one had them. I happened to go into the downstairs front bedroom, adjacent to the one I was staying in, when I saw some very long boxes! The postman had opened the bedroom window and chucked them in!

They were worth the unintended wait as they made the van interior look very smart and I'd get better night's sleep with blackout blinds. I wasn't like I was in a huge rush to leave though.

June is a stunning time in Jimena. The valley below the hillside town is brimming with pink Oleander bushes growing either side of the river in amongst the rocks. We did several walks by the river, as well as high up in the Los Alcornocales Natural Park, amongst the cork oaks. Jimena is a very magical and stunning place with a diverse history, from prehistoric cave paintings to Phoenician, Roman, Moorish, and Christian civilisations, that has now evolved into a singular vibrant Andalusian white town or as they say in Spanish, pueblo blanco, with the narrow, hilly, cobbled streets town that it is today. While I was in the first lockdown, I'd wished I'd been in Jimena instead of somewhere so urbanised and highly policed.

As it turns out, I would have hated it even more than where I had been under house arrest. Tom lived on the edge of town, so he thought he'd be able to sneak out for some fresh air and exercise from his back gate, along the farm track and out into the countryside. It turns out that no sooner had he closed his gate, than he saw the police waiting at the end of the track for anyone who tried to escape the town.

Not having a lot of police in the area, they upped their game by getting drones to patrol. So not only were people hemmed in with the police laying wait on the outskirts, but they had to put up with the constant buzz of drones going over the houses all day long. No peace and no privacy.

On the 13th of June, we left Tom's lovely old mountain village home and headed west for Portugal. I was heavy-hearted, I knew I'd see Tom as he regularly came to England to look after his elderly mother, but I did wonder if I'd ever see my beloved Jimena again. It seems funny writing that now, but at the time it really did look like the option to travel would be removed completely for the unvaccinated. Anyone who didn't want an experimental vaccine was demonised and made a pariah of society. With the likes of Piers Morgan and Esther Ransen saying we should be refused medical treatment.

Even months later in December 2021, when it was clear there weren't many more deaths than a bad flu season, Andrew Neil wrote a full page article in the Mail stating the vaccine 'Refuseniks' should be punished, our freedoms curbed. In Austria, people weren't allowed to leave their homes, unless going for essentials like grocery shopping. It's easy to forget just how bad it was for those of us who didn't want to be part of an experimental medical procedure.

Years later when the side effects and excess deaths are now well documented and even the BBC has admitted the vaccines were harmful (something I never thought I'd see), people still lash out at those of us who didn't take it. The abuse ranges from we 'should have tried harder to tell everyone of the dangers', and even that it's our fault they took it! There have been online influencers saying that anti-vaxxers were right and everyone else was wrong, and mockingly assuming that we were smug about that. No. Virtually everyone I know feels nothing but heart-broken that we couldn't reach people, and that many of us are forever watching our loved ones wondering if they've been harmed.

Those who didn't get vaccinated may have escaped being physically harmed, but emotionally it has been devastating for many. I've known people whose family tried to have them sectioned because of the concerns they raised over the vaccines. Others have lost their entire family because they refused to be coerced into taking it. Very occasionally, people have made public apologies for the way they treated 'anti-vaxxers', but those apologies are few and far between.

If a garden designer from Colchester could look at the figures and deduce the vaccines weren't needed in the first place, no one is going to persuade me that someone in the government couldn't have figured it out. And would they really have been partying when people weren't allowed to visit their loved ones in hospital, if it had been the deadly pandemic it was billed as?

Part of my discomfort leaving Jimena, (other than the large brown cow blocking the top of the road out), was that I didn't know what was going to be in store for me when I returned to England. Which was why I was taking a detour west into Portugal. There was something important I needed to do before I returned to England.

# 11

# Megalith Hunting, Portugal

I reached Alcoutrim in the Algarve, Portugal, just before dusk. It's situated right on the unmanned border with Spain. It is set back about 25 miles from the coast. My mission was to have a backup plan if I didn't like being back in the UK.

I always like to have a backup plan. I wanted to find somewhere I could live. I'd travelled through Portugal a fair bit on other trips, and always liked it. The people friendly, and service efficient. I knew I couldn't live in Spain again. Not that Portugal had been a great deal better. They'd been so compliant with all the rules and regulations they'd not needed to be quite so heavy handed with the police presence. For Portugal, at that time, it was much easier to get a visa.

I wanted to explore all the parts I'd not been to before, especially places which were a bit off the beaten tourist track. But also close to the border, so if I did want to get back and visit friends in Spain, it would be easy to slip across whenever I wanted. Spain also has much cheaper fuel than Portugal.

I drove up to the Evora area, and stayed a few nights, as it was a good location to explore the surrounding area. I also wanted to do some sightseeing. Portugal has a lot of Dolmens and interesting henge-like monuments. After my disappointment in the Dolmen in Antequera, I hoped I'd have better luck in Portugal.

Of particular interest was the Almendres Cromlech. It is considered to be one of the biggest and most important megalithic monuments in the world, much older than Stonehenge. It's estimated this was built between the 6th and 3rd millennium BC. There were a hundred, as the name suggests, almond shape, granite menhirs, ninety-five of which are left today.

There are various theories as to why it was built, most seem to believe for religious and ceremonial purposes. It's noted the tallest menhirs points towards the sunrise in the Summer Solstice and another the Winter Solstice. Some of the stones have curious circular engravings.

I'd been given a book when I was in Jimena by friends of Tom, who were ditching Spain in favour of starting a new life in Brazil. They were deeply concerned by what was happening in Europe, and decided Brazil would be a better bet. They were getting rid of a lot of possessions and invited me to help myself to books. I chose one called Points of Cosmic Energy, by internationally renowned geobiologist, Blanche Merz.

The book covers how she found proof that the earth is covered with magnetic lines, which she likened to meridians acupuncturists use in the body. Merz did years of painstaking research, travelling the world finding proof of these lines' existence. I've always been fascinated by earth energies ever since I did a dowsing course, and learned about Geopathic stress in my twenties.

In the training, I'd been taught how to use metal dowsing rods which would cross over one another whenever I was hunting for the bad energy lines known as 'black streams'. The negative energy could then be released with earth acupuncture by driving a spike into the ground. It was a fascinating course and quite something to witness a line of ten or so people all have their dowsing rods cross at the same time and then uncross once the negative energy had been released with the acupuncture rods.

Blanche Merz's book talked about Menhirs, Dolmens and the Hartmann Grid. She concluded Menhirs intensify points, where the Hartmann lines cross and act like a transmitter. It was a fascinating book to read while I was visiting all these ancient sites. I could feel the energy at Almendres Cromlech, and so could the dog. It felt like the sensation you get being close to a loud speaker.

Even though we arrived at half-past seven in the morning, in the middle of June, the temperature was already in the upper-twenties, not weather, Lena would normally run around in for any length of time. She got the zoomies like I've never seen before. I managed to stop her zooming through the centre where people aren't allowed to go in case of soil erosion, but she just took off whizzing and whirling herself around, thankfully well away from the monument, chasing her tail and barking. Good job we were the only ones there as it was so early.

It was nice to be focusing on something other than the end of the world as we know it. Throughout my driving through Italy, Spain and Portugal I was listening to the paid versions of the Crrow podcasts, where they'd discuss the work of Rudolph Steiner and the Mystery Schools and many fascinating subjects. Listening to those lifted me from fear to fascination. Just how much of the old knowledge had been suppressed? Little did I know at the time, listening to the Crrow podcasts would result in me ending up on a theatre stage in London three years later.

I found myself fascinated with why earlier civilisations would go to so much effort to carve and arrange huge lumps of granite into position? How did they do it? How did they know how to place them so precisely? So many intriguing questions that I would probably never get answers to. I enjoyed the mind exercise contemplating it all, nonetheless.

I spent the next few days thoroughly absorbed visiting as many of the megalithic sites as I could. Dolmen hunting was my new favourite past-time. Some were so far off the beaten track, I'd have never got there in a regular car. Four wheel drive was needed on several occasions. Interestingly, the Dolmens which had been the hardest to reach, had the most powerful energy. Was it because it had increased because there hadn't been hundreds of people visiting them? I had no idea but it was an interesting theory, and perhaps might have explained why I got nothing from the one in Antequera.

On the 17th of June I met up with a friend from Spain who'd also fled after the lockdown. She'd settled just outside of Lisbon as she too couldn't face the thought of another lockdown in Spain. It was lovely to catch up with her as she'd been one of the first to reach out to me when I started muttering on Facebook. I left the area the following day and found a smaller version of Almendres Cromlech, which was very overgrown. I didn't like the energy of this one, so didn't stay long.

I headed back towards the Spanish border to a place called Marvao, in the Parque Natural da Serra de Sao Mamede. There was a castle with spectacular views across the landscape, and it had a surprisingly lovely formal garden, which I duly photographed and made a video blog about for my garden design business.

I really liked the area, and it was the first on my possible Portuguese places to live list. I popped back into Spain to fill up with some cheaper diesel before proceeding north to the unusual mountain village of Monsanto, roughly halfway up Portugal.

Monsanto is a village that dates back to the Paeolithic era. It is littered with huge round granite rocks, the largest estimated at 200 tonnes. The whole village is built around them. Some are incorporated into people's houses. The weather had turned surprisingly cold and overcast, so I didn't stay long.

From Monsanto, I headed to the Serra da Estrela Natural Park, a place I'd wanted to visit for a while. It's a shame I didn't have better weather considering the time of year. It was still a stunning place to drive though as the layer of clouds clung to the top of the mountain peaks. Though perhaps most impressive of all is the sculpture carved into the rock face.

It's a carving of the Virgin Mary, known as Nossa Senhora da Boa Estrela which means Our Lady of the Good Star. It's 23ft tall, and was carved in 1946 by a local priest called António Duarte. It was created in thanks to the local shepherds who endured the harsh weather conditions, while guiding their flocks through the mountains. It was cold enough on an overcast day in June, I wouldn't have wanted to be up there in the winter months.

I camped at a beautiful family run campsite in Torrozeolo, Caovas. It had a natural swimming pool surrounded by a gorgeous patio area and borders brimming with soft purple and white flowers. The owner said to make ourselves at home and said I could allow the dog to run free, which is usually unheard of on campsites. They did only have one other family camping, and someone in the guest lodge. I parked the van on the upper level, which we had all to ourselves. There were tall umbrella pines offering shade that we didn't need with the overcast skies. But their presence gave the campsite a majestic charm.

Early the following day, I embarked on the four hour drive back into Spain to a place I'd wanted to visit for years. Las Médulas, which is west of Leon. I'd got to know Leon rather well with a forced stay of two weeks, thanks to a rather unfortunate accident. Because of the accident, I'd never made it to Las Médulas so it was wonderful to finally tick that box off of places I wanted to visit list.

It's a UNESCO World Heritage site. The area was used for gold mining by the Romans. All that remains is a surreal landscape of tree covered, red clay gullies, caves and red, clay-rich sedimentary rock peaks left over from the mining. The gullies were formed when the Romans mined the gold by pumping large quantities of water to break apart the mountains. I was glad I finally got to see the unusual landscape, and spent the morning exploring all through, and above, the area with the dog.

Next stop, up to the golden sandy coast of Donastia San Sebastian, at the top of Spain, right on the border with France. We stayed in a nice campsite on the hillside above the beach. But before we could continue into France, I needed to find a vet. And what a palaver that turned out to be.

In order to get a dog into the UK, they have to be wormed at least 24hrs before they come back, but no more than five days before arriving in the UK. I decided it would be easier to get her wormed in Spain because I have slightly more Spanish in my vocabulary than French. Besides, Spanish vets are usually less expensive than some of the other EU countries.

Third vet lucky, and twenty euros later, and we were on our way to France. Pays de la Loire just above La Rochelle is where we spent our first night. Beautiful sandy beaches, but no dogs allowed, but I managed not to see the 'no dog' sign until after Madame had a nice run along the empty beach!

It was here that I noticed the camper had a very strange tilt to it. It appeared to be separating from the cab. I wasn't sure what was going on, but I was nearly home, whatever it was would just have to get sorted out in England.

Our final night was spent in Lower Normandy near the intriguing tidal island of Mont Saint-Michel. It's a shame we didn't have the time to visit the 8th century walled UNESCO World Heritage site as it looked quite magical from the coastal walk I did with the dog before supper.

I'd opted to take the ferry from Cherbourg rather than coming back via Calais, as I'd heard they were particularly officious in Calais. Not to say they wouldn't be in Cherbourg, I had just hoped a smaller port might be friendlier. I had three things I was rather concerned about.

It was now 28th June 2021. I'd been in the EU a lot longer than I was permitted to be. I didn't know if a record of my previous passport would be tied into the new one. I'd flown to Mallorca in October 2019 and then to Malaga with the old one. I hadn't gone through passport control in Malaga, so the last time I had my old passport scanned was arriving in Mallorca.

My new passport had been looked at leaving Italy in the middle of March, but I couldn't remember them scanning it. In theory going from Italy to Spain wouldn't show up in the system as it was inside the EU, that's what I was hoping for.

But would it cause issues leaving France, or getting back into England with a passport which hadn't been used before? If it did, I wouldn't be allowed back in the EU for ten years. Which is in part why I did as much sightseeing as I could, just in case.

Then there was the issue of the dog. I'd never travelled back to the UK with a dog before, especially one with an EU passport. I knew they would be vigilant with the paperwork. I'd got everything I needed, but I was still anxious.

Then there was the issue of the van. The chap who sold it to me was selling on the behalf of his friend in Gibraltar. A little odd, but I didn't concern myself with it too much. After I purchased it, the man told me he'd sold a lot of things for his friend and listed all sorts of vehicles. Alarm bells rang slightly at this.

There are a fair number of drug dealers in that area. I know because I'd seen the matt black Rangerovers with blacked out windows being stopped by the police enough times. On one occasion they'd thrown a spiked chain across to stop the vehicle, and when I drove past, the car was surrounded by police in full body armour with what looked like assault rifles pointed at the driver.

I knew there weren't likely to be any drugs left in the vehicle if it had been used for smuggling, but would there be any traces left? I knew there would likely be sniffer dogs when I got back to England. So it's fair to say, I was feeling rather stressed. And so was the dog, she'd been quite poorly. The worm pills had made her sick, and then the day before I was due to catch the ferry I happened to read an article that said UK vets can no longer fill in EU pet passports because of Brexit.

This meant I had to find a vet to give her a rabies shot, or I'd never be able to get her back in the EU without having to get her a UK pet passport and have every single vaccine re-administered. The combination of worm pills and rabies shot made her have a very dodgy tummy.

I really wasn't looking forward to this crossing. Would I end up getting carted off by the police for being in the EU too long? Or would the problem arrive with UK passport control? And if the van had been used for drug smuggling and there were any traces left, I might have a lot of explaining to do at the other end. What would happen to the dog if I was detained? She really doesn't do being separated.

And what would the reception be from my parents when they saw the state of me, my odd looking van (now looking even odder with its comedic tilt), and my now very poorly looking dog?

I had a very bad feeling about this, a tight knot forming in my stomach as we edged closer and closer in the queue to the check-in kiosk.

# 12

# The Return

Out of my many worries, the first one to rear its head was the dog. The lady at the check-in kiosk took her time going over every single vaccine. She wasn't happy she'd not had an up-to-date Parvo vaccine. I had spent a ton of time going over and over the rules and regs for getting a dog into the UK, and I knew it wasn't necessary and told her so. They only have to have that as a puppy.

The next thing she decided was wrong was the date on the worm pills. Vets, it would appear, have similar handwriting to doctors. She had misread the swirly handwriting and thought I was two days out on the dates, and therefore could not travel. I told her she'd misread it. I'd paid cash and not thought to get a receipt. My anxiety levels were through the roof at this point, and we hadn't even gone through my paperwork and passport, which I was really sweating about.

Eventually she conceded that I was right about the date. Then I had to scan the dog's chip. Could I find the damn thing, no. I knew she had one, it was on the pet passport, but I'd never taken her anywhere. She didn't like the scanner coming near her, I think she could feel it. The kiosk lady said it's usually at the top of their neck but sometimes they move, try down each side of the neck. I did, and the machine beeped displaying the number when I got down her right side by her ear.

I was about ready to pass out when she put my passport through the scanner. If she'd been this bad with the dog, I didn't fancy my chances. And I had no excuse for my tardiness returning to the UK, other than a rather lame, but truthful, I simply didn't want to go back any earlier. The machine beeped as she scanned. She looked at me and then back at my passport. And then handed it back to me before going through my other documents.

And breathe.

I was shaking by the time I got back in the van, boarding pass clutched in a sweaty palm.

One passport control down, one to go.

I don't recall a thing about the overnight crossing, other than it being a lot easier, thank goodness, getting the dog on and off it. And this time we weren't last off the boat.

To begin with, it looked like I could just drive straight through and out, but I was pulled over as soon as they spotted the dog. The paperwork was meticulously gone through again. I'd taken the precaution of making the worm pill date a little clearer so that Madame didn't end up in quarantine.

There weren't any sniffer dogs, but the customs guy wanted to look inside the camper part as the window was too high for him to see what was in it. I unlocked the door and pulled the steps down for him. He had a brief poke about in the drawers and storage, saw how many clothes and cooking utensils and dog related items I had stowed, and got bored fairly quickly. I suspect if I'd had been a teenager or hairy biker dude, covered in tattoos they'd have pulled the van to pieces as it just looked dodgy. I made sure I did my best plummy telephone voice, to convince them I was just eccentric and not into drugs.

It was at that point I suddenly remembered the remaining magic mushrooms in the fridge. Had I remembered to bin them as I'd intended? Yes, I had done. Phew. No unintended drugs onboard, as far as I knew!

They eventually let me go, and by 6:30 am we were on the motorway in absolutely appalling driving conditions. It was tipping it down so much that the windscreen wipers could barely keep up with it. Welcome to the UK! Ah yes, I remember what English summers are like, it was all coming back to me now. This is why I'd hardly done any in the last ten years.

At this point in time the Covid -19 Track and Trace system was in place. I'd reluctantly filled in the paperwork and given it in at customs. As much as I wanted to tell them to shove it, now was not the time to take a stand. My father's knee operation was just around the corner, and I knew they needed me to be there. The rules were that I had to stay in isolation for ten days.

I'd agreed I'd stay on my parents' drive in the camper. They couldn't risk having me in the house because of my father's operation. The hospital had made it clear that if he tested positive, they wouldn't do the op.

The dog's tummy still wasn't good, and we had to stop seven times. I was worried she'd had such a bad reaction. She'd lost a lot of weight with the three days of an upset tummy, and her ribs were showing. It's hard keeping weight on her at the best of times because of how active she is. I felt that at least ten days of being largely confined to a campervan and the small patch of grass surrounding it, should enable her to put some weight back on.

Now whilst my mother is nothing like the character, Hyacinth Bucket, the expression on her face when she came out and saw the state of me, my van and my dog on her drive for all the neighbours to see, was quite entertaining. I looked like all her worst fears rolled into one.

My father also came hobbling out and stroked the dog with my mother saying, "Don't touch that animal, you might catch something!"

It was weird being back after so long and standing six feet away and not hugging them. It made things quite strained. I'd get meals prepared and left on the van doorstep. I whiled away the time working on my laptop from an extension lead plugged into the garage, and a long ethernet cable plugged into the modem through the office window.

Because I was still on Spanish time, I'd be up at five-thirty and would take the dog across the fields for a quick walk before anyone noticed. The day after, I received a phone call from Track and Trace asking if

I was in the location I had given them and if I'd come into close contact with anyone.

I replied, "Yes and no." They then said they would phone every day and possibly send someone out to check up on me, and did they have my consent to send the information they collected on to the UK Government?

I said I did not give my consent for them to do that. The operator seemed shocked. He'd clearly never had anyone refuse before. I said he was welcome to phone me as often as he liked, but I did not consent to having my information shared with anyone. He said, "well it is only going to the government so it's perfectly safe." I replied, "only if you trust the government and I no longer do." He didn't know how to respond to that.

He asked why not. I replied that I didn't know what they were going to do with that information and how long it would be retained for. He then suggested, if I wanted to, I could contact them and ask for my information to be deleted after the isolation period was up. I asked him why I would want to spend my time doing that, when I don't have to give it to them in the first place? I reiterated that he could still do his job and phone me whenever he liked, but my information was to be kept private, otherwise it would be a breach of GDPR.

He hung up and I never heard from him or anyone from Track and Trace again. No one came out to visit.

It was a very long ten days cooped up in the van, but I respected my parents wishes and understood their fear of my father catching something I didn't have and having his operation cancelled, which was scheduled for the week after my self-imposed exile ended. At least I would be able to drive him to the hospital.

Having so much time on my hands gave me a chance to inspect my camper. It turned out the latch attaching the camper to the frame had sheared off. I thought about all the off-roading I'd done in Portugal searching for megalithic sites. Some of them had been on fairly heart-stopping and deeply rutted dirt track roads.

I crawled under the van and discovered something even worse. There was an enormous crack going around three-quarters of the chassis, and it was right by the fuel tank. It was an absolute miracle that I had made it back without it completely snapping. It was on the verge of it. There was hardly any metal holding it together. There wasn't a worse place on the entire vehicle it could have broken. It would have been impossible to weld without taking the whole vehicle to pieces, and I wasn't sure how the camper would take to being detached, because I knew the floor had cracked in the crash.

I then realised it must have already been cracked when I bought it because of how rusted the crack was. I'd noticed the tow bar was curved. I'd assumed it was the design, but of course, I now realised they'd obviously driven into something with a lot of force to curve it like that, which must have cracked the chassis, and then my off-roading had made it worse. I filmed the issue and emailed it to someone who'd been recommended to repair it.

All the mechanics that had worked on the van had missed it because the fuel tank had hidden the crack. It's doubtful even the owner knew of the problem. I didn't know what to do now. I adored the van, it was still my favourite vehicle, but it was continually needing repairs. This one was one too far for me, so with a heavy heart I soon realised I'd have to sell it.

Once again I was stranded in a country without a vehicle or home. This was becoming a habit I could do without. I'd have to rent somewhere and buy another vehicle. My parents said I could use their old car which they'd purchased when they'd had the dogs, but they were going to sell that, so I wouldn't have it for long.

## The Long Road to Recovery

My father's knee surgery recovery was horrific. Although the surgeon said the operation went well, my father was in agony for weeks afterwards. And even after several months he wasn't doing well. By this time I'd moved into the spare room. I'd never lived in this house, but the room had my old single bed from my childhood home.

The dog was allowed in the house, but not in the lounge or upstairs. Her first time in the house didn't go well. No sooner had she come in, she saw my mother swat a fly with a rolled up newspaper, and seeing that act of violence, she took off back out of the house. I had to explain to my mother how sensitive rescue dogs can be.

It's impossible to know how she'd been treated at her first home, but one thing I'd discovered is that she will not tolerate any form of what she considers violence, either physical or verbal. Fly swatting needed to be a thing of the past. As it was, it took Lena a few months to trust my mother whenever she picked up a newspaper, she'd leave the room just in case.

She will also leave the room if anyone swears. It is like living with the swear monitor. Even if you swear under your breath, or in a joking way, she will either come over and tell you about the bad word you've just said, or she'll go out. I can only assume her first household was violent and that it started with swearing.

It took her about two weeks to win my mother over. Being an incredibly bright dog, she figured out the score very quickly. She knew precisely which one to focus her efforts on. She'd won my father over instantly, but my mother was convinced I'd brought home some disease ridden street dog, and they'd get something dreadful from her.

Having recovered from her tummy troubles, and now that we had a proper address, I was able to get raw food delivered, which she does much better on. She soon started to go back to her normal weight. Looking less like a diseased street dog, and back to her usual self. She set to work winning my mother over at every opportunity, as I knew she would.

I'd already had the 'Lena loves you treatment'. I knew first-hand how persuasive she can be. When

I'd gone to visit her at her foster home, she immediately jumped on my lap when I sat on the ground next to her, and started play-biting me and licking my face. Something I later discovered that she doesn't normally do with strangers. She knew why I was there, and did the perfect audition.

And when I had a test week fostering her, she was as good as gold. Didn't pull on the lead, didn't chase cats, nothing. I swear the day I signed her adoption papers she knew. Suddenly the lead pulling started, as did chasing seagulls, pigeons and cats!

## Therapy Dog

Something else we discovered about Lena is that she's very empathic and a great therapy dog. One morning, before I was up, my mother was upset and tearful because of the never ending pain my father was enduring after his knee surgery. When I got up, I found them both in the conservatory. Lena was sitting upright on her haunches, ears back, looking like a meerkat with one paw in Mother's hand, and the other paw on her heart, licking her tears away. If anyone she likes is upset, she will put her paw on their heart and shower them with endless affection until they are better.

I knew my mother didn't stand a chance holding out when Lena was on a full charm offensive. It helped that she only barks if someone comes to the door, and that she didn't join in with the neighbours dogs' dawn chorus. Though it did take until Christmas before she was allowed into the lounge. With my mother saying, 'it's just for Christmas day'. Uh huh! Needless to say she's still allowed in the lounge, and I have even caught them having the occasional sofa cuddle. Her grand'paw'ents spoil her something rotten. She has more toys at their house than at home. Though she knows upstairs is still off limits, and won't go up there even though she does at my house.

But anyway, at this point in time, I didn't have anywhere to live, and knew I'd need to figure that out. As awful as my father's recovery from knee surgery was, the one thing it did do was bring us back to being the close family we'd always been. My mother was quite poorly during my father's surgery, so when he came out of hospital I was his main carer, and they both needed a lot of help.

Having me around helping, and spending so much time together, enabled them to see that I hadn't gone mad, I just had a different view on the world than they were used to. It also gave me the opportunity to show my mother the data, like the Office of National Statics death figures, and have her see with her own eyes the deaths per capita in 2020 were lower than in 2013. I asked her, "Do you remember there being a pandemic in 2013? No, neither do I."

Bit by bit, they reluctantly came around to realising what I was saying was correct. It took a long time though, but when things I'd warned them about, which they'd initially dismissed, all started to happen, they could see I'd been right. Not watching the BBC anymore also helped tremendously. They still don't want to believe everything I've told them, which is understandable.

Despite not wanting to believe it all, my mother does surprise me at times. The other day, she phoned to tell me she'd been out for a walk and had noticed how many chemtrails there were in the sky. She said she could see a small plane going back and forth, creating a grid of trails in the sky. She mused that it would no doubt be overcast the next day. She wanted to know if I'd seen them where I was as well. I looked out the window, and sure enough, there they were.

I'd first found out about chemtrails back in 2018 when I had my Gaia TV subscription. Regina Meredith was interviewing a TV meteorologist who'd quit after forty years because of all the weather manipulation. He said it made his job impossible. He'd watch the satellite images showing a tornado, warn viewers it was incoming, and then later watch as the tornado disintegrated on his screen without having naturally run its course. The meteorologist mentioned that he'd got a flight identity app on his phone and would regularly use it to track flights. He'd see a flight allegedly heading to the UK or wherever, watch it turn around in the sky, and then see his phone identify it as a different airline heading to Phoenix! He said he was witnessing impossible things with the weather all the time.

When Regina asked why it was being done, he explained that if the 'money men' knew what the weather was going to be, it would give them a huge advantage in trading commodities. For example, they'd know there'd be a shortage of almonds or other crops. At the time, while I found him to be very credible, that part sounded like a bit of a stretch to me, and I didn't believe that hypothesis. However, it did make me start paying attention to the skies. The meteorologist explained that a condensation trail, known as a 'contrail,' dissipates quite quickly, whereas a 'chemtrail' lingers for ages, slowly spreading into a milky haze across the sky. Once I started looking up, I could see these chemtrails everywhere. It made me wonder how on earth I'd never noticed them before.

During the interview, Regina recounted a conversation she'd had with a doctor in upstate New York. He'd told her he'd started noticing an increase in the number of people showing Alzheimer's symptoms around the same time he'd observed spraying in the sky. Concerningly, he reported that he was now seeing symptoms in children as young as fourteen. He had somehow managed to find out who was doing the chemtrailing and what was in it. Fine particles of various substances, such as barium, aluminium (which has been linked to Alzheimer's), and silicon, often referred to as aluminosilicates, were allegedly being sprayed in these chemtrails. When he asked if any health assessments had been done, he was told that wasn't in their remit.

I'd told my mother about chemtrails when I returned to England, but she hadn't believed me, even after I showed her the Geoengineering page on the UK Government website! I even photographed them during an early morning dog walk. It had been a beautiful, cloudless blue sky, and two or three hours later, it was completely grey and cloud-covered. So, it was quite a turnaround for her to be phoning me about chemtrails!

Curiously, at the time of writing this, a lot of the spraying had stopped, and we'd had glorious clear blue skies for nearly a month. Then, just as I was about to publish, the announcement came that the UK Government had allocated £50 million to conduct experimental dimming of the skies. Why admit to it now when they've been doing it for years? Too many people noticing, perhaps? Curious.

**Like-Minded Souls**

By August I'd decided to go along to something I read about online called 'Stand in the Park'. Every Sunday people would meet at 10am in parks nearly everywhere in the UK. It was an opportunity to meet and talk to like-minded people. I was in desperate need of that, having left all my friends behind in Spain and Portugal. I'd lost touch with my UK friends over the ten years I'd been travelling, some I'd purposely let slide, others just drifted away and I had no wish to reconnect as I already knew their views were no longer compatible with mine from their Facebook posts.

I went to the nearest one to my parents' place in Colchester. There was a gathering of about twenty people. I went most weeks up until I moved. It was there I met someone who would become one of my closest friends and allies, Carinna. She didn't have time to attend often, but we immediately hit it off with a similar dry but quirky sense of humour. I remember thinking it was a shame she wasn't there regularly.

The third time I met her, she invited me to join a little side group that met every month, organised by her friend David, who I'd met a few times and liked. There were six of us in total and we'd hang out doing various things from yoga, visiting a biodynamic farm, games night at the university, playing some weird outdoor game which I'd not come across that involved throwing little pieces of wood or something.

It was so nice hanging out with like-minded people. It was also nice to be at a social gathering and not being the weirdest one in the room! We could discuss any topic, from alternative history to a particularly hilarious and memorable conversation on Shivambu (if you don't know what that is, you probably won't want to, especially the way my new group of friends described it). Though having since read a book on it, it's a fascinating subject!

**Farewell Wacky One**

I eventually sold my van. It was snapped up for its uniqueness in spite of the very serious issue. It sold within ten minutes of listing it on Facebook Marketplace. The interested party came over an hour later. I showed him all the problems I'd highlighted in the video and photos. He was in the motor trade and made me a good offer. I did feel quite bereft selling Wacky Races. The new owner kept in touch and true to form it had been a complete nightmare getting another chassis, so they had to get specialist metal plates to be welded on, which had to be shipped from Australia, which cost a fortune.

I'd made the right decision selling it. Now I had to find myself another vehicle and somewhere to live. Both of those proved to be much harder than they should have been. And I managed neither until the following year.

At the time, there was a shortage of second-hand cars and it took me seven months to find something which fitted my very specific criteria - a vehicle which was as government proof as possible. My long hunt and patience paid off, I got exactly what I wanted, a low mileage, reliable SUV, good MPG, ULEZ compliant, £35 annual road tax.

With the Absolute Zero directive of reducing the cars on the road by sixty percent, it was obvious everything possible would be done to tax people out of their cars. As of writing this, the government have recently raised road tax, but because my car was registered just before the April 2017 rule change, it is unaffected, even though it's diesel. They'll no doubt get me one day, but for now, it was a good buy.

The time delay in getting the car also meant that my crypto gamble paid off, and my 3K Euro punt was now worth £9K, and with the money I got for the van, I had exactly what I needed to buy the car. With a mileage of 32k, I'm glad I took my time. I got a good deal buying online from a dealership up north. I had to pay to get it delivered, but it was still considerably cheaper than buying down south!

Somehow Lena seemed to know it was our new car. I took her for a quick test drive around the block and when we got back she refused to get out! I opened the boot and she stayed in it for the rest of the day. She'd never done this in any of my parents' cars we'd been borrowing. Perhaps she was hoping for a road trip back to Spain! But I think she was perfectly happy in England, she had a new favourite past time...

Lena soon discovered the delights of puddles, not something she'd had much experience of in southern Spain. She loved running through and jumping in them, but most of all, lying in them. The muddier the puddle, the happier she appeared to be. I hoped this was a trait she'd grow out of, but alas no.

## Bad Apples

As well as saying goodbye to Wacky, it was also time to ditch my beloved Mac. I'd been a loyal Apple customer for twenty-two years, but I'd been so appalled at the way Track and Trace had been automatically installed onto people's phones, along with various other things, I could no longer be a supporter. There was no way I was going to go back to Microsoft, so I took the plunge and went over to Linux. Oh boy, I regretted that decision quickly.

Linux has taken me quite a while to adjust to. It's like going back in time ten years. I'm under no illusions, with the Linux Foundation receiving funding from the likes of Google, Microsoft and IBM to name but a few, it's not immune to big tech influence, but it's at least a small step away. With Apple agreeing to give the UK government encryption keys to people's iCloud data, I'm glad I've made the switch, as a matter of principle, even though I miss the ease of my Mac, which I still have, but don't use much. After I'd made the switch for the first time, I considered the symbolism of the bite out of the apple…

I also tried a Linux phone but that was so ridiculously bad that I gave up, and still have my old iPhone 8, which is gradually becoming more and more unusable because I refuse to update the operating system, not being prepared to accept whatever new levels of privacy will be breached with each update.

I've also switched over the bulk of my online shopping from Amazon to Ebay. I know Ebay is another corporate giant, but it felt better than solely supporting Amazon. Now that Ebay allow credit card payments, I was able to ditch Paypal too. Another company which had overreached with shutting down accounts of people who spoke out against the mainstream narrative. I've switched as many of my online payments as possible away from them. These are small acts, and no doubt insignificant to the companies in question, but if enough of us do it, a difference is made.

I tried moving my garden design videos from YouTube to Odysee, but even putting a trailer on YouTube I could not get people to make the switch and view on another platform, so reluctantly, I've stayed with YouTube.

## Preservation

Sorting out somewhere to live was a never-ending fiasco, which I won't bore you with. So while I waited for it to resolve itself, other than battling with the Linux operating system, I spent a fair bit of time learning about foraging and preserving food. I learnt about canning soup, dehydrating fruit and making a lot of jam and chutney. There was just one slight thing. None of us actually eat jam or chutney!

In my keenness to learn about food preservation, I'd got a bit carried away. My parents garage was piled high with preserved food. They were counting the seconds until I moved out and took it all with me. I ended up giving everyone I now knew jam that year. I've still got the chutney, but it's so old now that I daren't give it to anyone. Though Francesca visited last year and was brave enough to try it and lived to tell the tale!

Most of 2022 was spent learning to grow vegetables and regenerative growing techniques. Considering my career path, it turns out I knew very little about the soil. I was amazed to learn that plants can't feed themselves, it's the soil bacteria that make the nutrients bioavailable. How did I not already know that? Regenerative growing feeds the soil, not the plant. At the end of each growing season the soil should be replenished not depleted. The complete opposite of modern agricultural practices.

## Finally a Home

I eventually managed to get my accommodation sorted, and spent a lot of time going through all the belongings I'd had in storage for ten years. I could have sworn blind I'd never seen half of it before. But clearly I had as it was my handwriting on the boxes!

The exceptionally bland garden needed sorting out, it was dreadful. So, the first thing I did, was to redesign it. Since I didn't think I'd live in the house for long, I came up with a cheap and cheerful design that would suit possible future renters, rather than designing it to my own tastes. I would have loved to fill it with wildflowers and trees, but the dog needed a lawn, and most likely, so would whoever moved in next.

Because I wanted to keep costs down, I did most of the work myself. It was an unusually hot summer, and I ended up laying bricks for the lawn edge in scorching sunshine and temperatures nearing 30 degrees. Typical that the one time I could have done with our more normal, cooler English summer temperatures! A Lithuanian man named Marius, who had worked for my father when he first came to the UK as a 17-year-old, helped with the heavy digging and laying of paving, along with his friend Artūras. They just about managed to get it done before Marius and his wife returned to Lithuania with their son.

For Marius, going back to his homeland was bittersweet. He'd spent half his life in England, but in Lithuania, he had a house and land where he could provide a better life for his family than he could here. Helping with my garden, in a way, marked the completion of his time in England. My father had helped him a lot when he first arrived, and Marius was meticulous about doing a good job, almost as a thank you to my father for everything he'd taught him.

In late June, I flew back to Spain for three days, leaving the dog with my parents. There were a few things I needed to sort out at their house, and it was lovely to catch up with my closest friends and meet my friend's beautiful baby boy.

In the latter part of year, I managed to get an allotment so I would be able to put everything I'd learned about regenerative agriculture into practice. I'd been sharing my father's allotment, but he is someone who likes to rotavate the soil at every opportunity and did not approve of my no-dig plans to not disturb the colonies of soil bacteria. It would be good to have my own plot knowing it wouldn't be rotavated when I wasn't looking!

**Best Foot Forward**

The dog and I both managed to get quite nasty injuries and lost the whole of November as a result. Just as well it was both at the same time since neither of us could walk anywhere for several weeks. She'd managed to rip a back claw completely off. I nearly passed out when I saw what remained. She'd had a whole host of injuries when we returned to the UK. She also developed an allergy to either the grass seed or nettles and her face was blotchy and spotty.

England did not seem to suit her. Thankfully she recovered and the allergic reaction didn't return. Her pads did not fare well with UK flint. No problems whatsoever scaling mountains with sharp rocks in Spain and Italy, but running across a freshly ploughed field, she needed stitches the week after we came out of self-isolation.

So I was well versed in tending her, as the stitches were useless. I'd learned the hard way how vital it is to keep her wounds clean, and the sock and bandages the vet gave us didn't do the job.

My own foot was in considerably worse shape than the dog's, and I was in agony. I'd been sterilizing a Kilner jar I'd had in storage with boiling water, when it broke. It must have had a hairline crack I hadn't spotted as it should have been able to take the heat. It shattered, dumping the contents of freshly boiled water over my foot. It went through the top of my slipper and I couldn't get my sock off fast enough. Nearly the whole of the top of my foot was burned.

I didn't realise it at the time, but I'd done a lot of damage in the time it took to get the sock off. In truth I should have gone to hospital, as it later turned out I'd got second and third degree burns.

Luckily for me, I'd created an extensive natural first aid kit in the house after witnessing the shortages of pharmaceuticals in the chemists when I returned to the UK. Seeing how much pain my father was in and struggling to get hold of enough of the pain killers he needed, made me all too aware how awful it would be if there ever came a day when supply chains were seriously compromised. Because, after weeks of research, I'd purchased virtually every natural remedy under the sun, I was able to treat it successfully at home. But not knowing much about burns, I made a lot of mistakes which could have cost me dearly had I not read up and changed course with the treatment.

A tiny Aloe vera plant is what saved me, being both an analgesic and antibacterial. When mixed carefully with DMSO it saved me from needing a skin graft. That accident taught me a great deal about scolds, burns and first aid. The house is now full of Aloe vera plants. I did a video on the miracle-working remedies that saved my foot along with the Aloe. It's on the Resource page [RachelMathews.UK/accidental-resources](RachelMathews.UK/accidental-resources) along with a video of our high and low-lights retuning to England.

I used my time stuck inside while my foot healed to learn how to grow mushrooms indoors, as well as a whole load of other indoor growing experiments, with everything from lemons to potatoes. Some of my experiments were more successful than others!

December brought snow, lots of it, which the dog loved, her second time seeing it. I resumed the cold water therapy I'd started in Italy. I'd hated doing the Wim Hoff training in the shower, I'd much rather be in a cold plunge pool. Francesca and I started it after we'd climbed Monte Catello above Agerola, the mountain that's as high as Ben Nevis. Even after nearly a whole day of exercising, I'd still had to crank the heating up to 24 degrees, and I was unable to get warm when temperatures dropped in the evening. I decided it was time to toughen up.

I surprised even myself with my commitment and the changes it brought. I went from someone who couldn't keep warm, heating a house to 24 degrees, to someone who now has the heating set at 16 degrees. It didn't take long to adjust either. It certainly improves circulation and cold tolerance. No coffee is required to wake up if the first thing you do in the morning is a cold plunge in the garden!

## An Interesting Hypothesis

The events I'd read about back in 2020 were happening at a much slower rate than I had expected. It was both comfortable and uncomfortable at the same time. I was enjoying my time reading and researching alternative history, ideas and people. I read all the books I could find on Viktor Schauberger and his implosion technology, as well as his revelations about water, which tied in with a book I'd read by Gerald Pollack on the fourth phase of water a few years earlier. I also read Rudolph Steiner books, Nikola Tesla and others. They were much more interesting to me than reading all the doom and gloom.

When I read the works of these great people and the immense knowledge they had, I felt sadness that so much of it is lost to the world at large. For example, most people are aware that the cycles of the moon affect plant growth, but people like Steiner could tell you, from years of observation, how planets like Saturn and Jupiter affected plants. Just imagine the potential for humanity if we'd all been educated to that level of understanding on multiple aspects of life. Instead, we've allowed ourselves to be dumbed down by television and the like, to such a degree, few people know anything of value. What a waste.

Several people suggested that all the enormous rocks, like the ones I'd marvelled at in the various Dolmens I'd visited, had been made from a geopolymer and not carved. This can be an acidic or alkaline mix, similar to concrete. One YouTuber even had a go at making some, and it looked a lot like granite when it cured, and was as hard as rock.

If they are correct, it suddenly puts a very different spin on a lot of history. It's said that a French materials scientist called Joseph Davidovits had a theory that the pyramids were built from a man-made stone. He thought that a soft limestone had been dissolved and then mixed with lime and natron (a naturally occurring salt mixture) and then cast in moulds insitu. It is not a widely accepted theory, but it would be a lot easier than thousands of slaves carving enormous rocks and then hauling each one perfectly in place.

I watched videos a diving team had made in Florida after they discovered an underground water chamber, which stretched for miles. A sample of the water was taken, it had a unique composition, when tested it was identical to a spring in Texas.

There were numerous YouTube channels exploring underground, and finding evidence of what appeared to be geopolymer constructions. In some areas in and around Nottingham, they were in abundance. People were finding these hidden gems by looking on LiDAR maps, which are easily found online.

I started looking locally, and immediately found some unusual buried World War 2 air raid shelters. Excited by my first find, I started scanning further afield and a friend and I would go for walks with the dog to see if we could find anything of interest. We didn't on the few occasions we tried, before life went in an unexpected direction, but it was fun.

There's only so long I could spend reading about all the dark stuff that was either happening in the world, or about to. I'd got the gist, and it didn't seem good to be continually reading about things that may, or may not, happen. There's so much fear mongering online, it isn't helpful. Whilst some of it may be true, I think a great deal of it is designed to keep people in fear, or make them sound deranged if they keep warning everyone around them about things which never happen.

I was much happier reading and researching things that interested me. The things I was hearing on the Crrow podcasts opened up a whole new world. Along with the Mystery School teachings, and how much information has been hidden from us, I found myself wondering if there was any value in Gematria or Astrology? I started researching frequencies and the effects they have on water and the human body. Why is so much symbolism used? The questions were endless.

What I enjoyed the most was contemplating things I'd never considered before. I was viewing the world as if for the first time, questioning everything I'd ever been taught about everything. History books are written by the victors, his-story. How much is just that, a story? Just because we've been taught something is true, it doesn't mean that it is. Seeing things from a fresh perspective, for me, was fun. It enabled me to think about things in ways I'd not done before. I was enjoying expanding my mind in new directions. I've no way of verifying the majority of what I came across, but that is what made everything so intriguing.

Taking ideas as far as possible is an important part of creativity. By reading, listening and watching so many different theories from wide ranging sources, enabled me to thread together parts which overlapped, as well as make connections from completely unrelated topics and form new ideas about how the world works. There do seem to be unwritten rules to how this realm works. But I have not spent nearly enough time researching to warrant expressing the little I have concluded.

Nor would I get the time to continue investigating all that fascinated me. My life took a completely unexpected turn in January 2023 which took up all my time for the next two years. Talk about a plot twist that I would never have seen coming in a million years. Publicly, I like to blame Cheryl, who I'd met at the Stand in the Park in Colchester. As much as it is her fault, really the blame, as always, does lie with me.

# 13

# Unexpected

England isn't stunning like Spain and Italy, but it is beautiful, in a subtle, understated, very English way. Coming back after ten years away, I discovered I had a new appreciation for the cold, damp, wet and windy land I'd found so distasteful a decade earlier. I'd matured enough to appreciate and fall in love with the place and the people.

For several years before returning, I had noticed that I was missing the greenness of England. One of the reasons I'd even tried living in Jimena was because it had the highest rainfall in Andalusia and stayed lusher for longer. But it wasn't quite the right shade of green. Which might seem an odd thing to say, but I think I was beginning to miss England, but hadn't realised it yet.

I noticed I was missing England coming back on the BA flight from South Africa at the end of 2018. It had been £400 cheaper to fly to Spain than England, even though the flight stopped at Heathrow and I had to change planes to continue onto Spain.

Instead of the usual boring flight safety instructions they'd got a cast of well-known actors and actresses. I can only remember Michael Caine and Joanna Lumley now, but I remember it made me feel quite homesick. I'd really missed English humour. There's just something so dry, irreverent and funny about English humour that other nations don't quite have. I decided if there was any delay, instead of getting on the flight to Spain, I'd grab my case and get on the train to my parents in Colchester.

As it happened, everything was on time and I made my connecting flight. It was tantalising to have touched down in England, only to immediately leave it behind. But my life then was in Spain, and I soon settled back into the swing of it once I was back with my friends and walking groups.

After ten years of travelling and sightseeing, which believe it or not, can become boring. There had come a point prior to doing the life coaching, early 2019, where I'd realised I had a large fly in the ointment of the 'perfect life' I'd created. I had begun to become bored.

Having gone back through a gazillion photos to jog my memory prior to writing this book, and making the book bonus videos with some of them, I must admit, I'm struggling to see how on earth I became bored of that life, but I did. As enormously satisfying as teaching complete amateurs to quickly design gardens to a professional level is, life didn't have any real meaning. Business was easy. I really had created the 4-Hour Workweek existence, actually, probably less than that. I had enough money to do everything I wanted. I'd pretty much travelled to the point that I'd had enough of doing it.

I was beginning to question what was the point of being here? Not in a suicidal way, nor a depressed way. I just couldn't see the point of it all. That can be a problem with achieving everything on your wish list, now what?

I'd got a really busy social life, too busy if I'm honest for my introvert self, but I needed to fill my time doing something. I remember during a game of padel tennis, a friend of mine was incensed that I'd been doing a series of sneaky little dropshots that just squeaked over the net, which she couldn't reach no matter how fast she ran. Whilst her frustration amused me no end, I found myself observing with a mix of envy and intrigue. I couldn't fathom how she could possibly care so much. I didn't give a monkeys if I won or lost, it was just a game. Completely unimportant and not worth any emotional energy. In that moment it all seemed so utterly pointless. I felt I was just going through the motions of life.

Is this it? Why am I here? What is the point of all this?

When life had been a struggle, I had purpose to my day, but now I really didn't. I suppose I could have put more effort into my business and tried to make more money, but when push comes to shove, I just didn't care enough about making more. As long as I have enough to do what I want to do, I can't be bothered to try and get it for the sake of it. Which does rather make me a bit sloppy on the optimising sales front of my business. Any of the online entrepreneurs at my business masterminds would have been appalled! They were all about split-testing and optimising everything on their sales and landing pages, whereas I was, 'great, I've sold stuff, excellent, which mountain shall I hike up today!'

In hindsight, it would have been sensible to have put a bit more effort into the money making side of things with the direction the world is heading. Had I known then what I know now, I would have optimised everything in sight and saved like crazy, bought some land off-grid well away from everyone and everything, and taken my best friends and family with me. Though in truth, that probably wouldn't have worked out in the long run, there is no escaping this, it's global.

After my experiences in lockdown, I was ready to come home. It was such a relief to be able to speak my native language rather than butchering Spanish, Italian, Portuguese, or French so badly. Even simple things like going to the post office were a joy compared to the trial they'd been abroad. I'm fine as long as whoever I'm talking to in the foreign country replies using the exact phrase on the language learning CDs. The slightest deviation and I'm completely lost. When you first attempt to speak a foreign language, there comes a certain degree of boldness because you don't know enough to know how bad you are. But as you begin to gain awareness, then it becomes excruciating.

Living back in England, I didn't even seem to mind the English weather, once I'd got over my initial reaction coming back to torrential rain. Considering I'd fled for ten years to avoid it, I was quite surprised at how easily I adapted. Everyone around me was complaining bitterly, but for me it was almost a delight. When you've lived through forty plus degree summers with not a drop of rain for months on end, it gives you a whole new appreciation for the stuff. It also meant I didn't have to spend all my spare time watering the allotments. Nature did that for me.

It was also much easier to do cold exposure in England than it had been in Spain. I'd missed English seasons. As much as I adored the light levels in Spain, and the mostly clear, intense blue skies, there were several years I felt over stimulated in the winter. The light intensity was too much all year, but then I do have a Celtic ancestry, so I don't mind a bit of hibernation time. Truth be told, I crave hibernation.

In the winter months I don't want to leave the house at all, especially at night. So it took an extraordinary amount of effort for me to drag myself out on the fateful night of the 31st January 2023. Perhaps part of me knew what was ahead.

## A Fateful Evening

I'd had quite a battle in my head, before finally deciding I would join the others going to a public council meeting at the Town Hall. I didn't want to go at all, but persuaded myself by reflecting that I'd never been to a single rally in London, nor had I ever done any of the yellow board signs at the roundabouts or anything remotely proactive other than making anonymous videos and infographics. The nagging voice inside my head was, "Come on, you never do anything, just go. All you've got to do is sit there. It's not like you've got to speak or anything."

Because of the internal bickering about whether to go or not, I was now quite late. I increased my lateness by being determined to find free parking. Not something which is easy in Colchester. By the time I did eventually make it in to the Town Hall, I was half an hour late. I asked at the reception desk where the council meeting was and they pointed upstairs. I was told the meeting had been suspended, but that I could still go up if I wished, but there was unlikely to be a seat.

I could hear a lot of commotion coming from the floor above, something had clearly kicked off. It sounded like a lot of people had come to this meeting. I didn't know exactly what it was about. Someone had sent a document pack out online, but it looked so boring when I skimmed through it that I had decided not to bother reading it because they'd discuss everything at the meeting. If going along in the first place could be considered mistake number one, mistake two was not getting there on time, and mistake three was definitely not reading the agenda pack.

As I came up the stairs and rounded the corner, the commotion was even louder. How many people were in there and what was all the commotion about? I walked in and the room was packed. I only recognised a handful of faces. Who were all these other people? There wasn't a spare seat in sight. There must have been about thirty or more people crammed into the back of the high-ceilinged meeting room, with sage coloured walls and a luminous pea green ceiling adorned with white wood panelling, all talking at once. The council staff looked rather flustered and were trying their best to restore order and get everyone quiet. I heard a voice I recognised from Jef, who I'd met at 'Stand in the Park' ask, "When can we speak? We should be able to have our say!"

My friend Karena, yes, different to the other Carinna, who was also supposed to be coming but texted she couldn't make it, waved me over to the front row where she was sitting. She shuffled up on quite a large chair and there was just about room for me to squeeze in next to her.

I'd only just taken off my coat and got my backside on the chair when the young meeting Chairman, in an ill-fitting blue suit with a red tie, who looked like he'd only recently come out of short trousers, said over the speaker, "OK, two of you can come and have your say." I instantly had an awful feeling it was going to be me. I did half consider it, because it was clear things couldn't continue like this. But Sensible Me put that notion to rest by very firmly telling me, "Do not volunteer under any circumstance, you do not know what is going on!" Good point, well made. I won't volunteer. And I didn't.

My body flooded instantly with relief that I was not the appropriate person for whatever the hell was going on. I still had no clue what all the commotion was about.

And then mistake number four kicked in. Sitting right at the front of the room. Had I been there on time I would have tucked myself quietly away at the back. My earlier sense of relief vanished the moment I got a tap on my shoulder. It was Cheryl. "Rachel, will you do it?"

What!?

"Well, er, yes, I could do, but I don't know what's going on!"

Cheryl replied, "I'd do it, but I doubt they'll take my Dagenham accent seriously, but they'll listen to you!" I didn't entirely agree that they wouldn't take her seriously, but I knew what she meant. And I knew I could put my private school accent to good use when required.

I reluctantly agreed, but told her she'd have to tell me what to say as I'd no idea what was going on.

"Didn't you read the document pack?"

"No!"

"Oh!"

And with that the meeting resumed. I sat next to Jimmy who had volunteered to speak. I concluded that by the end of the meeting I'd know what was going on and I was sure I'd be able to contribute accordingly. That was mistake number five.

No sooner had I got to the microphone, next to Jimmy, than the meeting Chairman announced, "Right you've both got three minutes each to 'Have Your Say' (which was the name the Council had given to the publics' 'opportunity to speak' section of their meetings)!"

What now?! Oh hell.

I hoped beyond hope that I'd be able to glean something from Jimmy's contribution, which would enable me to work out what was going on. All I could remember from the flyer, which was shared in the group, was that the Council wanted Colchester residents to give up their second car, and eventually eliminate the need for a private car altogether! But what else?

Jimmy asked a series of questions about what happens if people don't want to give up their car, would they be taxed out of it with congestion charges? He received some fairly bland word salad, slightly patronising responses back. Cheryl had probably been right about how they perceived us, and the commotion earlier hadn't helped with that impression. If only I had half a clue about what was happening to be of use.

Then Jimmy asked about DEFRA. I tried to jog my memory, DEFRA, aren't they farming, or was it military? I'd been out the country ten years, I couldn't remember. But either way, what could DEFRA possibly have to do with bicycle lanes?!

I could sense Jimmy beginning to run out of things to say, and it was going to be my turn any moment. The responses he was receiving didn't give me anything to grab hold of to run with. If only I hadn't been so late I would have seen the presentation and known what was going on.

Although I'm not a deeply religious person in the traditional going to church sense, I did pray at that point. Well, more pleading than praying. I mentally shot out, "If you want me to do this, I am going to need help, and quickly!" hoping some force of Universal Intelligence would come to my rescue, because I had absolutely no idea what to say. I could not think of a single thing.

At the exact moment I could hear Jimmy wrapping up, Cheryl appeared next to me and discretely placed a neatly written post-it note, with three questions, on the table in front of me. Oh thank goodness. I just about had time to read them. And now it was my turn.

They were questions about a survey, presumably that had either been covered in the presentation, or the document pack. All I could do was wing it, and hope the Council Officer answering me would give enough information so that I could respond properly, though judging by how she'd spoken to Jimmy, I didn't hold out much hope.

The Council had done a survey to see if people would ditch their car for a bicycle. From the note Cheryl had written, it appeared they did the main survey at an eco-festival – hardly an unbiased crowd. I pushed them for details, and was given a very vague, 'we surveyed lots of different people at various events', answer. I pressed for more details. What demographic did they survey? A very vague response came to that question. They didn't keep a note of the exact demographic apparently, but they were of all ages.

I replied "So you're telling me that eighty year olds want to get on a bicycle?!"

"Oh yes, you'd be surprised how many older people were keen on cycling and with eBikes now, it opens cycling to a much wider group." Before I could press her on anything more the Chairman cut in to say that he'd generously given us more than our allotted time, and politely told us to go away, and that they were going to continue on with their meeting.

I'd done the best I could under the circumstances, but without being armed with enough information, I didn't feel I'd been of much use. We stayed to watch the rest of the meeting, and to our surprise there were some really nice councillors.

Councillor Moore raised her concerns over the eBikes, with the sustainability of the batteries and the horrific mining of cobalt using child slave labour. She reminded her colleagues that purchasing these was against the Council's anti-slavery policy. That seemed to fall on deaf ears with the Council, but not to the audience. She said the Council was in danger of becoming schizophrenic with wanting to attract more shoppers, but not wanting them to come in by car. Everyone started clapping and cheering as she raised such thoughtful points.

Later, another councillor took the opportunity to address us. He said how pleased he was that we'd come along, we were a breath of fresh air. He joked that he'd told his wife he'd be home fairly early, and he'd thought it was going to be a rather dull meeting, and thanked us for showing an interest and expressing an alternative point of view. He told us that he was delighted we were there, as it was good and healthy to get alternative viewpoints expressed. He said he used to be part of an activist group and came to so many meetings that eventually he became a councillor himself. He advised us to get ourselves organised and to come back to future 'Have Your Says'. I wonder if he's regretting that advice now? Because that is exactly what we did.

I'm fairly certain the Council had never experienced an evening like that before. They were used to lots of people turning up to contentious planning decision meetings, but not for the Environment and Sustainability Panel. As each councillor spoke, people would applaud if they said sensible things, so it became more like a night at the theatre, rather than a council meeting.

I later found out what all the commotion had been about. Whilst everyone, except me, had read the agenda pack, no one had thought to research what happens at council meetings. It would appear the public thought they could join in and give their opinions on what was being said. It was a public council meeting after all! No one knew there was an allotted time that the public could speak, and that was it. So when council officers had tried to shut everyone up, it hadn't gone well. They'd more or less all said at once, "The Council are supposed to be working for us, so why can't we speak?" That's the point when I'd arrived.

Afterwards, in the break, some of the councillors came up to us thanking us for coming, and remarked how it had made it easier for them to speak up. I'd not had any preconceived ideas about what councillors were like, and I'd been very pleasantly surprised. They mostly seemed nice, good people. We left that evening spirits high. Bumpy start aside, it had been a good evening.

Our view of the Council was about to change dramatically. The people behind the scenes were not happy about our appearance, and unbeknownst to us at the time, sent out an email to all the councillors the following day saying that we must never be allowed to do that again.

Then, on social media a couple of days later, the polite, young Chairman turned out not to be anywhere near so nice and polite when he wasn't in the room with us. And so the battle commenced…

# 14

# Doing Things Properly

The next day I watched the part of the meeting I'd missed on the Council's YouTube channel. To my horror it was all about eBikes, and replacing the Council fleet with electric vehicles, and a Rapid Transit Bus system, which would also be electric. At that time, all the EV fires weren't on mainstream social media, but we'd all seen too many videos of horrific fires on the alternative social media platforms. I was kicking myself, because if I'd have known, I could have spoken quite a bit about the dangers of them, and why it was inadvisable for the Council to be turning their fleet into EVs, as well as public buses.

I decided as I'd made such a hash of speaking that I would go back to the next meeting in a couple of month's time with a properly researched and written out speech. To get my own back on Cheryl, I asked her to do a speech as well! Plus, she had a friend who was high up in the fire service and he was deeply concerned about EV fires, as his son was still a firefighter. She was able to ask him to provide information which we were pretty certain these councillors wouldn't know, but needed to.

The more I started to research EVs, the more I realised it wasn't just the child slave labour for the cobalt that was bad, but how the lithium was extracted. All mining has an environmental cost, but lithium extraction is particularly awful. The more research I did, the more I realised it had been a blessing I'd been late to the meeting, because I now knew a lot more about the production process. EVs were the antithesis of green and environmentally friendly. I was really quite shocked.

I was also feeling physically sick every time I looked down at the giant lithium battery on my office floor, connected to a solar panel that I had in the garden, powering my office. It sounds ridiculous, but I was so sickened once I realised the true cost of making a lithium battery and the recycling issues, that I didn't use it for six months. Completely illogical. It did not make its purchase any less damaging by not using it, but I couldn't bring myself to go near it. I did debate if I should sell it, but in the end, decided to live with it as a reminder that I should have considered production, and not just how long the battery charge was. Besides, if the Net Zero initiatives I'd read about in 2020 happened, I knew I'd need it.

## Not Such a Nice Guy

The beginning part of the meeting that I'd missed, which someone filmed, showed a room full of people quietly sitting there with yellow A4 paper signs saying things like 'leave the car alone', and 'there is no climate emergency' etc. It was shared on Twitter, and picked up by one of the daytime GB News people. When they shared it, and it went slightly viral, things started getting interesting.

The Chairman of the Environment and Sustainability Panel replied that we didn't represent the views of ordinary people because we were a bunch of 'anti-vax, far-right extremists'. And to think he'd been so pleasant to us in the meeting.

When I arrived at the meeting, I did not see any signs about vaccines, only people wanting to keep using their car. So I'm not really sure what made him label us like that.

I responded to his comment asking why he thought our presence was anything to do with vaccines when we'd been discussing bicycle lanes? I took the opportunity to say that we were concerned about lithium mining, and uploaded a picture of a mine to emphasise my point. I also mentioned that we would put in a formal complaint if he continued being abusive on social media.

He did not take the opportunity presented to wind his neck in. Instead, he escalated his commentary, and diverted his attack because one of the concerned parents in our group wanted to rally outside Colchester library due to the drag queen story hour they were holding. On alternative social media there had been lots of reports of some of the drag queens being convicted pedophiles. Which, as you can imagine, was very concerning to the aware parents. Now, that's not to say the person coming to Colchester library was, but the parents in the group felt very strongly that adult entertainment should be for adults, not children. No one had anything against drag queens, they just felt it should be age appropriate.

When he saw the post on Twitter about gathering outside the library, he embarked on a series of tweets, which called the group 'homophobic, dangerous, far-right extremists', and a litany of other delights, and said we preyed on the vulnerable. Considering it had been my face on the public video that the Council had put on YouTube, I wasn't best pleased. Nor were the parents who were concerned about the children, and were highly displeased at being branded as homophobic. It was especially ridiculous as several of the group are gay!

I decided I would write to the Council Leader, and put in a formal complaint; this was unacceptable and highly unprofessional. The Council Leader wrote back immediately saying that he found it very concerning, and that he'd pass my complaint over to the Monitoring Officer, as it was he who dealt with the Councillor Code of Conduct complaints. I thanked him, and advised him to have a word with the councillor in question, as he was damaging the reputation of the City of Colchester, a title I knew they'd worked hard to get from being just a common town, previously. At this point, the councillor had even paid for his offensive tweets to be boosted, and as a result, had managed to get into a spat with the pop group, Right Said Fred! I mentioned this to the Council Leader, saying that it was getting embarrassing now.

The Monitoring Officer duly got in touch, and I put in my complaint. I didn't for one minute think the Council would endorse this sort of behaviour. I pointed out that he had "Councillor" written across his social media profile banner. He was also discussing members of the public, who had attended a Council meeting that he had chaired and that his behaviour was clearly council related and unacceptable. Several other people also put in a complaint against him. Complaints went in to Essex County Council, Colchester and the Labour Party, reporting his behaviour.

## Rally On!

On the 18th February 2023 I attended my first rally. We all chipped in to hire a coach and fifty of us went to support the people of Oxford against the Low Traffic Neighbourhoods (LTNs) which were being forced upon them as an experiment. Once in place, add in surveillance, Digital IDs and hey presto, you have yourself a 15 Minute City.

They are billed as, 'for your convenience', with everything within a fifteen minute walk, which would be wonderful. Where it gets concerning in Oxford, is it was proposed that people could only leave their dedicated zones in a car a hundred times a year. Every time they went over their allowance they would be fined £70! Though the scheme did allow for them to use the ring road without penalty, but what a pain that would be, having to drive all the way round when you just want to get from A to B.

A few thousand people turned up to support the people of Oxford, there was just one thing missing… the people of Oxford! Whilst the event had been organised by locals, we spoke to loads of people who wondered why we were there! Most had no idea what was about to happen to their city. It was truly shocking so many were clueless. We informed as many as was physically possible to raise awareness.

The council said they were only putting in measures to improve traffic congestion. Newspapers reported the 15 Minute City concerns were just conspiracy theories. Let's hope so! Regardless of whether they are or not, it was a lovely day out and I enjoyed my first rally. I had both Carinna and Karena with me and even managed to have a quick meet up with my lovely friend who was over from Portugal and happened to be in Oxford that day.

Back to business in Colchester, the Monitoring Officer said he'd get back to me regarding my complaint once he'd investigated. The weeks went by with no outcome. I checked the Council complaints procedure, and read that they had to get back to me within six weeks. I sent the Monitoring Officer a follow-up email to ask when we might hear back. He said that we would hear something in the next couple of weeks. I wondered if they were stalling as there was another Environment and Sustainability Panel meeting coming up in two weeks.

## The Art of Good Communication

In the meantime two ladies in Maldon called Katie and Janet, had organised a talk with Piers Corbyn, and a man called, David Charalambous, from ReachingPeople.net. I wasn't particularly interested in hearing Corbyn talk, but I was very keen to listen to Charalambous. He was a behavioural and communications expert, and his talk was all about reaching people and brainstorming how we could communicate with councils, and how to voice our concerns effectively.

Piers Corbyn was entertaining, and I warmed to him more than I'd expected. He had some surprising things to say about climate change, and handed out some info leaflets. David's talk was fascinating and insightful. He started by asking the question, "How many of you have managed to change someone's mind using facts and logic in the last few years?"

The audience gave a resigned chuckle. He went on to tell us that unless someone has the information already on the map in their mind, then you've virtually no chance of getting your point of view across effectively. He said, that it was, however, possible to put some information onto their map by tying it into something they already believe to be true. Asking poignant questions in the right way is also another good way of breaking through with people.

My biggest takeaway from what David told us, in the short time we had with him, was that it is possible to reach people with a different point of view to you if you go about it in the right way. That for me was game changing. It had been tempting to go back to the Council and tell them off for all their ill-conceived plans. After David's talk, I started writing my speech with a whole different mindset, but there were a couple of points I needed to put right at the beginning before I could write the things that might be on the map in their minds.

It took me two weeks to write that first speech. Not because I'm a slow writer, but in part due to the amount of research I had to do, so that I got my facts right, but mainly because of the time limit imposed on speeches. Colchester Council only allows public 'Have Your Say' speakers to have three minutes each. I had so much I wanted to say. I was determined to cram in as much as possible since I only had one shot at this. I was cursing about the time limit. My first attempt at getting in everything I wanted to say was fifteen minutes long. Surprisingly, the time limit later became our greatest ally.

I could feel anxiety rising every time I practised my speech to see if I was able to read out everything I'd crammed in within the three minute time span. What was I thinking? I'm not a public speaker. I'd never done anything like this in my life. I certainly wasn't the type of person to make a fuss, or dream of going along to the Council. But I was so concerned over the dangers these EVs presented, and then finding out how devastating for the environment they were, that I had been spurred on. I was incensed that something that was sold as saving the planet, could be so devastatingly damaging.

It's doubtful I would have done it had I not been so incensed. My sense of justice had kicked in enough to motivate me to do the unthinkable, reading out loud in public. Not something any dyslexic relishes. I must have practised reading that speech out loud a hundred times, or more. Every time a wave of nerves arose, I'd do some EFT tapping on it. This anxious state went on for two weeks prior to me setting foot back in the Town Hall. A lot of tapping was required.

I'd been tricked into attending EFT, or Emotional Freedom Technique training, many years earlier. I was told by the lady teaching it that it was something business owners and entrepreneurs were all learning to help them be successful. That caught my interest. At that time in life, I was listening to CDs from the likes of Tony Robbins, Brian Tracy, and many more of those kinds of 'success coaches'.

The first evening EFT lesson, three of us gathered in her living room, where she had a whiteboard set up to explain what EFT was. Opposite me was a big, burly farmer I'd known from my Young Farmer group days. I was amazed to see him. I didn't think he was the type to go in for self-development. When the demonstration started, I couldn't believe my eyes. Our tutor started tapping various places around her head and body, whilst muttering various statements.

It was all I could do not to burst out laughing. I looked across at the farmer, and he looked like a deer caught in headlights. Clearly he'd been tricked into attending, just as I had. I knew him to be ambitious, so she'd probably used the same lure to get him to attend as she had me. But what to do about it?

I couldn't just get up and walk out, that would be so rude. These days, I definitely could, but back then I was far too polite.

I stayed put, and did all the ridiculous tapping of various acupressure points around the head and body. Then something really weird happened. I started to yawn and feel my whole body relax. I don't remember exactly how our tutor described how EFT worked, but it was something along the lines of freeing trapped emotions which get stored in the body.

After the first class we were all given homework, and told to practice it. The final class was the following week. I did as instructed, and did notice things that I'd been stressing about, melting away. I returned to class the following week. The farmer did not.

EFT is quick and easy to learn, and you can release years of trauma. Some things take longer than others if there are multiple aspects. For example, a spider phobia you might tap on seeing a spider. You tap that out, but then as soon as it moves, you freak out. Tapping on moving spiders would need to be done. Then you might need to tap on touching spiders before a spider phobia completely clears.

Gary Craig started EFT in the 1990s. It is a simplified version of TFT (Thought Field Therapy) from the work of Dr. Roger Callahan. It's often just one of the acupressure points you tap which causes the emotional release, but rather than tapping a specific sequence, depending on the issue like TFT, with EFT you to tap all the points knowing that one of them will do the job, so no need to try and figure out a sequence like TFT. I have since read TFT is superior to EFT because sometimes the sequence of what you tap is important. You also don't have to think about each aspect of whatever is traumatising you, just the initial trigger will do, and the sequence takes care of everything else.

I told my mother about EFT, and suggested she try it. Wanting to learn more without going to classes, she purchased a box set of Gary Craig DVDs and we both watched tens of hours of him treating people with phobias, PTSD and all sorts of other emotional issues. It was nothing short of incredible watching him work. If those DVD's are available digitally, I'd recommend them to anyone. You could see the change in people's faces as years of trauma left them.

One of the most powerful examples, was a woman whose mother had purposefully poured a pot of boiling water over her when she was two years old, the scarring still showing on her body. She was deeply traumatised over it, as you can imagine. Before Gary started the session, the woman's face was contorted with rage, when she spoke, asking 'who would pour boiling water over a child for God's sake? A little defenceless child!'.

By the end of the session, which took about ten to fifteen minutes, she was calm and looked ten years younger. When Gary asked how she was doing, something he always did before and during sessions, she'd gone from a ten to a one on emotional distress levels. In a soft voice she said, "My mother wasn't well, she needed help." Her anger, remarkably replaced by understanding.

My EFT tutor had said emotional responses to past traumas were like having dirty windows, they cloud your vision of everything you see. You view all your life situations from the viewpoint of what has happened to you in the past. For example if someone hit you every time you spoke up as a child, you're unlikely to speak up as an adult. The rather blunt way I tend to describe EFT, is that it clears the shit off your windscreen.

The amazing part is, when it's gone, it doesn't return. You still remember all the things that have happened in your life, but they don't define you any more. EFT allows you to view them with detachment, and you release your emotional reaction to whatever has happened. It is an incredible tool, and I'm forever grateful I was 'tricked' into going along as it has been truly life changing.

So of course, it was my go-to tool for the situation I now found myself in, public speaking at the Council. I didn't care if my legs were shaking, I just didn't want my voice to. My one wish was to have control of that, even if the rest of me had turned to jelly, I wanted to sound in control. On the day, I could still feel my anxiety, so I really tuned into it, in between reading the speech out loud, over and over. Something most unexpected popped into my mind.

A scene from school played out during one of the rounds of EFT. It was from my third year of senior school. There was a girl who was being mercilessly bullied. I could never stand bullying, so, as usual, I stepped in to stop it. I always ended up with a backlash, but that didn't stop me. I had such a strong dislike of bullying.

On this particular occasion, most of the class turned on me for speaking up, including the girl I'd stopped being bullied. I couldn't believe it. I'd helped her, and she was so weak minded, instead of siding with me, she chose to side with the bullies. I don't think I stepped in again after that experience. It was odd, that of all things that particular incident should pop up now, but I did several rounds of tapping on it and the feelings subsided.

I realised what I was about to do was in some ways similar. I was standing up and speaking up about something I saw to be wrong. I also knew that what I had to say wasn't likely to be well received. How funny that trauma from my past that I'd all but forgotten about, was affecting me decades later. Once I'd tapped it out, I felt much calmer, and I knew I'd be alright on the night.

Before we gathered, I asked everyone in the group to make sure there weren't any disruptions this time, and I asked them all to remain quiet, otherwise I felt that we wouldn't be taken seriously, and that we would be viewed as troublemakers. If that's how they saw us, we'd never be able to reach them.

What I hadn't anticipated was what would happen before I even got a chance to speak. As it turned out, the Council were determined to be in control this time, and not allow a repeat of the previous meeting. They had a little surprise in store for us when we arrived that night.

# 15

# Take Two

Colchester's Town Hall, built in 1902, is a grand Edwardian Baroque style building which dominates the High Street. This third iteration includes a 192ft bell tower containing the bell from the original Moot Hall built in the 1400s. The tower is adorned with a statue of Colchester's patron saint, St Helena, which was donated by the industrialist, James Paxman.

The building facade is a mix of stone and brick, with pillars around stone alcoves containing life-size statues of prominent figures from Colchester's rich history, from Boudicca to Archbishop Harsnett.

Inside, the stone floored foyer is lined with large stone pillars escorting visitors to a central marble staircase which winds its way up to floors above. On our second visit, the foyer was also adorned with a welcoming committee of police and security staff.

This time, in order to enter the Town Hall, we had to be searched. The security guards were armed with scanners and set about scanning, prodding and searching everyone, and everything, that was coming in, with the police standing by in case there were problems. It was a little undignified to be treated like criminals, especially when the last meeting had ended on good terms, but everybody allowed the search without issue.

Cheryl enquired as to why we were being searched, and we were told it was to make sure there were no demonstration materials, and something about 'for everyone's safety.' When it came to my turn to be searched, as soon as my laptop was removed from its bag, all my EV fire posters fell out on the floor. The friendly older, portly security guard looked at them dubiously and asked me if they were work related, or something else. I replied indignantly, "I'm one of tonight's speakers!"

"Oh right", he replied and hastily shoved them back in my bag. I suspect he'd assumed I was a speaker the Council had invited. They often had experts come in with presentations. Phew, that was close. Those images were vital for Cheryl's speech on fires. Seeing is believing, after all. The amount of fire when an EV goes up is hard to imagine, it was critical those councillors saw it.

When I reached the top of the marble staircase, I was met by a Council Officer with a clipboard. He asked me if I would be speaking tonight, then my name. When I got into the meeting room, I noticed a lot fewer chairs than there were the first time we'd been there. It was odd there weren't more chairs as they were obviously expecting us. Perhaps they were purposefully keeping the numbers down. It turned out that that was the case. They'd got an overflow room set up with a large screen.

## Speaking Up

I was dreading speaking, the waiting was awful. I just wanted it over and done with. I started tapping the karate chop EFT point on my hand on the side of the chair. Cheryl saw what I was doing and laughed. She wasn't remotely bothered about speaking. Why do I put myself through these things, I questioned?

I suddenly started to panic that what I'd written was really lame. Should I have made it harder-hitting? Did I have time to re-write it? What should I write to make it better? It soon became apparent that there wasn't time, I would just have to read it out as it was. Making changes at this point could be disastrous.

The waiting is the worst part. The anxiety keeps building and building. It's a cross between waiting for a bad diagnosis at the hospital, mixed with going to have a tooth pulled out and hoping the anaesthetic has kicked in properly before they do it. I wanted to pace up and down to try and dissipate the nervous energy. All I could do were gentle tap, tap, taps on the side of the chair while Cheryl chuckled, knowing precisely what I was doing, and finding my ever-increasing anxiety levels amusing. She mouthed "You'll be fine." Easy for her to say.

Jimmy was also speaking again. He had a short speech asking questions on how they'd reached their conclusions regarding air quality. I could see him reading his, over and over like I was trying to do.

A text message arrived from Carinna saying that she was running late, but on her way, not to worry, she should just about make it. She was the backup speaker in case I passed out.

The meeting started, and my heart was racing and my palms, sweating. Tap, tap, tap. Breathe. Tap, tap, tap on the side of the chair. I decided I should probably stop doing that, it was beginning to look like I'd got a nervous tick, or extreme dislike of council furniture. The meeting started at 6pm with all the councillors and officers introducing themselves. Then the minutes of the previous meeting were agreed. Next up was the 'Have Your Say' part. Showtime.

The first speaker was a man who wanted the Council to do more to attract cyclists to Colchester for environmental and economic reasons. He wanted them to install bicycle hangers so people could safely store their bikes.

Then it was my turn to read out what I now considered to be the lamest speech ever. I would have to read it at a million miles an hour because of how much I'd packed in. Here is what I read out to a packed meeting room in the Town Hall on 21st March 2023.

*"Good evening. After the last meeting a Councillor here branded us as a group of dangerous far-right extremists!*

*In reality, we're unaffiliated individuals who are collectively very concerned about environmental issues and government policies, and we're hoping you can help us with our concerns.*

*In the past, I've taken government advice and purchased a car I hated in order to do my bit for the environment!*

*That was when diesel was considered good, until of course, it obviously wasn't!*

***Now*** *the government say that **electric** vehicles are good for the environment....*

*Considering how many times governments u-turn on what is good and what isn't... have members of the panel independently researched the environmental impact of making the batteries for the proposed electric bikes, scooters, buses etc?*

*Do you know that in order to extract lithium, a single mine can use over **5 thousand** tons of sulphuric acid, **per day**. To remove the acid, over **3,000** gallons of water is used **per minute**.*

*Every year, that single mine produces over 350 million cubic yards of **permanent** waste laced with sulphuric acid & radioactive uranium.*

*That information was provided by the US Bureau of Land Management about a mine in Nevada...*

*And they anticipate what's left of the water supply, in the area **indigenous people rely on**, could be contaminated for an estimated **300 years**.*

*Cobalt is also required for rechargeable batteries...*

*In the last meeting Councillor Moore asked about ensuring the Council use ethically produced batteries. Your professional standards require you to adhere to ethical principles, so have you researched this further?*

*Are you aware that unfortunately it isn't possible, because 70% of Cobalt is mined using child labour which is mixed-in at the factories with the 30% that isn't...*

*Professor Kara from Harvard University,* a *slavery researcher, who visited these supposedly audited eco-mines in the Congo, where children work and die in unimaginably awful conditions says...*

*"**There is no clean cobalt.** There is not a single company on planet earth that makes a device that has a rechargeable battery in it that can reliably and justifiably claim that their cobalt isn't coming from sources like that."*

*Do not support this corporate greed and exploitation, especially when there **are** good green alternatives to EVs. And if there aren't electric vehicles to charge, then the large, ugly power lines marching through our countryside won't be needed either.*

*And considering most of the electricity used to charge EVs is **not** from renewable green sources, clearly, anything with a lithium battery, which can't be easily recycled, isn't green!*

*So for the record, we do not consent to public money being spent on **any** lithium battery operated vehicles which will cause an exponential increase in mining devastation.*

*So no matter **how** enticing the financial incentives are, can we have the Council's **absolute assurance** that you will do what is **right** and **not** allow yourselves to be pressured by the government into any actions that do more harm than good for the environment?*

*Thank you."*

No one on the panel wanted to tackle answering that lot, so the Chairman asked the Environment and Climate Emergency officer to respond to the concerns I'd raised. His response was that the making of any vehicle has an environmental impact. It was at this point I was caught on the hop.

I didn't know I would get a chance to respond to their response, so I'd got nothing prepared. When the Chairman asked me if I'd like to have an extra minute to respond. I replied, "Traditional vehicles do not pollute the water supply for three hundred years in order to make a battery". That part was fine, it was what came next that I shouldn't have said.

I told him there were greener alternatives to EVs like hydrogen vehicles because I'd seen a video of JCB who had developed a hydrogen engine for all their machines. What I hadn't done though was to fact-check how green the production of hydrogen is since I'd not anticipated I'd get to speak about it, that was on my to-do list. Once the video went on my YouTube channel, I was inundated with people telling me hydrogen isn't as green as billed. That was deeply disappointing.

Next up was Cheryl with her speech on the fire hazards. I hoped my speech had sowed some discontent about EVs, and now Cheryl could go in and give them grounds for divorce.

*"Have the panel considered the dangers of electric vehicles in their planning, and has a Fire Service approved safety plan been created for dealing with the fires?*

*A freedom of information request shows that in London in the last 5 years there have been over 500 fires caused by the batteries in electric vehicles - over 200 of the fires were cars, over one hundred electric bikes, over 60 scooters, 19 buses & 10 HGVs fires.*

*The following information comes from a fire expert who holds a senior position in the Fire Service, training fire crews nationally and abroad.*

*The Fire Service require the burnt out vehicles to stay at the fire site for 24 hours due to the fact they can reignite and explode. But if it's inside, the whole building has to be shut off for 48 hours.*

*Sometimes a hole has been dug and filled with water and the car or scooter pushed into it until it goes out. We have enough issues with pot-holes, let alone car size ones!*

*Is there a plan in place if there's a fire at an electric charging station or multi story car park & how long these would need to be shut for, bearing in mind the number of electric vehicles that could ignite if one catches on fire?*

*Who would be responsible for the shut down of the area and would the Council compensate any businesses that have to close for 24/48 hours?*

*If an electric refuse lorry caught fire on a housing estate, have evacuation procedures been put in place to get people away from the toxic fumes?*

*Is the panel aware that whilst it's the Fire Service's responsibility for the polluted water run off, they admit they aren't able to secure this toxic waste water, so would the Council take on this responsibility? It can take 30,000 litres of water to put out an electric car fire...*

*The Fire Service are soon issuing new electric vehicle fire regulations, do your safety measures meet up to these new regulations?*

*If not, we request you draw up safety plans with the Fire Service in accordance with the new regulations for the existing electric scooters and any fleet vehicles. And immediately remove the scooters until that revised safety plan is in place, and public safety can be guaranteed.*

*As councillors and council officers, you have a duty of care to the public. The fire hazards of electric bikes and cars etc, are well documented. Which means any officer that recommends EVs and councillors that authorise their use to the public, could be held personally liable, as they have violated their duty of care, and indemnity insurance is unlikely to cover this.*

*With all these points in mind, unless you can guarantee they are 100% safe, we request that you don't go ahead with more electric vehicles, as we feel they are of great danger to the public, and will eventually have to be scrapped, which will waste millions and won't help the environment. Especially as there are safer, greener, alternative options available."*

Their response to Cheryl was slightly better, they acknowledged they did need to look into it more. And the Chairman added that he believed that the Council did liaise with Essex Fire Services, and that they were usually good at checking things.

While Cheryl had been speaking, several of us in the audience held up A3 posters of various EV fires I'd managed to get past security. The Council staff came over and asked people not to hold up the posters, so they put them down. I didn't. It was too important. The councillors needed to see just how bad these fires are. I continued to hold mine up.

The surly, younger and leaner, ex-army looking security guard, who was dressed in a sharp-looking, dark navy pinstripe suit, decided that since I wouldn't comply, he would come around behind me and tap me on the shoulder to get my attention. He couldn't walk around in front of me because he would have been on camera. He started to insistently tap on top of my right shoulder. I ignored the firm tapping and it soon turned a bit more forceful. He started to push his finger into my shoulder.

It didn't matter how firmly he pushed his fingers in, I wasn't letting go of the posters. Those councillors were going to see those images. He tried pushing his fingers quite deeply into a pressure point, where the neck joins the top of the shoulder. In theory it should have been enough to make me let go but it was my right shoulder which was so tight from playing tennis in my youth, and now too much time spent using a mouse at the computer, that his efforts couldn't get through the tight muscles. Had he put that much pressure on my left shoulder, I suspect I would have shrieked out.

He then resorted to trying to grab the images, but that turned into a game of cat and mouse. This is a game I'm good at having spent many hours tormenting the dog with her toys, moving them out the way just when she thinks she's going to get them. I kept slowly moving the posters from one side to the other depending on which side of my head he was lunging at them from. Eventually he had to give up because it was beginning to cause a scene, which annoyingly no one behind me thought to film! I could feel another complaint to the Council coming on. Not that they'd addressed the first one!

Next up was Jimmy...

*"How much influence does the panel have with Essex highways? And are the panel able to voice environmental concerns on our behalf to Essex, or is that something we need to do directly?*

*The Council reports its emissions in terms of tonnes of carbon dioxide equivalent, shown as $tCO_2e$. Can you provide me with the data used in the Methodology published by EcoAct, which shows how they arrive at this figure, and has it been independently verified?*

*Have the panel calculated the amount of $CO_2$ that will be produced making all the electric vehicles they propose, and scrapping the existing ones, compared to just using the existing fleet?*

*Can the panel provide the data they've used to calculate how many cars would need to be off the road, and using cycle lanes to make a noticeable difference to air quality in Colchester?*

*The data the Major of London used recently - stating there were 4000 deaths a year from air pollution were incorrect - when a member of the public did a Freedom of Information Act request to the Office of National Statistics, it turned out to be just **one** death in the last 20 years - which was a child with a rare form of asthma, and it couldn't be exclusively put down to traffic pollution.*

*With regards to the proposed bike lanes and electric bikes scheme, we request that the Council do a full consultation with the public - asking only 800 people when they are out for the day, is not a proper consultation. Colchester has nearly 200k people in the area, asking less than 1% is not democratic.*

*Especially considering the cost of living crisis - people should be fully informed via newspapers & website. You need to find out ahead of spending millions building cycle lanes, if they are wanted and will be used.*

*Regardless of whether it's down to Colchester or Essex - our roads are in appalling condition, wrecking people's cars and endangering lives, so a priority should be to repair the roads that the majority use, and not spend millions on the minority, no matter how well intentioned.*

*Thank you."*

The Council said they would email us back with answers to our questions. Finally, the ordeal was over. I was mightily relieved I wouldn't ever have to do that again. I would rather have been at the dentist, at least you get anaesthetised there!

I was mistaken about the ordeal being over, it wasn't quite. There was the wild-card, Ian. In my anxious state, I'd forgotten about him. He was part of the group who did the yellow boards around town. He'd come up to me before we went into the Town Hall and said he'd decided to speak as well. I eyed him suspiciously, and said, "It's not anything conspiracy sounding or confrontational is it?" He smiled and told me it would be fine!

I probably should have pushed him a bit more to find out exactly what he was going to say, but I was in too much of a fluster. Besides, what could I do? I may have been leading the charge, but I certainly wasn't in charge. We were a collection of individuals, it wasn't a group with a leader, it was just people coming together. I'd just suggested we go back and do things properly and others had agreed. He'd been sitting right in front of me at David Charalambous' talk, so hopefully he'd follow his advice on communication.

His opening statement was a question for the Chairman. "Your strategic plan for Colchester 2023 and onwards, is all based around what you see as a climate emergency in your lust to achieve Net Zero. It's now more important than ever that all councillors must fully understand what this means. There is other information you need to consider. If you knew that man-made climate change was not true, would you still go ahead with this strategy?"

It was at this point the Environmental and Climate Emergency Manager burst out into a slightly-laughing, big grin. Ian continued on about Agenda 2030 and 15 Minute cities not being grassroots initiatives, which is true. He told them about Absolute Zero, and how shipping and flying would cease, and that we'd all be living in a digital prison, with our data collected and used against us tied into digital IDs and Central Bank Digital currencies. Again, all true, but there are ways of saying things, and judging by the look on the councillors' faces, they'd dismissed everything he was saying.

It was the antithesis of David's advice, confrontational and challenging them on firmly held beliefs. Not to mention dumping too much information at once. If only he'd worked with the rest of us, a few tiny tweaks to ask questions, instead of making statements, would have made what he said very impactful and he would have had the best speech of the night, rather than being laughed at and dismissed.

I was not a happy bunny. If I'd known he was going to say it like that, I would have pulled out. I felt it completely undermined what we'd all just done and the days of painstaking effort which had gone into it. The councillors and officers were looking bemused and probably now lumped us all together.

I was also annoyed that he hadn't said he didn't think our speeches were hard hitting enough (something I, too, had worried about) when we'd met a few days earlier to run through the speeches. I made a point of asking everyone if they were happy with our speeches, because what we said represented them. At the time he didn't say he wasn't happy, but later decided it needed to be done differently. Which is fine, it's not like I knew for sure the 'gently, gently' approach was the right way, but it seemed a good idea to take the advice of the communications expert. It was the lack of communication that had annoyed me the most. People are free to do things however they please, but it would have been nice to discuss it.

## Bad Behaviour Brushed Under the Carpet

The day after the meeting, we received emails from the Monitoring Officer about our complaints. He and the Council's allegedly 'independent person' felt that since the Environment and Sustainability Chairman had deleted his comment, they didn't see anything wrong, especially because he was acting in his private capacity and therefore it wasn't anything to do with the Council. He was entitled to express a personal opinion.

I responded that the councillor in question had the word Councillor before his name on his social media profile, it was also in his profile banner and he was discussing members of the public who attended a council meeting that he was chairing. That was clearly done in his capacity as a councillor. But they wouldn't budge on it. So I informed them that I would be putting in a complaint to the Ombudsman (which of course went nowhere, even though they agreed the comments were libellous, they had no powers to get the councillor to make a public apology, or any apology for that matter).

I also informed the Monitoring Officer about the incident with the security guard pushing his fingers into my shoulder, which technically, was assault. I suggested he give the man in question some proper training, as he shouldn't be behaving like that with the public. I said I would leave it with him to sort out in a manner he felt appropriate.

The following day, I made a video using the footage of the meeting so that we could put it on social media and get awareness of the EV fire hazards out to the general public. So few people knew how bad they were at this point in time. I did not include Ian's contribution and told everyone why. It did annoy some as they thought he'd done an excellent job of giving it to them with both guns. Which he had, but the aim was to go in gently to get them to listen to what we had to say, not go in guns blazing. I made him a separate video which he could share however he wanted.

The clip of our January meeting, which had gone viral on Twitter, didn't have any of us speaking (thank goodness), it had just been of people quietly sitting there holding yellow A4 posters saying things like 'Let's improve public transport not force restrictions on people'. So the video I was making would be very different. I peppered the footage with all the relevant images and documents we'd dug up from our research to back up what was being said.

## Great Minds Think Alike

Unbeknownst to us, three weeks earlier, a group of people in Thetford had called a public meeting and got their councillors to attend. It had been filmed and it showed several members of the public speaking their minds to the Council about their proposed Net Zero plans. The video had gone viral, but we didn't see it until after we'd made our March 21st meeting video. Had they seen our viral clip from January and been inspired to go to their Council, or had it been coincidental? We didn't know, but it was great to see others taking similar action.

Then it turned out, the week before we had gone in for our second council meeting, Sandi Adams, the lady who'd been so instrumental in connecting the dots for me in the interview I'd seen in the first lockdown, had gone into Glastonbury Council and her speech had gone viral. Again, we didn't know about that video until a while after our video was released.

So within three weeks of each other, three completely unconnected groups of people had chosen to go into their local councils, film it, and then make videos. Collective consciousness in action, perhaps? I usually got about two thousand views on my small Successful Garden Design YouTube Channel videos. It only had twelve thousand subscribers so I wasn't expecting many views, especially on people going to a council, but I was very wrong.

I suspect that because of our January council meeting clip, combined with the viral videos Thetford and Glastonbury made in the two weeks prior to us, an audience appetite for watching ordinary people standing up and speaking at the council had been created. So when I released our video, much to my great surprise, it took off.

The day I released it there had been about two hundred views, which was pretty decent, but when I woke up the next day, my inbox was inundated with YouTube comment notification emails. When I looked, it had over five thousand views. Gosh, that was more than I was expecting and all within twenty-four hours. I began to feel rather uncomfortable. I'd never been someone who likes being in the limelight.

I'd forced myself to make videos for my garden design business back in 2009. For a good couple of months when I started writing online garden design courses, I did consider whether I could get away with teaching people garden design by just filming my hands drawing, and never actually showing my face on camera. I could be like the Wilson character from Home Improvements. You never saw his face, he was always half behind the fence whenever he spoke to Tim 'The Toolman' Taylor. In the end, I thought that would be ridiculous, so I forced myself to speak to the camera, as uncomfortable as it was.

By the following day, the viewing numbers had shot up to twenty thousand people. Now I was feeling really uncomfortable. I'd not prepared myself for this. There were hundreds of comments. People were so shocked EVs were not only devastating for the environment, but also so dangerous with the fires, not to mention how awful the child slave labour aspect is. Many people were asking why the BBC weren't covering this. Someone even suggested we tell the Prime Minister! A few EV zealots bit back, but mostly people were as horrified as we'd been when we found out EVs were anything but green.

This is part of what had made me so incensed. It was the people who care most about the environment, and had paid extra to purchase an EV, who had to live with the inconvenience of charging, and who had been completely conned. It was like Covid vaccines all over again. Good people being told to get them for the sake of others. Do the right thing, stop polluting the planet, whilst doing the exact opposite. I'll be blowed if I was going to stand by and do nothing, especially with the quantity of various electric vehicles the Council planned to buy. On their shopping list was everything from scooters, cars, waste trucks to buses.

Within a few weeks the video had over two hundred thousand views on YouTube and was being shared all over social media.

When we eventually received the Council's email responses to the concerns we'd raised at the March meeting, they were rather surprising. They seemed hell bent on carrying on, regardless of all the information we'd given them. I had naively thought that people working for the Environment and Sustainability Panel would care about the environment. We had numerous exchanges with the officers back and forth, getting us absolutely nowhere.

## Fresh Start

Council elections had come and gone in May, and a whole new Environment and Sustainability Panel was created. Not getting the responses we were expecting from the council officers, there was only one thing for it. We'd have to go back and do it all over again for the new panel.

By this time, I'd discovered far worse things about other so called green technologies, so they would have to go into the speech as well. I hoped I'd find speaking easier, and it would be third time lucky. Oh if only. About halfway through, it turned into my worst nightmare and then just kept getting worse… and that was after I had another run in with the security brute.

# 16

# Great Green Deception

Not only did I find out that most hydrogen production isn't anywhere near as green as billed, something far worse came to light. Once our March 2023 council video had received over a hundred thousand views and comments kept increasing, several people asked me if I'd looked into wind and solar.

Noooooo not solar as well. I had a giant solar panel in my garden powering my office. I'd been a supporter of wind and solar since my mid-twenties. I even had a whole page dedicated to that alternative energy on an 'eco page' on my first garden design website, because I felt so strongly about it. Back then, it was because I'd seen all those haunting images of the BP oil spills. Seabirds and seals slowly dying, covered in black, gooey, oil. Those images broke my heart.

At the time, it had not occurred to me to look into how solar panels were produced. It was an emotional response to a tragedy. I felt bad enough about the lithium battery, I really couldn't face solar being as bad as well. Surely it couldn't be.

Coincidentally, at that exact time, the 'Geoff Buys Cars' YouTube channel did a piece on how bad solar panels are. Geoff had already done a great video about EVs, which had been very helpful for my first proper speech as he'd linked to a New York Times article, which then in turn linked to the lithium mine specifications pdf. That's how I was able to find out how many thousands of tons of permanent toxic waste is created and water is used.

Geoff and I had exchanged numbers after the first video went viral, so I texted him and asked if he could send me the details from the Ethical Consumer Report he'd based his video on. Again it was dreadful, with forced labour camps, it's almost impossible to buy a solar panel which doesn't have slave labour somewhere in the supply chain. Although one could argue, that also applies to a lot of goods. With the production of solar panels, there is the added issue of silicosis for the forced workers from not having adequate PPE.

Then there's the issue of recycling, something I'd not given a moment's consideration to. I'd been too caught up in the idealism of how wonderful it is to harness energy from the sun and wind. And it is a lovely idea, it's just not in reality when you factor in all the mining and resources and forced labour it takes to build these things. The more I researched the reality, the more sick to my stomach I felt. Wind turbine blades can't be recycled because they are made of fibreglass and resin, so they end up in a landfill. With their relatively short lifespan, and size of up to 351ft, it's a colossal problem. They also shed microplastics, which get into the soil.

As YouTuber, engineer and climate researcher, Paul Burgess, points out that they don't even supply adequate amounts of electricity, and many of the parts have to be replaced within ten to fifteen years, which means it's not cost effective to maintain them. He likened them to Trigger's broom in 'Only Fools And Horses' when Trigger proudly states he's had the same road sweepers broom for twenty years, and then goes on to add that it's had seventeen new heads and fourteen new handles!

Doing the research for that third council meeting was thoroughly depressing. But as councils have been instructed to not refuse planning for what's considered critical infrastructure, I knew it was important to share what I'd discovered. These so-called green solutions are not remotely green. And no one was more devastated by that than I.

Our email correspondences with the Council were getting us nowhere. It was clear they were going to do as instructed, no matter how much contrary evidence we provided to the officers. Our only hope was that the new Environment and Sustainability panel would be genuinely concerned about the environmental impact of what the Council were doing. But just in case they weren't, I wanted to up our game a bit, give them one more chance, and then serve them all a notice of liability in their personal, private capacity if they continued down the EV path.

Colchester was already littered with electric scooters and eBikes. There were plans for one hundred more. Having seen the fires and read that an eBike battery catching fire is the equivalent in explosive power of six hand grenades detonating, we had to do something. None of us had enough experience to do the paperwork correctly, and this wasn't the time to try and guess at it. So I asked around the various groups to see if anyone knew of someone with the necessary knowledge.

A gentleman by the name of Terry was given my contact details, as I was told he might be able to help. He'd wanted to speak to me anyway about what we were doing in Colchester, as he was planning on doing the same in Ipswich. We arranged to meet up in Colchester. He said he'd bring a couple of Associates with him who were very knowledgeable about the law.

Terry arrived at the pub we'd chosen with two men. Lance and Brian, at first glance, an unlikely pairing. Lance looked like an accountant. Brian had a powerful build with tattooed arms, and looked like he could handle himself. Having run landscaping crews on building sites where I was often the only woman, surrounded by men even bigger than he, several with criminal records from their misspent youth, I wasn't remotely bothered by his tough guy appearance. In my experience, the bigger and tougher they look, often times the gentler they are, though I wasn't about to label Brian as a big softie. He might not have appreciated it.

Lance was very personable and had a nice way in his communication style. He told me they were part of a constitutional law group called the Peace Keepers. I'd heard of them already, as Cheryl had spoken highly of them. He explained a bit about what they were doing to challenge councils by asking them to evidence their claims of liability regarding Council Tax. He explained that they have no issue with us all contributing towards the costs of running things, but they feel that the law should be followed, and that there should be an agreement, a meeting of minds. He told me councils do not have any more powers than we do as individuals. We cannot go around demanding money with menaces, and neither can they. They felt that the public should agree to what we want to pay for.

Then we got chatting about what we'd been doing at Colchester. Terry had sent them both the video. I explained I wanted to serve the Councillors and the Officers with a notice of liability in their private, personal capacity, I wanted to know if they could they help with that?

Brian hadn't said much up to this point. He looked at me and asked, "Then what?"

"I don't know!" I replied. "Won't that do?" I naively asked.

He laughed and said there was no point in serving notices if we didn't have a plan of what we were going to do next. Apparently the Councillors and Officer would just ignore them anyway. I thought that if someone served me a Notice of Liability, I would think twice about littering the streets with devices which could explode and cause harm to the public. He then went on to explain that we didn't need to serve notices. In many respects we already had by going into the Council and getting our concerns on public record.

## Punch Time

I told them I felt my speeches lacked punch. I didn't feel they were strong enough to get them to change their behaviour. Lance said he could help with my next speech, and would add some things that would make them take note, or at least some wording which would make the Monitoring Officer do so.

I felt a bit deflated as I'd got my hopes pinned on a 'one and done' scenario. OK this was the second time doing it properly, but I thought this would be a great way to finish it. And I knew from a viral video point of view, the look on the Councillors' and Officers' faces being served a Notice of Liability would be a winner.

I explained that I didn't really have the time, or inclination, to keep going into the Council. It was taking a ridiculous amount of time with all the emails back and forth, and I had a business to run. I asked Lance if he had the time to write the speeches if the others wanted to continue? I knew Carinna was keen to go in and have her say on a multitude of topics. He said he would be happy to work on what we wrote, but that he wouldn't have time to write them from scratch, which was fair enough.

As disappointed as I was about the serving notices idea, there was an equally huge sense of relief having them there with us. It felt like the cavalry had arrived. I was quite surprised at my reaction. I've never been a girly girl who's needed a big strong man to come and rescue her (unless it's something I can't physically lift). I'm usually very self-reliant and capable. Analysing it later, I realised I had been leading the charge into the Council, and I was having to use a lot of masculine energy to do so. It was making me feel unbalanced in the process.

Having very strong male energy there with us had enabled me to relax back into my natural feminine energy and thus restore balance. I no longer needed to fill both roles. It was fascinating to experience. We already had plenty of wonderful men in the group supporting us, and they'd often say things like, 'we're right behind you ladies, go get 'em!' But with Lance and Brian, it felt like they were beside us, not behind us, and energetically that made a huge difference. For the first time in my life I had a real understanding of the importance of balanced male and female energy synergistically working together, and how much power emanated from that.

It became a fascinating dynamic for me to experience. I realised that with a lot of men, I would pussy-foot around subjects so as not to offend their egos, a skill I'd had to master quickly running my parents' landscaping business. With Lance and Brian, I found myself saying exactly what I thought, with no filter. It was wonderfully freeing to not be concerned about how they'd take something I said. I don't know how much they appreciated unfiltered full-blast Rachel, but instinctively it felt the right way to be. There's no games then, just honest communication, and that feels very empowering.

We soon found that we brought balance to one another. When they wanted to take a stance on things which felt too aggressive, Carinna and I would give them the female perspective and a gentler alternative to consider. When we were too soft, Lance would say, "Rachel, no more nice, middle-class language. It's time to go for the jugular", or words to that effect. And he'd be right. I'd half felt those times I'd needed to be more forceful, and he would give me the nudge, which helped me get over my more feminine leanings of not wanting to create conflict.

Working with Lance and Brian took our speeches to the next level, and it was so comforting for me not to be constantly second guessing everything I wrote. I'd do the first draft, then send it to Lance. He'd send something back, which I would then put into my own voice. Though I didn't interfere with anything which was law related. He would put the punch into what I was writing. I don't think I would have continued with what eventually turned into Council Watch, had it not been for Lance and Brian always being there supporting us.

There's so much talk about toxic masculinity, but when men come from a place of power, they don't dominate or talk down, or try to appease. Problems arise with weak men and/or weak women - that's when it becomes a battle of the sexes. There has certainly been a push to emasculate men over the past few decades, as well as make women more masculine. It unbalances the population and the more out of balance people are, the more easily they succumb to coercion.

There certainly are times when masculinity can be toxic, as we found out when we next went to speak at the Council…

## Aggression

On the 22nd June 2023, we returned to the new Environment and Sustainability Panel. There were a lot of councillors we'd not seen before, and the room once again was packed. Lance and Brian came with us along with what looked like half of Colchester. There were so many people they had to open up the overflow room. Once again, I asked everyone to be on their best behaviour before we went in. I immediately ended up not taking my own advice, as there before me doing the searches, was the security guard, who looked ex-forces, who'd pushed his fingers into my shoulder.

There had been another incident involving him when Carinna had gone in on the 6th of June to ask the Scrutiny Panel to look into why we hadn't had responses to some of the concerns raised at the Environment and Sustainability Panel in March. The searches had been quite rough, and not done with the levels of respect that they had been on the 21st March. I had not expected him to be on duty after I'd reported his behaviour to the Monitoring Officer.

They clearly hadn't taken my advice about properly training him. Cheryl was the last to be searched. She was at the back of the queue, as she was with her mother who is vaccine injured and has trouble walking. The security guard was invasive with the search. He picked up the scanner without asking Cheryl if she consented to being scanned, nor did he check if she had any medical conditions or equipment which might preclude it. He waved it on her front and back, over her arms and down her sides. She had her feet together, and he put the scanner in between her ankles and used the scanner to press into her legs to indicate to part them. He brusquely said, 'open your legs', and then went up and down her inner thigh with the scanner touching at certain points, making her feel very uncomfortable.

He then went to her bag, looking in every single pocket. He got out confidential paperwork, looked at it and started reading it. Then he got her makeup bag out, opened it, and rummaged through before putting it back. No one else received such an in-depth search. Because she had been a speaker at the last meeting, and she felt harassed, as though she was being targeted.

Whilst there hadn't been anything sexual about how he'd behaved, his inconsiderate use of the scanner between her legs, touching all up in her business, was unpleasant. And as she said to the Councillor in front of her, when she got upstairs and sat down, "What happens if he does that to a women who has experienced sexual abuse?"

Cheryl put in a formal complaint, but it hadn't been answered in the three weeks that elapsed.

So when I came face to face with him the moment I walked through the door and he went to scan me, as you can probably imagine, things did not go well. I told him he wasn't going to scan me after how he'd treated Cheryl. He looked shocked and denied anything happening, I also reminded him about the time he pushed his fingers into my shoulder - he didn't deny that. I told him he'd crossed the line, and I wasn't going to have him search me. I marched past and got a few feet before being stopped.

It was at this point that I could hear Lance quietly recommending that it was important I delivered my speech and to pick my battles. I acquiesced, but told him he had better not do to me what he had to Cheryl. He protested that he hadn't done anything wrong, and that it would have all been captured on the CCTV camera above us. I said that we'd mentioned that in the complaint which had been put in against him. He did look genuinely shocked when I'd accused him. I suspect he was just rough handling Cheryl and probably hadn't even noticed he'd inadvertently touched her inner thigh with the scanner.

He scanned the front of me but when he got down to my ankle, the scanner went off. He grabbed hold of my trouser leg and yanked it up to see what had set it off. I immediately pulled my leg away and told him, "You do not touch me. If you want the trouser leg pulled up, you tell me and I'll do it, or you ask if you can. You've not been trained for this and you need to be." He glared at me but said nothing. He then went around the back of me and took ages. I told him to hurry up, I didn't want to be cooked with the scanner. I couldn't hear or feel anything, so after quite some time I grabbed my bag and walked off up the stairs.

He yelled after me that he hadn't finished. I replied. "Well I have. You had plenty of time to scan me, you should have done it quicker." And with that I marched off up the stairs. He immediately took off after me.

I managed to make it almost to the top of the first flight. His pinstripe suit was so tight it inhibited him taking big strides, so he ended up doing a rather mincing run with little steps to get up the stairs in front of me. It was all I could do not to laugh watching. At this point he got right in my face standing on the step above me, snarling that he wouldn't let me go any further. I very calmly informed him that he could not prevent me from attending a public meeting. The exchange went back and forth about it being a condition of entrance, and me repeating he could not prevent a member of the public attending a public meeting as set out in the Local Government Act of 1972, with neither of us budging.

I could hear Lance, still in the foyer, call my name in a slightly questioning fashion. "Rachel?"

I'm a Taurean, backing down isn't one of my strong points, especially when there are matters of principle at stake. I still didn't budge, even though I knew Lance was right. I realised that I had plenty of time to get in there, so I decided that I might as well see how this would play out. Eventually the Door Manager came over to intervene. I explained that the guard had had plenty of time to scan me, I'd stood there ages, and as far as I was concerned, I'd been scanned and enough was enough. He told his colleague to stand down and that he would handle things from here.

He was very polite and courteous, so I allowed him to continue where his colleague had left off. I eventually got up the stairs a few minutes later and took my seat with Lance and Brian not far behind me. The Chair of the meeting this time was a woman. I tried to sum her up, and wondered if she'd be better than her predecessor. I had the feeling she might not be.

As it turned out, my evening was about to get considerably worse than the set-to I'd just had with the doorman. I was about to have a big, unpleasant battle on several fronts, one of which was most unexpected.

# 17

# The Warrior Within

I will admit to having a bit of a strange fascination with the council carpet in the Grand Jury Room at the Town Hall. By the end of 2023, it occurred to me that with the hundreds of hours I'd spent watching council meetings, I'd spent more time looking at the council carpet than I had the carpet in my own living room. I'm not entirely sure why it fascinated me to the degree it did. There's certainly been a few occasions when it held my attention more than the meetings I was supposed to be watching.

The carpet in question was black with large orangey-red geometric patterns forming a grid. At first glance it looked like hop-scotch size squares, which are set out at an angle, making them appear diamond shaped. On closer inspection they were octagons with finials which gave the appearance of squares. The design alternated, with two distinct patterns inside the octagons that looked like something a kaleidoscope might make. I could not decide if I liked the design or not, that was probably part of the fascination. The other question that my carpet staring elicited was 'where do you buy carpets like this'? Is there a specialist carpet shop for listed council buildings?

I also found myself wondering if there was any significance with the squared octagons linked together with circles. Octagons have been tied to Christian symbolism, where eight represents resurrection and regeneration. Squares tend to symbolise stability and order in the earthly realm. Circles represent unity and eternity. The carpet designer may have had lofty ideals but sadly, if there was purposeful symbolism, it was clearly lost on the current councillors running the show.

Contemplating meaning into council carpets was a sure sign I'd spent far too much time watching and attending council meetings than was healthy. Talking of which, on the particular evening of my third fateful council meeting, whilst there were moments when my run-in with the security guard had been quite amusing, it was still not a great way to start the evening, especially as I really didn't want to be there at all. I was feeling rough. Really rough.

I'd got a migraine which was getting progressively worse with each passing minute and it had affected my hearing, something I'd not experienced before. I was now completely deaf in my left ear. It was blocked, and I felt like I was half underwater. I was also really thirsty. I'd had a quick bite to eat at my parents house when I dropped the dog off. My father had made a Shepherds Pie, but had put too much salt in it. I'd drunk nearly all my water by the time Carinna arrived.

To make matters worse, the meeting appeared to be delayed. Council Officers were coming up to the Chairwoman whispering in her ear. I could hear a bit of a commotion coming from downstairs. I guessed exactly what was happening. Everyone had had the same reaction to the security guard that I'd had. I hoped there wasn't going to be trouble.

I was in no position to sit in judgement, having ignored my own advice about being on best behaviour. I could hear it all kicking off downstairs, secretly pleased that they were putting up more of a fuss than I did. I hadn't liked acquiescing. That security guard should not have been on duty, nor conducting unlawful searches. There are strict guidelines for searching the public, and he clearly wasn't trained.

Eventually the noise became louder as I could hear them all coming en masse up the stairs. By the sounds of things they had done exactly as I had, but in numbers walking past security. They were now all outside the door, and we could hear the Council staff telling them that they must be searched. An elderly lady asked why she should be searched, why was she considered a danger to anyone? Another person said the Councillors were supposed to be serving the people, not having them searched.... and so it went on.

It was clear that the public in attendance did not, and would not, be searched, so the Council staff put them all in the overflow room. All this delayed the meeting by half an hour, which didn't make any of us happy. By this point, I felt like I'd got someone trying to drill my eyeball out whilst I was half underwater. I just wanted to curl up into a ball and be magically transported home.

I was the second on the list to speak, so at least I'd get it over and done with quickly. Having someone else speak first gave me time to assess the new Chairwoman. Once she started speaking, she seemed nice and she let the gentleman in front of me (an Alderman) overrun his three minute slot quite considerably, which made me relax as I knew I had crammed so much into my speech that there was a good chance I might overrun by a few seconds.

I did a few taps on the chair on the karate chop EFT point to settle the last of my nerves down before it was my turn. I wasn't sure if the sickening feeling in my stomach was from what I was about to do, the migraine, or the excessive salt in my rushed dinner. I just wanted it to be over so I could go and lie down in a darkened room.

Lance had helped me put some punch into the ending. You'll probably be able to work out who wrote what! Unfortunately for me, there was a rather major glitch which meant I wasn't sure if I'd make it to the end…

## An Unexpected Torture

Halfway through speaking my mouth had become so dry that I was struggling to get my words out. I hadn't got any water left. I'd never experienced anything like this before. My mouth was sticking to my teeth. I now not only felt like I was under water, but sounded like it too. There was no moisture anywhere. It was making speaking virtually impossible. I briefly closed my mouth and swallowed, losing precious seconds, but it made virtually no difference. I didn't know what to do. I wasn't going to be able to carry on for much longer, every word becoming harder to say.

I'd often heard people talk about how dry their mouths became when public speaking, but I'd never experienced it. Was it the salt, or was it a new symptom my body had created to stop me speaking? I was well aware I didn't want to be there doing this, it felt like my body was doing everything it could to make sure I didn't. I was in really bad shape, and the stress was making my migraine worse. Being deaf in one ear didn't help. Was I sounding as bad as I thought I was? I couldn't tell. Any moment I knew I might not be able to utter another word. What the hell was I going to do?

It's not like I could start doing EFT, besides this wasn't fear, I'd tapped that out. If this wasn't because of the salt, it was likely that it was a subconscious reaction to doing something that I really didn't want to do. I'd not thought to try EFT on doing something I didn't want to do. This was different to the usual negative emotions. I was doing something completely out of character. My spirit was more than willing, it was just my personality which was resistant.

A new Me had been born that night. Initially, out of belligerence with the security guard, and the cat and mouse games on the stairs, and then fuelled by some residue anger from how Cheryl had been treated. This new Me was a Warrior, and was taking over. Once I got up the stairs there was no more anger, it had been replaced by an icy calmness. My predominant Sensible Me had been usurped, and was now second in command. The other Mes had not agreed to this. It was like having the military move in and take over. Warrior Me had not yet been integrated into my personality. It was clear the new arrival was going to be trouble, she'd already killed off Timid Me. Who else would be culled?

It was this which was causing a disconnect, and mid-speech was not the time to self-analyse and pick which tool in my life-coaching tool box to sort it out with. I just had to get my damn words out. Somehow.

Here's the speech which turned into the hardest of my life. Though remarkably, it didn't sound anywhere near as awful on the audio recording as it had to me at the time. Despite my difficulties, I'd managed to make my words reasonably clear. It just sounds as if I had a slice of lemon wedged in my mouth in some parts.

## Rachel Speech 2 - Green Energy Deception

*"Good evening.*

*I've been a supporter of green energy and a keen environmentalist since my twenties.*

*My office is solar powered. So I was mortified to discover that a single lithium mine causes millions of tons of waste every year, laced with sulphuric acid & radioactive uranium, polluting the water supply for 300 years. Not to mention the unacceptable human costs with child labour to mine cobalt.*

*When I researched which solar panel to purchase, I did **not**, for one minute, consider if it would be made by people trapped in razor-wire enclosed labour camps, being exposed to large quantities of quartz dust, which causes silicosis!*

***Please note that** The Ethical Consumer organisation report that it's hard to avoid forced labour in the solar panel supply chain.*

*Wind turbines, which last about 20 years, consume a colossal amount of resources & energy to manufacture & install (not to mention the blight and bird kill). They require diesel engines to start them up and then gallons of oil to lubricate. And they can't readily be recycled.*

*Solar panels are also extremely difficult to recycle, costing more than the production of the panel. And lithium batteries pose steep challenges too.*

*Add to that the human suffering, which we've all unwittingly been part of just by owning a laptop or mobile phone, which is minimal compared to what's required for an EV or solar farm. These so-called green, or ethical solutions, aren't solutions **at all**, just very good marketing from the 1.5 TRILLION dollar-a-year climate change industry (that's 4 billion dollars a day by the way!).*

*None of us can undo what's already been done, but what we can all do is make sure this doesn't escalate **exponentially**, with fleets of unnecessary EVs, and acres of solar farms eating up precious farmland.*

*It would be helpful if anyone would actually define what they mean by green? If they mean better in all respects, which is a reasonable suggestion, then in retrospect we can clearly see that the current offerings are not really better than our existing energy solutions, and in many regards much worse.*

*Knowing the true cost of the so-called green technologies, I cannot in good conscience support this Council as you embark unwittingly on faux-green endeavours.*

*At the last meeting, I informed you of the inhumane nature of cobalt extraction. So you may no longer claim ignorance as a defence. To continue to support any form of slavery through spending public money is negligent, in so much as once you are made aware of a harm, your first act must be to stop. And then to investigate.*

*And this is why I am here today. I am providing you with the knowledge that many of these well-intentioned projects that you are keen to pursue, are actually harmful, and as such, must be halted, and then either properly investigated, or more simply and less costly, dropped altogether.*

*After all, your own code of conduct obligates you to act and take decisions impartially, fairly and on merit, using the best evidence and without discrimination or bias, and you are specifically required to **not** misuse Council resources.*

*Finally, do Council agree that it is your obligation to always seek the best available knowledge? And, should it so transpire, that any policy, howsoever well-intentioned, may subsequently prove harmful, then the Council are obligated to stop?"*

I just about made it to the last sentence when the bell rang, I was going to go a few seconds over but I was on the home stretch, I just had to get the last few words out of my bone-dry, barely functional mouth. Halfway through that last sentence someone somewhere spoke, I think. It was hard to tell in my semi-deaf, migrainey, parched-mouth state. Determined to finish my speech if it was the last thing I did, I continued until the end.

People in the audience behind me told me to keep going. I turned around and said, "I've finished, what was the interruption?"

It had been the Chairwoman who'd interrupted me, and she replied that I'd gone over my allotted time. She said that she'd mentioned at the beginning that I only had three minutes to speak. It's entirely possible that the normal, easy-going Rachel, if she hadn't have had the run-in, playing cat and mouse with the security guard, might have apologised for running over time, but that wasn't the Rachel in the room that night.

The version of me that was there was the proverbial bear with a sore head, in a lot of pain, already pissed off from the hassle of getting in the room and she was in no mood to be interrupted, especially when it was such a difficulty to speak in the first place. I was in a rather indignant, 'now is not a good time to mess with me,' mood, with the unknown quantity of Warrior Me at the helm.

I responded that I was on my last sentence and she'd allowed the gentleman before me to over run by at least thirty seconds or more. When we checked the replay she'd allowed him to run over for 1 minute 12 seconds, and she'd interrupted me after 6 seconds over time. I informed her that it needs to be rules that apply to everybody, not just the ones where you don't like what the speaker is saying.

It was rather annoying that I couldn't speak properly, as it came out rather lacking the force I felt inside, but perhaps that was for the best! The Chairwoman said she respectfully didn't dislike what I was saying, it was the first time she'd heard it. She had stopped me in the interests of keeping the meeting moving smoothly.

I could hear Brian behind me saying to read it again. So I reiterated my final question so the Councillors heard it this time, and without interruption. A Council Officer responded saying that they do always consider new information as it comes to light, and then another one gave me the usual word salad response. He did add that they'd looked at hydrogen, and they had found that it was at least double the cost of EVs, and therefore they didn't consider it viable.

I started to reply that if they invested in these substandard technologies it would increase the quantity of them, whereas it would be better to wait until real green solutions come along. I was then interrupted by the Chairwoman yet again.

She told me that I had made my contribution. I replied that I get an extra minute to respond. She told me I didn't. It was her first time as Chair, so she double-checked with the Democratic Services Officer, who confirmed that I did indeed get a chance to respond. She apologised, and asked me to please carry on, but before I got a chance, she addressed the audience behind me. She asked them to show respect to the Board, who were doing their best, and trying to have a meeting where everyone could engage respectfully.

All things considered, the quiet murmurings behind me had been very controlled. I was amazed how good everyone had been. If the positions had been reversed, I'd have had a hard time keeping my mouth shut. I was very proud of them all for having done as I'd asked. Also, having seen how it had been in the first meeting, compared to now, everyone was as good as gold. I was concerned her speaking down to them could kick things off. So I immediately jumped in and said, "I think they are being very respectful." I waited a moment to let that sink in with the Chairwoman and then continued.

"As I was saying, unless you have really good solutions, ultimately you are going to waste money. You'll just get EV points everywhere, and then the Government will turn round and say, oh these are no good. So you'll end up wasting money. And you are investing in slavery, which is unacceptable. If it was your family who had children crushed to death down these mines, would this be your answer, that it's too costly to find alternatives?

Especially when no one here can even fully explain what the climate emergency is."

I told them that, by the Council's own admission, they did not have a definition for what the emergency is. So the Council's actions had sprung from an emergency that no one there was able to define. I added, "If you cannot clearly define the emergency, how will anyone possibly know when it's over? Or rationally, impose any Policy response without knowing? The emergency needs to be properly defined and evidenced if you are to get the public onboard with your associated proposals."

I then got up and went back to my chair. Next up was Carinna. She did not look happy, and to my great surprise, within a few words I realised that I was witnessing something I'd never seen before. Mama bear, Carinna, and she was cross. Even though I'd held my own, she did not appreciate the ill-mannered interruption mid-sentence, on top of the disrespectfully loud conversation during my speech. I say cross, but we both do anger in a very controlled middle-aged women-in-cardigans kind of way.

The moment she sat down she opened up the mic and stated, "I'd appreciate not to use any of my time to just point out while you are voicing your opinion on respect, two of you were sitting having a conversation that I could hear whilst the previous speaker was talking. So if we could have a level playing field, in terms of not two-tier system-ing, and expressing respect both ways, that would be much appreciated."

The Chairwoman acknowledged what Carinna had said. I later found out that it was she who Carinna was referring to, regarding talking. That telling off was a turning point. I felt a shift in her demeanour that I hadn't been able to achieve when we'd locked horns earlier. It also helped that there was a bit of humour, when someone from the audience had made a comment after Carinna had demanded a level playing field, she turned around and told them, with a twinkle in her eye, "No heckling, please!"

Carinna then delivered the speech she'd written, and Lance had tweaked.

*"Good evening.*

*On 6th June, I asked the Committee to scrutinise why the Environment and Sustainability Panel are continuing with environmentally harmful plans; why is Council ignoring documented safety concerns?*

*Shipping companies are starting to ban EVs because of the fires that can't be put out. UK companies have banned their use on trains and buses.*

*Will Council confirm that serious fire safety concerns are not valid?*

*Has Essex Fire Service been consulted by Council, as suggested by Councillor Lee Scordis, with regard to the management of toxic run-off from EV fires?*

*Please identify, explicitly, which Council Officer will be accountable for compromising public safety?*

*We've highlighted these dangers. If you choose to continue acting negligently, liability rests with Council, but also privately as individuals. Why should the taxpayer foot the bill?*

*We have requested a public forum, and do so here again. Council must evidence their climate data, and their claim of a man-made climate emergency.*

*Most people don't know the full extent of the Net Zero plans. Few have read the Absolute Zero & IPCC reports and are blissfully ignorant of how much our lives will radically change if recommendations go ahead.*

*A few examples from these reports;*

*By 2030, UK airports close except Heathrow, Glasgow and Belfast, which close by 2050.*

*By 2030, 50% less lamb and beef production... had you noticed we're being conditioned to eat insects?*

*Fossil fuels completely phased out by 2050, but don't worry, you'll have a rather generous 3 item clothing allowance per year!*

*And so it goes on.*

*France has already banned internal flights where rail alternatives exist.*

*If you expect the public to willingly go along with losing our entire way of life, our livelihoods and our freedom, then you absolutely must conclusively prove it's necessary. Anything less is insane.*

*Not just cherry-picked data the IPCC put out. Full chart data showing everything, including the inconvenient ice core sample data, which shows $CO_2$ levels over 5 times greater than they are now, with much higher global temperatures, with no detriment to the planet. This is referred to as a dissenting opinion.*

*I'm not a climate change denier. I can conclusively confirm from the empirical data that climate change does exist... I'm pretty sure I was taught that at school. The onus is on Council to prove these effects are man-made.*

*Phasing out of petrol and diesel will restrict the people's freedom to travel. Can Council confirm the constitutional basis by which either they, or central Government may act in any of these respects?*

*It seems that the servant seeks to control the master, can you evidence that Council may?*

*Thank you."*

The Chairwoman said she would get back to Carinna within seven days and gave her word this would happen. In Carinna's one minute response, she told them something that nearly made them all fall off their chairs.

"I'm not sure if you're aware of the Public Accounts Committee Report that came out recently, but the two years prior to Boris Johnson becoming Prime Minister, the fraud and waste from the Government was 5.5 billion pounds. The two years Boris Johnson was in power, that had escalated to 21 billion pounds in fraud. So we are here to make you guys accountable for what you are doing, and make them accountable, because the way we are watching things pushed, on a lack of evidence and just all through PR, is not acceptable. We will not accept being forced into restrictions that are all claimed to be about the environment. When you actually check the data, climate change is real, the earth has been much warmer than it is now, in fact, the deserts are greening because of the increased $CO_2$. So we do need to look at all the data."

Later in the meeting several of the councillors said they had been reflecting about what we had said and how concerned they were about the supply chains of these so-called green tech. Councillor Laws said he thought that our challenging of the green tech had been interesting, and that things might sound green, but the pylons they plan to put across our beautiful, tranquil countryside needed to be fought because they were going to ruin it. And if we were covering land with turbines that require oil for lubrication, and then the materials and energy to build them, they do have a destructive nature. Councillor Laws said that he was all for green tech, but that we did need to look at the destructive unintended consequences.

Councillor Lissimore asked for a full lifecycle, including recycling of what the Council were buying, but it was met with a lot of resistance, saying it would take too long. Councillor Dundas chimed in to back her up saying that we did need to know that what they were doing was green and not just box ticking.

I felt completely done-in by the time we left the Town Hall that evening, and was so glad that I'd never have to do that again. The biggest battle hadn't been with anyone at the Council; it was the inner one. I was going to have to sort this out and find a way to integrate this new Me, and soon. It was such a big change in my personality that even my own mother didn't recognise me.

Some months later she asked, "Have you had a slip-in or something, take you over?"

"A what?!"

"A slip-in. Some alien being who takes over a host body!"

"No! I am not even going to ask what you've been watching on TV to ask that question!"

"I could never have foreseen you doing all this when you were a child." She remarked.

Well, no, me neither. Although when I pondered it further, a few days later I decided she was wrong. There were signs. I could never abide bullying as a child. And what we were all going through now was the ultimate in bullying. The world's richest people, steering governments to enforce rules which would take away people's freedom, and destroying the earth under the guise of saving it, for greed and control. I'd always stood up to the bullies at school, so it wasn't surprising I was doing it as an adult as well.

The surprising part was how I was going about it. A method that was very much out of my comfort zone. But then, I've always done that which makes me uncomfortable, it's how we grow. So all things considered, it wasn't entirely out of character, even though it looked and felt like it.

What happened as a result of that Council meeting changed all our lives, but none more so than mine...

# 18

# Going Viral

The next day I made a video of the Council meeting, again putting in all the supporting images backing up everything that was said. I shared it on Twitter, as I thought that's what had caused the first video to take off. I really hoped this one would, as I felt it was a much better video. We'd managed to cram even more into three minutes than I ever thought possible. I also had a feeling the 'handbags at twenty paces' at the end of my speech, and the beginning of Carinna's, would make it compelling viewing.

As much as I still didn't want to be in the limelight, I had realised, after the success of the first video, how important it was to educate people about how environmentally harmful the so-called green tech is. The comments showed just how shocked everyone was, and how so many of us had been sucked into believing it was good for the planet, just because of good marketing. I braced myself for another viral video...

Nothing happened. It was a complete flop. Barely two thousand views compared to over two hundred thousand of the first one. Even now, two years later, it's only managed fourteen thousand views. What a pity. Never mind, must just be luck of the draw.

## Lift Off

Five days later, all hell broke loose in an unexpected way. Several people, with bigger YouTube channels, got hold of the video and made a video voicing their opinions as they showed their audiences the footage. 'Tousi TV' had nearly seventy thousand views and 'We Got A Problem' nearly sixty thousand.

There is something surprisingly compelling about watching these council meetings. You'd think it would be exceptionally boring, but when edited down to their essential moments, they are fascinating. It's the mix between councillors who've been trained to think and function in a way which defies all logic and common sense, versus members of the public speaking plain English, rationally presenting information and facts, which the Council then completely ignores because it's not inline with their agendas. At times their answers defy belief, others are nothing short of farcical. It's reality TV that leaves viewers gobsmacked.

After the YouTubers, then things got really crazy. A Twitter account called The Stark Naked Brief created a thread of the video. https://bit.ly/twitter-stark Twitter threads only allow short videos on free accounts, so the video was split over several posts. The first two-minute clip of my speech had over half a million views. This caused several influencers like @Bel_B30 to pick it up. The two that I saw had six million views in a weekend.

For weeks, and even months, afterwards, I could not escape my face on Twitter. Thankfully, I was not tagged on the versions the influencers shared. Something I am forever grateful for, judging by the frenzy the half a million views in the original thread I was tagged in caused.

From there, people shared the video on Facebook, Instagram, Tik Tok and all the alternative video hosting platforms. Wherever I looked, there I was. It's impossible to say how many times that video has been viewed now, but I wouldn't be surprised if it's over a hundred million views, judging by how many shares the two influencers I saw had. It went all over the world. When US actor Rob Schneider shared it, he got 2.6 million views and sixteen thousand shares https://bit.ly/twitter-rob. Who knows how many views and shares the sharers got!

Twitter influencers like James Melville and June Slater shared the video clip repeatedly and June put it into several of her YouTube videos. Philly J. Lay, the No. 1 Wellness podcaster, also repeatedly shared the video. Thanks to them, and others, the momentum and sharing of the vital information kept going for over two years.

At the time, I was still processing what had happened in the meeting and was working out how to integrate the new Me who was emerging. I was wiped out for days afterwards. So much so that I bundled the dog into the car and we went camping for a few days in Norfolk. I craved some beach time and it was wonderfully warm at the end of June that year. It wasn't quite the relaxing break I had envisioned because of the number of comments and shares. I should have just put the phone down, but I couldn't believe my eyes. It just kept going and going and going.

It was both deeply uncomfortable and exhilarating. It was also very weird reading some of the comments. I was referred to as a 'green woke leftie' and a 'dangerous far-right extremist' – not by the same person, obviously! One person even accused me of being a cult leader! Another likened me to presumably, King Cnut, albeit with a bit of a typo! It was fascinating watching people's vastly different interpretations. I was either Devil's spawn, or an Angel incarnate, depending on people's point of view.

My many years as a garden designer had trained me well. During the design process, you are creating a new entity, it's your baby. But ultimately it's not yours, you pass it on to the homeowners who commissioned it. Invariably, people always make changes, and sometimes not for the better. I'd trained myself to put my heart and soul into my work, but to immediately let go afterwards. I'd done my part, it was over to others now, and the garden would take on a life of its own. I did the same with the videos. I detached myself from them completely. They too appeared to have lives of their own.

It wasn't about me. It was the message that was important. I was just the hosepipe which delivered it, just like I was as a designer. The work isn't me, it just flows through me. I was rather annoyed when I realised that was what I was doing after about ten years as a designer. My ego wanted to be the big 'I am' as a garden designer. The only slight issue was that my ego couldn't design a garden if its life depended on it.

The number of times after I'd just qualified, the design would only come once I'd mentally given up. My mother used to call me 'Eleventh Hour Productions' because I'd always tell clients I'd be back in two weeks with their finished design. I'd spend twelve of those days trying frantically to design, and wouldn't be able to do it. But as soon as I let go, the design would come.

Then, when I found myself running their landscaping business, there simply wasn't time to spend days at the drawing board. I'd be lucky if I could get ten minutes without an interruption, or some disaster that I'd had to go and sort out. I taught myself to get out of the way quickly. I had no choice.

About ten years after I'd qualified, when I had escaped the family business and had my own design and construction company, I had a client who wanted a contemporary design. Something I'd been hankering to do for a long time. I set about looking at garden pictures for inspiration, but in those days there were very few on contemporary gardens. I was on my own for this one.

I set about my process of getting my conscious mind out the way so my subconscious could do its stuff. What came out was a surprise. It was incredible, and nothing like anything I'd seen in a book, so I knew it wasn't an amalgamation of ideas. I was overjoyed. I'd finally made it as a garden designer. The design was amazing. But the more I looked at what was on the paper, the more I realised that I did not have the skill to do what I'd just designed.

So where the hell did it come from? It was a freaky moment. I'm not being modest, I really didn't have the skill to produce that design. That was when I realised the designs were coming through me, not from me. All I had to do was sit still and shut up long enough to get them out. That's the bit I'd got good at. This really annoyed my ego; when it realised all I was doing was holding the pencil!

Well, that isn't entirely true. The designs would come, but I still had to make them work in a practical sense. Decide how high the pergola should be. Make sure the lawn shape could be mowed, that kind of thing. I was constantly switching back and forth between creative flow and practical. I was doing the boring bits and the creative design part I loved so much was coming through me from who knows where.

I think that is why creative endeavours are so fulfilling. We connect and align with the universal creative consciousness. A flow state I suspect we are meant to always be living in, but we're usually all too busy being busy. So those moments of pure creativity are glorious. Time stops, motion does not.

In creative time, I can design an entire garden in a matter of minutes. During the process, I lose myself completely in it, feeling I've been there forever. It's always a surprise when in reality it's only been a few minutes. I think that's why creative people can be hopeless with time in the real world. You're so used to being able to do vast amounts in the creative world, you have no concept of actual time when you're out of it. The things you think won't take long, invariably do when you're not in the creative world.

Once I got over my huff about not being quite the great designer I'd hoped I was, then things got even freakier. After a while, I would be doing a design and then I'd find myself doodling something else. Something I knew would not be right for that garden. I didn't know what to do with it. I showed the clients anyway because that is what had materialised, just in case they wanted a second option. The clients would say, that's lovely, but no, we prefer your first plan.

I would then find the idea that didn't work in their garden would be perfect for the next one. The freaky part was I hadn't met those clients at the time the idea came. I always used to meet one customer at a time because I didn't want the overload of ideas taking on too many projects at once brings.

This would happen over and over. Then it started extending to two or three clients later. Sometimes I'd get a design idea for a client I would meet months later. This happened with a very contemporary garden I designed for a client in New York. I had envisaged a modern floating patio with under-lighting, I wondered which client it was for. The moment I saw the architect's plans for the modern house three months later, I knew immediately the floating patio was for them. It worked perfectly.

Clients would be amazed. They'd tell me afterwards that they couldn't articulate what they had wanted to me because they couldn't visualise it, yet I had managed to create their dream garden. They thought that I must be psychic! I'd smile, whilst muttering under my breath, nope, I just hold the pencil and shut up long enough for it to land. When it came to creating my online garden design courses, I reviewed all the designs I'd done and came to see patterns. I'd always use design shapes which would make long gardens look wider and wide gardens look longer and from there I was able to create a teachable formula that anyone could use.

The council stuff felt very much like it was happening all over again. I felt guided and directed. I used the same process for writing speeches as I had with gardens. I got out the way. My conscious mind had to be a bit more present than designing gardens because it's words not pictures and I had to get my facts right. But the process is the same. Get out the way and see what flows. It's like I put my busy mind on pause and then the creative flow happens.

I do believe there is a creative, intelligent, consciousness in the universe and that it flows through me all day long. I feel very connected to whatever it is. Some may call it God, spirit, higher self, whatever, I do not profess to know what exactly it is at this point in time, but I know it's there. I'm on a very narrow bandwidth with what comes through. It's not like I'm able to get next week's lottery numbers, but, once in a particularly heightened emotional state, I did get something different to a garden design download.

## The Grid

I wasn't completely awake, but I wasn't asleep. I was in that twilight zone of consciousness. I saw an infinite grid in my mind's eye. It was fine red grid lines, with quite a dark blue background. We were all connected to this grid. I didn't see people, but felt the consciousnesses connected to one another through the grid, and knew who was around me.

I had an awareness that we were closely connected to those nearest us on the grid, but not necessarily by blood. It was also timeless. There were consciousnesses on the grid who'd perhaps been the love of our lives at some point in time, but in this current plane of existence we either hadn't met yet or they were just a helper, our paths crossing in a meaningful way but not permanently. It felt like such a strong connection on the grid and so much love everywhere.

The message was that we're all connected, love is always there, especially to those in our soul group surrounding us on the grid. If the relationship ends on this plane, it matters not, the connection is stronger than what happens here. You just have to connect to the Source, which was visually represented by the grid in my mind. It was trying to show me that there were stronger connections than the earthly ones, and that I wasn't as alone as I felt at that time. Each one of us on the grid has a role to play. The grid is made up of us. Threading us all together like an infinite net of consciousness. People come and go, but the grid does not. It's infinite.

It was a powerful experience, and I was in a discombobulated state for several days afterwards. Lots of tears. At that point in my life I felt very alone. Never really having much in common with those around me. It felt like I was always looking through a window watching everyone at a party, but never being part of it. I found it hard to connect to people. I felt like I was a different species. Always the square peg, never fitting anywhere. I laugh when I look around me now. My life is overflowing with fellow square peggers. There are millions of us. Can't go anywhere without bumping into another square peg these days.

The 'Aware Square Peg Society' is growing by the day, as one-by-one more light bulbs come on. Shame it took so long. But then that aloneness and disconnection from the world at large was the tempering of our characters. Forging the strength required to not follow the madness of the crowds. The more you can be in the flow state, the easier it is to find others and connect.

## Following the Flow

I've learned to follow the flow. I was drawn to do Mark Attwood & Abby Wynne's Self-Publishing Masterclass even though I didn't even know if I'd be writing another book, or what it would be about if I did. I enrolled anyway, because I just had the feeling I should. At the time, I had no spare money and it was intellectually unjustifiable. It's a very good course by the way, I highly recommend it, especially if you want to get out of the Amazon publishing traps. From doing the course it's helped me immensely with this book! You likely wouldn't be reading this if I'd followed my intellect instead of my inner direction.

The afternoon I received the phone call from Charles Malet asking me to speak at the UK Column event in Bristol, I was filming a video, so the phone was on silent and I missed his call and it went to answerphone. Bristol is a long way and I had nothing to talk about other than Council Watch, which I'd had enough of. If I'd spoken to him, I may well have said no. About five minutes after I had listened to his voice message, the downloads started.

Big chunks of what I should say landed in my head. I rolled my eyes and muttered to myself "I guess I'm doing it then". Things I'd not thought about before arrived, seemingly out of nowhere. The concept of the two lands, with a population with integrity who did not tolerate tyranny, was born.

By the time I phoned him back in the evening to say that I would do it if I could find a dog sitter, as my usual ones were out the country, information and ideas were pouring down. And continued to do so for the next three weeks, right up until the event. I had so much material that I could have filled the entire morning.

What was interesting is that I wasn't the only one getting those downloads. Doc Malik, another brave soul who spoke up raising concerns during Covid, was the first speaker, just before me. He was a tough act to follow. In his inspiring speech he had said many of the things I was going to cover. Just like in London, when Matt, Richard, Clive and Janey had all said what I was going to. I adjusted my speech accordingly, grateful I was on second this time, so I still had loads of material left.

When I got off the stage and later bumped into the good Doc, he said he couldn't believe I had spoken about the phrase 'The meek shall inherit the earth'. He was going to say the same thing but had not had a chance to look up the dictionary meaning like I had, so he left it out of his speech.

What were the chances of two people deciding to pull that particular phrase out of the Bible at the same event? Very high in my world, we're all connected and receiving the same information, which is why, for all future events, I will try to avoid being the final speaker. And if Doc Malik and I are ever speaking at the same event again, I'd better try and get on before him, just in case!

I'd told the Bristol audience that the one phrase which had stood out to me from Sunday School was 'the meek shall inherit the earth' and that as a small child this had fascinated me. I found myself wondering when and how this would happen, but most importantly, it lodged in my brain that you don't have to be a thug in this world, in fact, it's better if you're not.

When I'd looked 'meek' up the Cambridge Dictionary had said, 'quiet, gentle, not willing to argue or express opinions in a forceful way. Miriam Webster was worse, 'deficient in spirit or courage.' These did not feel right to me, so I researched further. The origin of meek comes from an old Norse word meaning gentle, but a fuller understanding comes from the Greek, 'praus' which translates to strength under control.

I finished that part of my speech by quoting Aristotle, "A meek person doesn't shy away from taking a stand. Rather, the stand is taken at the right time, with the right people, in the right way." That's more like it.

With my garden design downloads, I'd had to keep a notepad by my bed because they'd always come in the middle of the night. Eventually I mentally asked, 'can you wait until I get up? This is exhausting!'. The downloads immediately stopped, and then every morning as soon as I'd get into the shower, they'd start up.

Whilst doing the self-publishing masterclass, I had felt drawn to writing again, and I intuitively knew I'd know what my book would be about after the Bristol event.

Those of us who are tuned in are all getting the same ideas at once. I've lost count of the number of people I know who are writing books right now on what's happened in the last few years, and what we can do moving forward. I will be surprised if there aren't massive overlaps in the messages we all put across, albeit done in slightly different ways, each one of us attracting slightly different audiences.

It took me six months to write my first book but I knew this one would take about a month. I cleared my diary, because I knew once I started the writing process, it would flood out. That's exactly what happened for ten hours a day. Writing started on the 8th January and three weeks and eighty thousand words later I'm three-quarters of the way through, so I'm on schedule. Yes, I have to go back and polish, but the bulk is there.

Early January, I was asked to speak at an event at the end of February. I agreed, but no downloads came. I thought it was a little odd, but I was also relieved not to be getting a constant stream of things to say for weeks on end popping into my mind. Perhaps it was because the event was so many weeks away and I was busy brewing this book.

Three weeks before I was due to speak, the organiser told me they were worried about having me publicised as a speaker because it was a council-run venue and they didn't want to run the risk of the event being cancelled, so would I mind just coming as a guest and not a speaker. Of course I didn't mind, I'm very happy not to do public speaking! Was that why I didn't get a single download, because it was never going happen?

The organiser offered to announce to the audience that I was there so people could come and talk to me in the breaks. No! Don't do that. If I'm not a speaker, I'm more than happy to quietly sit at the back without anyone knowing I'm there! As it happened, I wasn't able to go at all as my mother was very poorly that week and needed a lot of assistance.

It's always amused me, doing Council Watch (how that evolved, I will get to shortly), how many of the life skills I had developed for completely different things have come in handy. Learning how to make and present videos for my business. Learning copywriting, communication techniques, persuasive sales page writing. Learning how to be relatively calm in stressful situations. The list goes on.

Is there a big angelic sorting office in the sky that's trying to combat evil forces, and as soon as one of us shows signs of awareness, they shout, "Here's one! She's finally got the level of awareness required. She can do videos, writing, has life-coaching training, is reasonably calm under pressure and has a wickedly sarcastic sense of humour."

"Right, deploy that one to start Council Watch. She'll need a good sense of humour for that!"

"She's not remotely interested in politics."

"Even better!"

Or is it the other way around? Did we develop all those life skills because one day they'd be needed for this?

Whichever way around it is, all my life skills have been thoroughly utilised in ways I never imagined. I was able to use the same detachment I did with gardens over the now viral videos. It no longer mattered what people said or thought about me. I'd been steered to do all this, and I knew it. Which is why I'd mentally shot out on that first fateful Council meeting back in January – "If you want me to do this, you're going to have to help me, and quickly!"

People rarely see us as we truly are anyway, even those who we think know us. Everyone projects, it just happens more when people haven't met you and happen to watch a video. Qualities which you either don't possess, or have in small amounts are projected onto you in bucket loads. That's why knowing thyself is so important. It allows you not to get caught up in the noise.

Both Carinna and I know exactly who we are. If people saw how much faffing and fiddling went into our first speeches, and even now sometimes, I don't think anyone would be impressed. It's not like we can just speak like that in real life without anything pre-written. If we had that ability, then I'd be impressed. But we don't. To be that concise takes hours, sometimes days. The finished videos have been edited so the fluff-ups are mostly out, and then with the pictures added to back up what is being said, which gives a more polished performance than is reality.

So when people come up to us and say they could never do what we do, we always say, yes you can. If we can do this, anyone can. Our main superpower, if you want to call it that, is that we are determined and persistent. But then we are both Taureans, that helps! We succeed because we won't let things go. Well, I say we, Carinna is actually more determined at making sure we chase things up to their completion than I am.

The Council rules of only allowing three minutes to speak worked in our favour. Determined to get as much as we could in our allotted time, we've both learnt to write in a way that jam packs all the points we want to get across. And guess what that makes? Great videos. That's what helped them go viral. People have the attention span of a hyperactive flea these days. Packing a ton of info in two or three mins, with images, is what made it a winner, along with the unusualness of people talking to their councils in this way.

The number of comments we've had under the videos appreciating the calm, non-confrontational delivery of information was unexpected. With TV soap operas all screaming at each other, always argumentative, I was surprised that calm, middle-aged women in cardigans would resonate so much.

It took a few days for me to become calm and completely detached from the videos and all the comments. To begin with, I was like a deer caught in headlights. I was struggling to wrap my head around six million views in a weekend.

Suddenly offers for interviews started to come in. The first was from podcaster Tom Nelson, the producer of Climate The Movie. When he said what he did, and how much he loved the video, and would I like to be on his climate podcast, the old default Rachel took over and immediately said no!

He'd really caught me at a bad time as I was a total deer in headlights when he emailed. I felt I couldn't possibly go on his podcast, I didn't know anything about the climate. I also didn't want to be in the limelight. It was bad enough I couldn't go on Twitter without seeing my face splattered up and down the feed, the last thing I wanted was more publicity. He was very insistent, but I kept saying no. This was getting out of hand. Besides, I'd said what I needed to in the Council meeting, what else was there? I'd be a dreadful guest, especially to a predominantly American audience, so I stuck to my guns with a firm no. I did eventually say yes a year later, once I'd got over myself, and I'm glad I did as Tom is lovely. We even managed to meet in person when he came over to London a few months after the interview.

There were several other interview offers, but all were met with a, 'no'. Once I had calmed myself, and got as used, as one can be, to seeing my face splattered all over Twitter, there was one interview I did say yes to, along with Carinna, and that was with Richard Vobes, but only because Carinna and I liked his videos and we thought it would be nice to talk to him. I also thought that if we did one interview, then we wouldn't have to do any more. After all, it's not like we would need to go back to the Council now they'd been informed about how bad the green tech was. Stop laughing.

We enjoyed chatting to Richard, he made the process relaxing and not the ordeal we'd thought it would be. Carinna is less keen on online interactions, and requested that I do all the talking and that she'd chip in whenever she had something to say. In real life, it's the exact opposite, and people are always surprised she's the chatty one when it appears like she barely gets a word in edgeways in interviews. People thinking Carinna is the quiet one amuses her no end.

I think it was through Richard Vobes that Carinna and I were put in touch with Sandi Adams who'd organised a Net Zero debate in Glastonbury on 7th July. She'd seen our Colchester Council video and invited us to attend her event. Although it was quite a drive, we decided we'd go along as it might help us with the Council; their email responses had come through and it was clear they were going to continue with their EV ideas regardless. Their email responses regarding EVs all came down to $CO_2$, something I knew plenty about with regards to plants, but absolutely nothing with regards to climate.

There had been many advantages to my ten year Digital Nomad lifestyle other than the exciting places, people, food and glorious weather I'd experienced. Not being near English TV or newspapers meant I'd missed all the fear-mongering regarding climate change. I genuinely had no clue, and therefore no strong biases. I had a suspicion there may be some exaggerations, because I'd seen all the Agenda 2030 stuff thanks to Sandi's work. In order to move us over to Stakeholder Capitalism, Net Zero was essential. But I didn't know any of the science on either side of the argument.

I'd started to read up on $CO_2$ being the main cause of global warming, and it all sounded plausible to my ignorant mind. But was the amount of $CO_2$ that man made tipping the balance and heading us into catastrophe? I didn't know, so I was interested to get what I assumed would be a different perspective to the mainstream narrative I'd been reading. I wasn't, however, expecting to hear what I did, and sat there open mouthed, in a state of complete disbelief...

# 19

# Climate Catastrophe or Con?

There were a couple of glitches getting to Glastonbury. Firstly, the event was on a Friday and we had to go via the UK's largest car park, the M25. Carinna had a client in the morning, so we couldn't leave until lunchtime, and the event started at 6pm. I didn't have a dog sitter, and it was scorching. My original plan to leave the dog in the car during the evening event wasn't going to work, I'd have to sit outside with her, and hope I could hear the talks through the window. We also needed to get to the campsite I'd booked and set up the tent before we could go to the town hall for the evening event.

We just about made it in time. It was a stressful drive through the endlessly snarled traffic, and Carinna had to put up with quite a lot of swearing from the driver. We arrived at the campsite, hurled everything out of the car, and put the tent up in record time, once I had remembered how to do it. Then it was everyone back in the car and the hunt for the Town Hall. I knew there was a car park right outside as I'd googled it, but it was small. If we weren't able to park there, it was going to be a bit of a nightmare.

Thankfully we did manage to grab one of the last spots. I left Carinna with the dog, and went in search of Sandi, who had our tickets. I was ravenous, but would there be time to grab a bite to eat before it started? I knew I wouldn't last three hours of talks if I didn't eat first.

I found Sandi, we gave each other a big hug and had a brief chat. It was so wonderful to meet her after all this time. She'd played such an important role in enabling me to see my way out of the woods, when all I could see were trees. There was an instant bond, as I find with so many of the people I've met along this crazy journey since 2020. You're on the same page in so many ways, it's like you've known each other forever.

Sandi told me there was a slight delay getting started because the Council had insisted on security for the event. I told her about the issue with the dog. She suggested I ask if I could bring her in. It was so hot, the back doors by the stage were open, along with all the windows, so I knew I would at least be able to hear what was going on, even if we weren't allowed in.

Getting back to Carinna, I suggested we risk a quick pub meal. If it wasn't done on time, we'd have to ask for a takeaway. We went to the first pub we found, which was more or less opposite the Town Hall. Ordered what we thought would be quick and hoped for the best. There was a fair sized queue to the event, so we hoped we'd manage to get fed before it all started.

We just about managed to stuff our faces and get to the Town Hall just as the Net Zero Debate was about to start. I asked if I could bring the dog in because it was too hot to leave her in the car, and to my surprise they said yes. In fact, there were several dogs inside already. We got our seats at the back of the room, and I placed Lena's furry blanket on the wooden floor in front of us. I hoped she'd get the idea and go to sleep on it.

She wasn't used to crowds and had never been to an event like this, so I wasn't sure how she'd react. She was too interested in everything around her to lie down, but she did sit on her blanket. I just hoped she wouldn't get bored and start yowling to go. She's a fairly quiet dog, but when she's had enough of something, everyone soon knows it. Not too dissimilar to her human, in that respect, now that I think about it!

Sandi started the evening, and introduced the mayor, Indra Donfrancesco, who would be the first speaker. The evening was supposed to be a debate on Net Zero, but no one, other than the Glastonbury Mayor, had been willing to speak on behalf of man-made climate change. She had involvement with Extinction Rebellion and Earth First and spent her time waffling about how many wonderful carbon saving things the council had done, but she did not back up what she said with any evidence.

Unfortunately, she didn't stay to hear the other side of the argument, but some of the other councillors did, and afterwards they said they had learned a lot from the evening.

The next speaker was climate researcher, Ralph Ellis. He'd published several peer-reviewed climate papers on the modulation of ice ages, from procession and albedo feedback mechanisms. Ralph is a polymath (brilliant at a lot of things) and an interesting man. He'd been an airline pilot, computer analyst, author and historian to name a few. He was also an entertaining public speaker; I appreciated his dry wit, which certainly helps with a topic like climate change.

His talk was on climate 'mis-' and 'disinformation'. Right out the gate he stated that his papers were controversial because they say that $CO_2$ is not the major feedback agent in controlling temperature. He said he wasn't going to talk us through his entire paper, but he would show us one graph from it.

He put the graph on the screen, and it showed eight hundred thousand years of temperature data and $CO_2$, with all of the major ice ages. It clearly showed $CO_2$ and temperature are in lockstep together. He told us that some scientists have assumed from this that $CO_2$ controls temperature. On the graph you could see why.

But Ralph said, "Correlation does not imply causation. You need some evidence for causation." He then went on to point out the finer details of the graph, and to my surprise it showed high levels of $CO_2$ when the earth cooled, and low levels when the earth warmed.

What?! I was having trouble wrapping my head around that. My eyes were showing me the complete opposite of everything I'd read online about $CO_2$ and global warming. Before I could properly process what I'd seen, he was on to the next slide, showing something he said would be familiar, called the Hockey Stick graph. I had seen this one. It showed the sharp increase in temperatures in the last few decades.

The graph showed a thousand years of temperature data derived from tree rings. Ralph said that tree rings are not a good proxy for temperature, but never mind. He then moved onto the 'Climategate emails'. They were between Michael Mann and several other apparently well-known climate scientists I'd not heard of.

The emails stated that they had done Michael Mann's 'nature trick' of adding in real temperature data to the last fifty years. By stitching the two different data sets together it hid the temperature decline. Ralph showed us the original tree ring data chart. The chart showed six hundred years of tree ring data, and you could see the temperature bobbing along fairly consistently, and then in the mid twentieth century it declines, which of course is not what climate alarmists want people to see.

Ralph quipped, "It's called the tree ring divergence problem. Trees were able to record the temperature data accurately until the 1950s and then suddenly they don't! And if you believe that, I've got a bridge to sell you!" The audience laughed.

He then showed us that in order to hide the temperature decline, you just chop the graph off before the temperature dip and then replace it with recorded temperature data, and, hey presto, you have a sharp increase, and the hockey stick graph is born. Two completely different data sets stitched together.

For Ralph, the climate alarmism started with this disinformation, and it's continued ever since. He then showed us a whole series of charts and data, with everything from tornadoes to forest fires. All things we've been told are getting worse.

In every chart he showed, things were not getting worse when you looked at the full data set. In fact, the opposite. There are fewer tornadoes, hurricanes and forest fires than there were if you go back to the early 1900s. But if you start the charts after the 1940s, then it looks like things are getting worse.

It was so eye-opening. All the charts I'd looked at online showed everything getting worse. It hadn't occurred to me to get a longer range chart. But then I'm not a climate scientist. Why would it? I'd assumed that was the chart and I had no idea when records began on such things.

Next up was melting sea ice, which is, according to the alarmists, all going to melt and flood us. Ralph showed us the charts. Arctic sea ice has been melting for the last 40 years, and it's decreased by about twenty percent. But in Antarctica, the ice has been increasing for 35 years, up until a big storm in 2017 which broke up the ice, but it's been recovering and increasing ever since. So why the disparity? $CO_2$

is a global gas, it should affect things equally. Ralph said no one actually knows.

Next up was the threat to polar bears. We all know they are being wiped out because of climate change. Wrong. They aren't. He showed a graph from Dr Susan Crockford, a zoologist who's been studying polar bears for thirty-five years. The data showed that polar bear numbers have been increasing for sixty years! In fact they've quadrupled. As Ralph pointed out, organisations like the BBC have a lot to answer for. The journalists must have come across the real data.

The clincher for me was the next part of Ralph's speech, and he'd only been going for about ten minutes at this point. It's well-known that 97% of climate scientists agree with anthropogenic (man-made) global warming. Once again, no they don't. Ralph gave us a breakdown of the actual data from a paper by John Cook and others.

They took nearly twelve thousand climate papers, and of those 66% expressed no opinion on whether man is responsible for global warming. So those papers were rejected. Out of the remaining papers, 3% rejected global warming completely. So you could say 97% support global warming. But if you dig deeper into the paper, it said, only 24% supported some man-made global warming. Ralph himself said as a $CO_2$ sceptic, he'd be included in that 24% because there has been some global warming, but we don't know precisely what is causing it.

Digging deeper into the paper only 8% supported anthropogenic global warming (AGW), i.e.

it's our fault. But going deeper still only 0.5% explicitly supported the IPCC anthropogenic global warming. Governments around the world use the IPCC reports to base their climate policies on. Ralph said that if you don't agree with anthropogenic global warming you don't get grants.

The IPCC are the Intergovernmental Panel on Climate Change, notice the governmental part of the title. Climate science, as I was to find out later when I did a deep dive into the science, and even went on a climate course to study it fully, is political, not scientific. Climate researcher, Paul Burgess who has appeared on GB News, has made a video where he shows what happens inside the IPCC, and how the reports are made. The scientists write the full reports, and then politicians from each country vote on every word that goes into the policy maker's summary, which is all that most people read, with sometimes startling differences between them.

According to the Dutch, award-winning science journalist, Marcel Crok, the IPCC have already cherry-picked some of the data in their scientific reports before the politicians get their hands on it. In a recent talk Marcel gave to our climate course group, he cited an instance where 52 out of 53 peer reviewed papers dealing with 'normalised disaster losses' saw no increase in harms that could be attributed to climate change. The IPCC highlighted the single paper that claimed an increase in losses. Marcel said that paper is flawed, yet it's the one the IPCC chose to use.

Marcel is the co-founder of the Climate Intelligence Foundation (Clintel) which he set up in 2019 with the emeritus professor of geophysics, Guus Berkhout. They have created a declaration stating there is no man-made climate emergency, which has been signed by thousands of professors, scientists, including two Nobel Laureates. The declaration can be seen on their website: https://clintel.org/

The IPCC claims there is an acceleration in the rate of sea-level rise in recent decades. Clintel has shown this claim is flawed, because the IPCC ignores decadal variability in sea level. Marcel said there were many other similar instances he and others have uncovered, so many in fact he co-edited a book on them called The Frozen Climate Views of the IPCC.

Ralph's talk continued with all sorts of fascinating facts and figures about $CO_2$ and how different levels affect plants. He also talked about $CO_2$ deserts, not something I knew about. Apparently the Gobi Desert was caused by low $CO_2$ levels, it wasn't to do with lack of water. In the Jurassic era, $CO_2$ was at 2,500 ppm, which is six times higher than now, and the biosphere was fine.

The rest of Ralph's talk was about energy production, and just how flawed renewables such as wind and solar really are, and how impossible reaching Net Zero is. It was an enlightening talk and can be seen on the UK Column website, as they filmed the event. Just search for 'Net Zero Debate Ralph Ellis'.

## If You Can't Beat Them, Join In!

By now, the dog had settled on her blanket and seemed quite content to stay put so we made it to the end of Ralph's speech without incident. But as soon as the applause started up at the end, she sat up and looked at me with her head tilted to one side. I knew instantly what was about to happen. I could see the quizzical furrow of her brow as she tried to work out what was going on. She'd never heard applause before, and didn't know what to do.

Because I was clapping she looked at me as if to ask what she should do. With her options limited, I knew it was going to be one of two things, howling or barking. I'd never heard her howl, so I guessed at barking, and sure enough out came an excited and loud "WOOF, WOOF, WOOF!". The more the applause, the more she barked, which was fine because the applause covered the sound of it. But when the clapping stopped, she did not.

"WOOF, WOOF, WOOF"

"Shut up!"

"WOOF, WOOF, WOOF"

"Will you stop barking!"

She was on a roll now she knew noise was required. She is very good at that particular noise and continued, caught up in the excitement of her noise-making and eagerly wagging her tail.

"Woof, Woof... Woof"

In desperation, I put my hands around her muzzle and demanded she stop. A final muffled little 'woof' escaped through my fingers as she eventually got the message. This happened every time there was applause, she thought she had to join in. And every time she didn't take the cue to stop when the applause did. UK Column must have loved this during their filming.

There were a few video clips played between speakers, and Ralph was followed by Peter Taylor, who is a science analyst turned environmentalist, who worked as an advisor to the UN, and governments both locally and across the EU. His particular area of expertise was computer modelling of ocean and atmospheric systems. He'd published numerous works in scientific journals, and had written books, as well as lectured at many leading universities. If I listed everything Peter has done, and his extensive qualifications and experience, it would fill the rest of this book.

His book, 'Chill, A Reassessment of Global Warming Theory' goes deeply into analysing the science of climate change, and from that he concludes that the earth's cooling will be much more of a problem to us than its warming. His talk wasn't as concise as Ralph's and veered off more into the politics of good people getting driven out if they don't follow the narrative of man-made climate change, which I wasn't as interested in. I wanted to know more about $CO_2$, Ralph had really whetted my appetite on that subject.

During the break, a couple of ladies came up to us and said they'd seen us on the Richard Vobes Show. When I stood up, one of them exclaimed, "Oh you're so much smaller than I imagined!" like she had seen me as some big bruiser in her mind's eye. This amused Carinna and I no end. Even pint-sized people can stand up for their rights, and as I think I may have said at the time, "All good things come in small packages!"

At this point, I decided to put Madame back in the car (the dog, not Carinna!); she was getting restless and trying to get on my lap for a cuddle. It was now cool enough, at well after 8pm. She'd be more comfortable in her car hammock than her fluffy blanket on a hard wooden floor. It was just a matter of her getting out of the room without her usual excited barks at going somewhere.

"WOOF, WOOF, WOOF!"

"Will you shut up!"

When I came back, Carinna was chatting to another lovely lady who'd also seen us interviewed on the Richard Vobes Show a few days earlier. As she left to go back to her seat, she handed Carinna an envelope and in it was some money for our travel expenses. How lovely! We were both really touched.

She couldn't have known how much the council stuff had taken over our lives, to the point I'd almost stopped working to do all the emails, speeches and videos. We gave ten pounds to Sandi for the tickets as we knew the Town Hall hire hadn't been cheap, and then the rest went towards the diesel.

After the break, Ian Jarvis spoke about his concerns over 5G, and Sandi finished the evening speeches with her talk on Agenda 2030, and how corporate communism was being rolled out and how we mustn't allow it.

The evening finished with a Q & A with the panel, and MP Andrew Bridgen was there and said a few words, too. So whilst it hadn't been the debate everyone had hoped for, it was still a great evening and we were glad we'd made the effort to come. We chatted to Sandi briefly afterwards, and promised to keep in touch. I also met the event organiser, Eli. He invited us to join in his monthly Zoom calls with people around the country, as he thought what we were doing in Colchester should be done in as many councils as possible. We said we'd be happy to join in.

We headed back to the campsite as it was getting dark. It had been an exhausting day, sleep came easily to us all. We woke early the next morning to a very strange distant indistinct yelling. The three of us were crammed like sardines in my allegedly three to four person tent. I can only conclude they either use Pygmies, or stacked positioning when determining tent sizes.

The dog was happy, she'd made herself cosy in the middle. As soon as she saw we were awake, there were loud thwacks with her tail and she immediately rolled over with legs in the air demanding tummy rubs. Rolling from one side to the other, making sure she got equal amounts of Carinna cuddles, as well as Rachel cuddles. It was like watching a furry windscreen wiper going from one side to the other, determined to get her cuddle quota before we left the tent.

We had breakfast, and decided to walk up to the top of Glastonbury Tor, which was just above the campsite. The Tor is a hill that's over five hundred feet high enabling three hundred and sixty degree views across the Somerset Levels. The tower is all that's left from St Michael's Church. The weather was the complete opposite from the previous day, it was overcast, slightly drizzly and the outside of the tent was covered in large beads of water. I hoped the sun would come out and evaporate them by the time we returned.

As we got near the top of the Tor, the yelling we'd heard earlier suddenly became a lot louder. It was coming from inside the 14th century tower. There was a man sitting down rocking back and forth shouting at the top of his voice, "I am Lord Jesus Christ.

> I am Lord Jesus Christ.
> I am Lord Jesus Christ.
> I am Lord Jesus Christ."

Each time he yelled 'Christ' it came out like a strangled shout. Was he re-living the crucifixion? It certainly sounded like it. We circled around the tower, not wishing to disturb him. As we got around to the back of it, we could see some bare feet belonging to jean-clad legs poking out as the shouting continued.

As readers of my first book will know, I have had my fair share of strange encounters when travelling, but nothing quite like this. He sounded distressed. What should one do in this situation? Should we leave him in anything but peace, to get on with it, or ask him if he was OK?

I knew what I wanted to do, get the hell out of there. But then I'm not a people person. Kind-hearted Carinna, on the other hand, most definitely is, and so is the dog...

# 20

# Giggles in Gloucestershire

Anyone who's seen 'Kick-Arse Carinna' in action at the council might think I was being facetious, referring to her as kind-hearted, but I wasn't. The council-slaying version comes out of nowhere the moment she steps foot in the Town Hall. The Carinna we all know and love is nothing like Council-Slaying Carinna.

She's the kindest, gentlest of souls, with a strong sense of social justice, who is always there for anyone who needs her. She has an endless supply of hugs, whether you want one or not.

During a reprieve in the shouting, spying a pair of bare feet, the dog decided she wanted to investigate the owner of said feet, and dragged Carinna in his direction. Carinna managed to steer the dog away from going through the Gothic arch to him, but in the process she caught his eye and cheerfully greeted him with, "Morning!" And then none of us knew what to say after that. Awkward.

Then it started to rain. So all four of us - Carinna, me, Lena the dog and the bare-footed man identifying as Jesus, ended up huddled, still not knowing what to say, inside the Tower, which could only part-shelter us because it doesn't have a roof. The three humans and the dog just standing there with that very English special half smile reserved for awkward situations with strangers. The bare-footed man took this opportunity to take a break and took out a banana from his purple rucksack on the stone seat inside the Tower. I could see a whole bunch of bananas poking out and wondered if he was in for the day. I was hoping it wasn't his last supper.

    Mercifully for us all, it was the quickest of quick downpours, so we bid him farewell and descended the opposite side we'd walked up from. This wasn't as steep as the back path we'd clambered up on the way in. On our descent, Carinna told me she'd woken up around 5am because of strange noises. She'd been trying to work out what type of animal it had been. She now realised it hadn't been animals she'd heard, but the bare-footed man. He'd been up here since before dawn. By the time we reached the bottom field, we could hear his shouting resume.

"I am Lord Jesus Chriiiist!"

    I've no idea what the man identifying as Jesus was going through, but it sounded like he was desperately trying to banish his demons. I sent him a silent prayer and hoped he managed to find the peace he so clearly needed.

By the time we'd got across the field at the bottom, we popped out by the Chalice Well and weren't a million miles away from the town centre, so we carried on going. We bimbled around the town going into all the quirky book and crystal shops, eventually landing in a nice modern tea room which allowed dogs. We had our drinks and a bite to eat before heading back to the campsite to pack up and get back on the road. We'd enjoyed our flying visit and spirits were high.

The journey home was much easier than the one getting to Glastonbury and we managed it in about four hours. We were laughing most of the way home. I don't remember what had set us off but once we start, it can go on almost indefinitely, as the people at the next event in Gloucester discovered a month later.

## Glamping in Gloucestershire

Sandi's friend Eli, who'd helped her set up the Net Zero event and who had been in charge of the PA system, had invited us to be his guests at a yearly three day event he organises called the Shine Seminars, held in marquees in a field on the outskirts of Gloucester, near Westbury-on-Severn. No dogs were allowed at this one, so at least there would be plenty of room in the tent. Carinna had brought her huge family tent, and I'd got mine as a backup in case we weren't able to get her more complicated tent up.

The speaker line-up was fantastic. We were really excited about going, and Sandi was going to be there, along with a whole host of other people we'd got to know through doing the council videos. We drove up nice and early on the Thursday, and got there without too much hassle mid-afternoon. We got Carinna's tent set up OK, but there was a bit of mould in it near the base so we decided to set mine up to sleep in and just use hers as a day tent because, unlike mine, you could stand up in it.

The laughter started in the first lecture we attended. We were crammed into one of the smaller tents of the venue. I don't recall what the speaker's subject was, but I remember she was a lovely lady who kept getting interrupted by people butting in with questions or comments. There was a woman who seemed determined to show everyone she knew more about the subject than the person speaking.

At one point there was a technical issue which needed to be resolved, so whilst the crew were sorting out the PA system, the woman who knew more than everyone else got into a loud conversation with a man across from her, who also seemed to know his fair share of everything. I watched the passive-aggressive game of spiritual one-upmanship exchange go back and forth.

The part that started my internal giggling, and led to great difficulty keeping a straight face, was when it turned into, 'I've read more advanced spiritual books than you'. The man had played what I assumed was the trump card of having read the Bhagavad Gita, I think it was. I eagerly awaited her response. Had she read it too, was it going to finally silence her or could she trump that?

The woman decided she could definitely trump the Bhagavad Gita. Her choice was most unexpected and had me in near convulsions to the point I had to tell Carinna, "I'm just going to stretch my legs, back in a minute!"

She had already seen my shoulders moving up and down trying to contain the soon to be uncontrollable laughter which was bubbling up. She'd caught the energy of it and wasn't far off herself having been equally amused at the one-upmanship peacocking display, so she followed me out. Though she didn't know precisely what had been my tipping point.

One of the many wonderful things about Carinna is I rarely have to explain what I'm finding funny. She is the one person who immediately gets it and often starts to laugh before I do; she knows when I'm going to find something funny.

The lady's indignant retort to the Bhagavad Gita was to inform him that she'd read The Celestine Prophecy!

Now don't get me wrong, The Celestine Prophecy is a lovely book from what I can remember of it. It was the first spiritual book I read in my late teens. So the association in my mind was like the spiritual equivalent of the Ladybird books you read in junior school. It's where you start, which may well be doing the book a great disservice, but nonetheless, that's where it is in my head, which is what made it so funny, as I never would have picked it to trump books like the Bhagavad Gita.

Once the laughter started, like the drive home from Glastonbury, we couldn't stop ourselves. Everything kept getting funnier and funnier. The pinnacle of amusement came from an incident involving the composting toilets. I won't go into the details because it wouldn't be fair on the third party involved. It had been along similar lines to the book incident with spiritual one-upmanship, only this time quite literally backfiring spectacularly. Anyway, this one incident made us laugh so much that we didn't manage to walk past the toilets from that point on without becoming doubled over with laughter.

Every time we said to each other, "Right, we can walk past the toilets without laughing this time." Only moments later one of us would break and start laughing, which would inevitably set the other off. We must have looked like a constantly inebriated real pair of Essex girls. Our awareness of this made it even funnier because neither of us drink. Which of course led to more laughter.

I've noticed life does seem to like to reflect back to us that which we need to work on in ourselves. After the second spiritual one-upmanship incident, I started to wonder if that was a character trait I sometimes exhibited? I wasn't sure, but I made a mental note to myself anyway, 'don't do that!' From then on we didn't have any more of those types of encounters. All the people we met were lovely and a joy to spend time with. The laughter continued throughout, largely due to the fact that it was impossible to get from A to B without passing the composting toilets.

Funnily enough, one of the things the person had said to us just prior to the unfortunate incident was, you always remember the toilets at these kinds of events. I'd thought that was an odd thing to say because I couldn't recall a single toilet of any event I'd ever been to. Though obviously, now I can. She certainly made sure we'll never forget those composting toilets!

It was a good job our tents were well away from everyone else's because the laughter started each morning around five-thirty and didn't stop until nine or ten-thirty at night, once we both collapsed from giggle induced exhaustion. This went on for three days. It was also a good job none of the others from Colchester had come with us that weekend or we'd had driven them insane.

We clearly needed the release after months of stressful council encounters. It's not pleasant doing battle at the Council and the Colchester Council are polite. Some of the other councils we've watched people deal with are awful.

The weekend away did us the world of good and we booked Eli in for an Indian Head Massage as a thank you, with a lovely practitioner who had a stall at the event whom we'd met in the mobile sauna. That was our favourite place, we went in day and night. It wasn't great weather at the beginning of August that year, and it had tipped it down so much that Carinna's tent flooded, making us very grateful we'd got my backup tent along with the log burning stove sauna, which was heaven.

It was probably the best trip away I've had with all the laughter, like-minded people, camaraderie, interesting lectures, conversations, and the wonderful sauna. We left feeling renewed and restored. Ready to do battle the following week. On the journey home, Carinna decided to put our time to good use, and between us we wrote her next council speech while I drove.

This time Carinna wanted to complain to the Council about the unlawful searches, and to our surprise, when we arrived, there weren't any. We were impressed that the Council had stopped them. Had they actually taken onboard the unlawfulness, or had they decided it was pointless paying overtime to security when people just walked past them? We were asked if we wanted to speak, but we both said no, turned around and walked out again.

That was the most pleasant trip to the Council yet. We went to the park instead as it was a lovely warm and sunny August evening, shame we hadn't had that weather in Gloucester. Carinna then spent the next half an hour beating me up in her professional capacity as a physio-terrorist whilst I lay on the grass grimacing. She swiftly sorted out all my aches and pains, much to the amusement of passers-by seeing the contorted grimaces on my face as she pressed, prodded and released the results of my poor computer posture, from hours spent making council videos. The 'average' video was usually between twelve to twenty hours of work. With everything else I was doing behind the scenes, most weeks were thirty to fifty hours on 'Council Watch' matters.

# A Verbal Spanking!

September we were back again to the Council, with Carinna chasing up the Environment and Sustainability Panel on why she hadn't heard back from them in the seven days they'd promised. She'd got a corker of a speech and was going to go in guns blazing, but there was a bit of a glitch when we arrived; the Democratic Services Officer said they had sent a response. He rushed downstairs and printed it off for us.

We had just a few minutes to go through it and completely re-write the first chunk of Carinna's speech, to deal with the new information. We were still frantically writing when they tried to start the meeting. Just as it was due to start, there was a technical glitch with the livestream, the delay gave us just long enough to scramble sense into the speech. That was a close one. Carinna adapted beautifully, as always.

The officers gave her the most ridiculous answers about why they hadn't answered the freedom of information requests. The look on my face was an absolute picture when one of them said he didn't feel he needed to respond to follow-up questions as they weren't in the form of a Freedom of Information (FOI) request. The next officer said he hadn't responded to my last email because he couldn't see any questions in it.

I did a nicely sarcastic video pointing out that questions are the sentences with the little question marks on the end of them! I showed him the seven or so he'd missed, and said I would put extra large question marks in all future emails so he didn't miss them. The email discourse I had with him went on for nine months. It can be read in the Council Watch Dropbox folder, email no.2. I started off very politely and you'll soon see the point at which my patience ran out.

The upshot of our exchange provided us with the following information: no one in the Council has any clue about what the parameters of the climate emergency they declared are. They do not have any evidence of the man-made climate emergency other than the IPCC say temperatures must not rise 1.5 C.

The Council think our concerns about Absolute Zero aren't warranted as they don't 'believe' these things will happen, even though it has been debated in the House of Lords, and they were all in favour of it. When the councillors voted to declare a climate emergency, they were not given any evidence from which to make a judgement, and were left to research it for themselves in their own time. I wonder how many did?

Part of the problem with discussing climate are the other things which have been attached to it, namely pollution. There is no question that a lot of human activities aren't ideal for the planet. We pollute, and damage, with almost everything we do and no one rational wants to do that. So as soon as you start to challenge anything climate related, you immediately hit a brick wall of people's noble ideals over not wishing to pollute.

The two issues are so firmly welded together in people's minds that they cannot separate them. $CO_2$ is synonymous with polluting car fumes, so of course EVs sound preferable. Even if you tell people the rise in $CO_2$ is helping to re-green the deserts and we've been at historical lows for centuries, with the highest being almost 8000ppm, they cannot grasp it being anything other than a pollutant, when it is in fact an essential gas of life. None of us would be alive without $CO_2$. It came perilously close to that dropping past the point of no return when it came down to 182ppm at the end of the last glacial advance. Had it got to 150ppm you wouldn't be reading this and there would be no life on earth.

Far more concerning than $CO_2$ is how much plastic we pollute the planet with, chemical contamination of our streams, rivers and seas, deforestation... the list goes on.

## Back to Bad Form

Disappointingly, the security searches were back at the front door. Had they not expected us at the Cabinet meeting, is that why there was no one there? Were they just putting on the searches when they knew we were coming? The police were also there again. All this for two middle-aged women in cardigans with a posse of pensioners, coming along to support us! So in October, Carinna went to the Cabinet meeting to point out the unlawfulness of their searches.

One thing had changed, at least this time they had hired very polite and professional SIA trained staff, which as a licensed premises, they should have had in the first place. Our ex-forces looking friend at the front door was nowhere to be seen. We had the option to be searched by women, and could refuse the scanner. So it was a better level of search, but it still shouldn't be in place as a condition of entry.

We were told they'd received a legal opinion on the searches and that they are lawful. We asked for a copy of this legal opinion and to this day, one has not been provided. This was October 2023, Carinna keeps asking, refusing to let this go. In January 2025 she was still pursuing this elusive legal opinion. My recommendation is not to hold your breath on it ever being provided. The point of the perseverance is to make sure those who have taken an oath to serve the public do so, and don't make up rules to suit themselves to the public's detriment.

## Full On

We decided to up the ante a bit and go along to our first Full Council meeting, which are held quarterly. On the 20th October, I went in with an important speech. The whole Council were going to have a second vote on their self-declared 'Climate Emergency' and whether to push the Government for more money to help them reach their Net Zero targets.

I covered renewables and EVs. Carinna did the Absolute Zero report, and Cheryl was back with us after an absence due to serious illness in the family. She covered air quality. There was talk about making the whole of Colchester a 20mph zone. She'd got her hands on Colchester's air quality report, and it showed only one road with a problem, and another was due to ongoing roadworks.

She asked them if there is any evidence that slowing people's journey's down by a third or more improves air quality? She said that whilst it was rational to have 20mph zones outside schools and playgrounds for safety, there was mounting evidence that elsewhere the slow zones increased accidents. This was due to driver frustration, and carelessness from drivers and pedestrians, that the slower speeds caused. This was from an analysis of government data from the Institute of Advanced Motorists. They said that serious accidents on 20mph roads increased by 26%, with a 29% increase in serious injuries. She went onto tell them about councils who regretted putting them in, but now couldn't afford to remove them.

When it was the Councillors' turn to speak, the blue team [Conservatives] were supportive of what we'd conveyed, and said hearing another point of view was like a breath of fresh air. Councillor Sunnucks said that decisions should be made from an engineering perspective, not a campaign one. Councillor Lissimore said she'd investigated the mining of rare earth minerals, the production and recycling after what we'd said in the Environment and Sustainability Panel, and that she could not in good conscience vote through something where they didn't know the effects of what they were replacing existing technologies with.

Later on, one of the Green councillors spoke and finally admitted that EVs may not be perfect, but they were better than the alternatives because of the reduction in $CO_2$.

The first time the 'Climate Emergency' was voted for, all fifty-one councillors voted it through unanimously. This time seventeen voted against it. Were they just playing politics or had we changed some minds? Perhaps both? Who knows. But it was a step in the right direction of getting them to think about the pollution and recycling, which is never discussed on mainstream media.

## Counteracting $CO_2$!

We'd now reached the part that I really didn't want to do, not that I particularly wanted to do any of it. Brian had already said to me a few months earlier, "You're going to have to address $CO_2$ soon." I was very resistant because it meant I'd have to cross the line into climate science, and I'm not a scientist. I really didn't want to go there. I'd hoped that common sense would kick in and the blindingly obvious, that the green technologies are not better than what we have now, many are arguably worse, would have dissuaded the Council from carrying on.

The next Full Council meeting was in December. That gave me time at least to thoroughly research the subject. The other reason I didn't want to touch climate, is because it's such an emotive subject.

There's been years of daily fear-mongering embedded into people's hearts and minds, which I'd missed because of travelling. For me, it was very easy to research with an open mind, but I knew the audience wasn't going to be remotely open-minded and I'd be branded as a climate change denier, which I'm not. I can read a graph as well as the next person and can clearly see the climate has always changed throughout the entirety of the earth's existence.

Before we had to face Full Council, we had another nice road trip planned. On the 11th of November, Carinna and I attended an event in Stroud where Sandi Adams was speaking alongside the brilliant author and podcaster James Delingpole, MP Andrew Bridgen, and others.

We arrived early as we needed to speak to Sandi regarding some information she had that would be helpful for our next council speech. Sandi was nowhere to be seen, so Carinna and I waited in the large, virtually empty venue. It was a beautiful old church, though it seemed rarely used, judging by the number of windows with missing glass and the pigeons coming and going as if it were their home! A few people were milling about, getting things set up for what was soon going to be a packed venue.

Andrew Bridgen was the first to arrive. He looked around the room and, not seeing anyone he knew, came over to where Carinna and I were sitting. He introduced himself and joined us. I must confess, other than knowing he'd been speaking out in Parliament, calling for an inquiry into the vaccines, I didn't know much about him. I was quite surprised when he told us he'd had two vaccines, which had caused him all sorts of health problems ever since.

He shared some of the things that had happened as a result of his speaking out—everything from no longer being able to get car insurance and trouble with bank accounts to leading Tories advising him to quit pursuing this course of action or it could be very bad for his health. I could quickly see why no one else was willing to speak out.

It wasn't long before the crowds arrived, and Andrew was mobbed by well-wishers. We wished him good luck with his speech and went in search of Sandi.

It was a wonderful day, full of inspiring people and speeches, though we didn't manage to catch up with Sandi properly until the end. She gave us the information we needed, along with the contact details of the experts she'd had at her Net Zero debate in Glastonbury, as we planned to organise a similar event in Colchester.

In the run-up to the Full Council meeting, I read climate papers and watched video after video on climate science. Poor Ralph Ellis, now that I had his contact details from Sandi, got the brunt of my endless questions as I wrote my speech. He kindly agreed to read through it to ensure I'd got all my facts right. Carinna didn't have the time to write her speech, so I created the outline for her and ran it by Ralph as well.

It's funny, the Full Council meetings should have been the most intimidating. Fifty-one councillors are seated in the large council chamber on the first floor of the Town Hall, with its imposing high, domed ceiling with large ornate pillars with gilt tops and horseshoe-shaped wooden panelled bench seating and stained glass windows oozing grandeur and officialdom. The Mayor runs proceedings, and is perched high above the councillor bench seats, in a raised panelled seating area at the back of the room, with extravagant gilt framed artwork hung behind on the primrose yellow walls, with the crest above, that is painted onto the wall.

For some reason, I didn't find it intimidating, which surprised me. Perhaps it was the fact that in full Council you 'Have Your Say' standing, while the councillors sit in front of you. Or perhaps I'd just become accustomed to this unexpected role I found myself in. That doesn't mean to say I wanted to be there. I didn't. I'd have still rather gone to the dentist, but at least I wasn't remotely intimidated.

I was, however, still suffering from the dry mouth syndrome which had plagued me from my third speech onwards. But now I knew it was likely to happen, I was at least able to make sure I had ample water and would drink it at every opportunity. I could at least make it a good way through the speeches before the inevitable dry mouth struck. It wasn't as bad as the first time, but it was still unpleasant to have to deal with that, as well as the ordeal of speaking - never knowing if the warrior within would be rendered wordless.

I'd psyched myself up for this one. Having Ralph go through everything I wanted to say made me a lot more comfortable than I would have otherwise been. His input got me over the fact that I had no scientific qualifications. I'd also spent so much time researching that I understood what I was saying, to a degree. What I know now makes that first $CO_2$ speech rather poor in construction, but it was a good enough start for someone who previously knew absolutely nothing.

There was however one wildcard none of us could have anticipated, which turned the entire evening into a complete farce, and once again, the police were called. For once, it wasn't anything to do with our presence, which made a nice change. But it did mean I was standing there like a lemon at the podium for half an hour waiting to speak, which did not help my performance anxiety in the least!

# 21

# Vexing $CO_2$

Because none of us knew anything about councils, after that first fateful meeting, we started to watch the meetings that the Council livestreamed to YouTube. This helped us get a feel for what the councillors were like. I purposely didn't look up which team each councillor was batting for so that I could evaluate them individually, rather than bracketing them together with their allotted colour rosettes, although it was fairly obvious with most.

Between us, we watched virtually every single Council meeting in 2023. Some of those meetings went on for three to four hours. Thank goodness YouTube has the facility to increase the video play speed. In November, I'd had the startlingly stupid idea of creating weekly highlight videos from their meetings. We all knew what was going on, but the rest of Colchester didn't. The idea wasn't the stupid part, it was thinking it wouldn't take me long to make them.

I ended up spending all my time making videos for the new channel I'd created, Colchester Council Watch. I added a playlist which featured all the Council accountability videos I'd made, which were on my Successful Garden Design YouTube Channel. It was dreadfully slow to get the viewing figures up with the new channel, but I knew it was necessary to have a content-specific channel, otherwise my garden design one would be taken over.

The night of the Full Council meeting, Carinna and I were sitting waiting in the pews in the far corner of the room. Lance was also planning on speaking, but was running late. A gentleman with dark hair and wearing a dark green Georgetown University sweatshirt came and sat next to me. He introduced himself as Gordon. He said he'd been watching our council videos and had decided to come along and join in the fun.

I asked him what his topic was, and he replied he was going to give them hell about their fraudulent council tax demands. I had a slight feeling of discomfort. Whilst he seemed a very pleasant easy going guy, my concern was not knowing what he was going to say and if it was controversial, which I was fairly sure it would be from the topic and glint in his eye, whether the Council would assume he was part of our group. I had a tough enough speech that night as it was without another wild-card incident.

As I've mentioned, it's the waiting that's the worst part with doing these council speeches. Once you're there, you just want to get it done and go. I'd seen the speakers list, and knew I was on fairly early, but what I hadn't noticed, at the time I'd glanced at it over the shoulder of the Democratic Services Officer, was that Gordon's name was before mine.

He'd told me he hadn't got anything written down and wasn't entirely sure what he was going to say. This increased my tension somewhat. When it was time for him to speak, I wished him luck and immediately got my camera out. I had a feeling this should be filmed. For some reason, I know not what, the main council chamber isn't set up for livestreaming video. That is only done from the Grand Jury Room where the smaller meetings take place. All that is available at Full Council is a very crackly audio. So it was down to the Council Watch camera crew, which is basically any of us with a phone, to capture everything.

Gordon very calmly started his speech with, "This Council is not a council, in fact that is deception. If I'm not mistaken under the statute of fraud, that's a criminal offence. You're a corporation, a registered corporation, just like the UK Government. Just like Parliament, they have no authority over the public. They're the same as Tesco, the same as McDonalds. So when this body asks people to pay council tax, they have zero authority whatsoever. Yet they harass people, demand that money, and that money goes to where? A central fund. That money after it has gone into the consolidated fund, does what? It buys weapons, it supports genocide."

That was as far as he got when the microphone beeped. He'd been cut off. The deputy Mayor, who was standing-in that day, is deaf and she was having to read the subtitles projected onto the screen at the side of the room, so she was a bit behind with what he said. She'd been advised by the people sitting next to her to stop proceedings because the speaker was being vexatious.

Gordon replied, "Well let me move onto history then." And started to try to tell her about the Magna Carta and Bill of Rights, but she cut him off again, saying she couldn't see how what he was saying was relevant. She'd cut him off before he'd been able to tell her, so it was not surprising she couldn't see the relevance.

He told her the Bill of Rights was relevant because it says that no fines or forfeitures can be burdened on the people. He told her that it is still current legislation, but before he could get much further he was shut off again and the Council staff started moving in on him. Staff appeared either side of him asking him to leave. Gordon refused. The Mayor asked him to leave the building. Again, Gordon refused. To their credit, several of the councillors were unhappy about how a member of the public had been treated and one called a Point of Order to correct unacceptable behaviour. Councillor Hagon said, "the gentleman should be allowed to speak regardless of whether we agree or understand what he was trying to say."

Gordon returned to his seat and then my name was called. I got to the lectern but there was such a commotion that I couldn't start. The Mayor asked me to standby. The police had been called. Gordon was back in his seat surrounded by council staff all urging him to leave. Gordon knew his rights and did not budge.

The meeting was adjourned and we all stood around waiting until the police arrived, which they duly did. The police were very professional and also realised Gordon knew his rights, and sensibly they didn't try to remove him. There was nothing they could do, so they just had to stand there for decoration.

Councillor Barber came over to apologise to Gordon for the way he'd been treated, saying that if they had thrown him out, he would have left the chamber. It was good to see some of the councillors felt as strongly as we did over the injustice we'd all witnessed.

All this meant I was standing waiting there for nearly half an hour. When the meeting did re-start, there was a lot of chatter and everyone was on their mobile phone no doubt texting all and sundry about what had transpired.

It's doubtful the majority heard a word I said. Though, now I know more about $CO_2$, mentioning the percentage in our atmosphere is a poor argument, one which showed I didn't understand the subject enough at that moment in time. So probably just as well few of them listened to the following:

### Rachel – $CO_2$ Speech 7th December 2023

*"Good evening.*

*At the last Full Council meeting, the slave labour & environmentally harmful production methods used for green technologies were justified because of the reduction of $CO_2$.*

*The millions of tons and parts per million that we hear about are hard to visualise - to put it another way, $CO_2$ makes up just 0.04% of our atmosphere, most of which is naturally occurring.*

*$CO_2$ is a fascinating gas, its capacity to affect temperature is inversely logarithmic - the first two hundred parts per million make the biggest impact. To paraphrase Dr William Happer at Princeton University, think of it like a coat of good **red** paint on a barn. The first coat you really notice, but the 2nd, 3rd & 4th make very little difference to the saturation of colour.*

*Dr Happer quantified this by saying that increasing $CO_2$ from 400 to 800 ppm will only increase heat that gets returned to the surface by less than 1%.*

*In the Jurassic era, $CO_2$ levels were 6 times higher than now, with no detriment to the planet. If anything, recent levels have been dangerously low, only 30ppm away from plant life extinction.*

*The famous graph illustrating a correlation between $CO_2$ and temperature fails to clearly show the time lag of up to **700 years**. And the most crucial part is $CO_2$ rises A F T E R the temperature increase! Data shows when $CO_2$ is high, the world cools. And when low, the world warms. This counter-intuitive response strongly suggests that $CO_2$ is not the driving force, and other feedback agents are.*

*It is clear the science is not as settled as we've been led to believe. Is all the child slave labour and 300 years of polluting indigenous peoples' land and water really justified?*

*But what about the melting ice sheets in Antarctica?*

*Only the western side of the continent shows signs of melting, the eastern side is gaining ice.*

*Curiously, the ice on the western side is mainly melting **underneath** the ice sheet. Do you really believe that this is due to fossil fuelled cars and flatulent cows? Or is it more likely that it might have something to do with the large number of active volcanoes under the western side?*

*There is a world of difference between being "well informed" by the mainstream media, and **properly** well-informed. So we are delighted that Councillor King has agreed in principle to a public discovery meeting where expert speakers will present evidence that the Council should have considered prior to acting.*

*But better late, than never!*
*And we invite you all to participate.*
*Thank you."*

Next up was Carinna speaking. We'd had the behavioural expert David Charalambous take a look at the Carbon Literacy training that the councillors are put through, or, as we re-named it, Carbon Illiteracy training. Sandi Adams had told us about it and how highly manipulative it was. We knew the councillors hadn't had the training yet, so we wanted to get in ahead of any of them doing it.

We'd been a bit smarter with Carinna's speech; giving the councillors a good reason to listen to it. For hers at least, they did actually listen. We'd emailed them ahead of time to download an app so they could see the graphs and charts she referenced in her speech, since we're not allowed to bring any additional supporting material in to the council.

*"Good evening.*

*I'm here with a proposal which will save you two days of online training tedium, and save the public, in more ways than one, from having to pay for it. Councillors everywhere are being encouraged to undergo Carbon Literacy training, the content of which raises some concern.*

*This training states the current $CO_2$ levels of 420 parts per million are the highest in 800 thousand years. Indeed, but why does the training not show all of history; flip to Fact 6 on the Inconvenient Facts app; 550 million years ago $CO_2$ was nearly 8,000 parts per million. Our current geological period has the lowest average $CO_2$ levels in earth's history.*

*The training claims that extreme weather events & wildfires have increased since 1980; the long-term data shows the opposite trend. Talking of trends, are you starting to see one here? It very much depends on when you choose to start the data from, as to the picture presented.*

*The training says there's scientific consensus that global warming is occurring. Inconvenient Fact 30; only 0.3% agree with the IPCC. Inconvenient Fact 27; the IPCC warming projections are from computer modelling, which have overstated the warming by up to 3 times.*

*It continues with unsubstantiated claims and cherry picked data; this itself is unacceptable. What is worse is how councillors are encouraged to manipulate the public using psychological and psychosocial techniques to affect behavioural change. Using deceptive data to get to a desired result is both morally and ethically wrong.*

*An expert in behavioural psychology has looked at the training and was very concerned by influencing behaviour through public policy to manipulate how people identify. He warned that once people are trained, indoctrinated into ideas, they will not question them. The training wants you to target and influence vulnerable groups on every aspect of their existence, from what to eat to how many children to have. Do you want to be used to manipulate people like this?*

*The public do NOT want the Council consuming our money and our minds with yet more propaganda! We'd prefer you learn open, accessible information, direct from experts who aren't on anyone's payroll and do not serve interest groups. Which is why we have called for a public debate, where we may elevate our concerns, and get evidence-based answers directly from the experts.*

*In appreciation of the Council's financial difficulties, we suggest charging a nominal entrance fee to help cover costs, and would note in passing that the savings Council will make from a proper understanding of the matter, runs into millions!*

*Thank you."*

Councillor King, the leader of Colchester Council, responded by saying it wasn't true that they were manipulating people. They were 'following the science'! But he very generously acknowledged that the Council's understanding of 'the science' had been enriched by our contributions! He'd already agreed in principle to having a public Net Zero debate, which is why we'd both pushed on it at the end of our speeches.

He said to leave it with them and they would see what they could do with regards to a wider public discussion.

I was standing next to Carinna at the microphone, and before she had a chance to respond, I chipped in with, "Could we have your word that you will not use this Carbon Literacy training then, if you do not wish to manipulate the public? Last night Ben Plummer in the Environment and Sustainability Panel said this training would be rolled out to everyone. The title of it alone should give you a clue as to how bad that training is. Carbon Literacy training could be for pencils or diamonds, it should be called at least the right name, Carbon Dioxide Literacy training! So that just shows you the standard it's written at! It's an absolute masterpiece in manipulation but it is utter propaganda and should not be rolled out to everyone."

Unsurprisingly the Council leader was not willing to give us that assurance. I've no idea if the 'Carbon Illiteracy training' did get rolled out or not, but at least every single councillor there had it their minds about how manipulative it is and how poorly put together. It felt a satisfying evening for the Council Watch team.

As we left, I said the thing I have said to Carinna after every single council meeting. "Well I'm glad I won't ever have to do that again!" Normally she says nothing, just raises an eyebrow with a knowing little smirk. This time she challenged me on it. "You know that's unlikely to be true, don't you?"

My immediate response was to hold my hand up and say, "No! Don't say it. The only way I can get through doing these is to tell myself I won't ever have to do this again. Play along!". It was at this point that we ran into Gordon again, which was a surprise as he'd left about an hour before us. His car battery had run flat. He didn't know anyone else to ask as he was new to the area.

We all went to my car and I drove us to where he'd parked and got my jump leads out. Gordon was proving himself to be quite a delay causer! His battery wouldn't come back to life. We waited a good fifteen minutes but eventually gave up and drove him to his lodgings, he'd have to sort it out in the morning. Then finally, I dropped Carinna off back at home and went to collect the dog from my parents.

Whilst Council Watch operate in a very considered way, and Gordon had more of a gung-ho approach, he had probably done more to highlight the error of thinking within the Council than anything we'd done in the nine months prior. The way they treated him really highlighted the inverted relationship people have with all levels of government. They think they have authority over us, when in reality they do not.

In what other walk of life would any of us tell our bosses what they can and can't say and do? We wouldn't, well, not if we expected to keep our job for any length of time. So who was it lurking in the shadows of the Council instructing the officers and the councillors on what to do and say?

We all wanted to know, so Lance and Brian went along to the Council Scrutiny Panel to find out.

Here's what Lance said, "I'm here this evening to ask a few questions with respect to events last Thursday, when a member of the public attempted to communicate what is a clear and present problem - public dissatisfaction with our governance arrangement.

A month or so ago at Full Council, the Mayor stated that Council supports freedom of speech. Why then did the Deputy Mayor eject freedom of expression from the public forum of 'Have Your Say'? At the beginning of that meeting, the Deputy Mayor, newly announced that the public may not say things that are 'scurrilous, vexatious, improper or otherwise'.

Since when are things that the hearer may find annoying, not to their liking, grounds for silencing? The Council's Constitution makes no reference to these restrictions, only that the public must not be violent, abusive or threatening to councillors or officers, or wilfully harm property of the same. So who, and under what authority, was the Mayor guided to insert these arbitrary rules? And who was it, and what reason, did someone advise the Deputy Mayor to deny the gentleman the right to have his say on what are serious concerns that impact us all? Precisely where did all of that come from?

I have taken the trouble to listen back to what he stated that evening. Aside from one claim that he made with respect to the billing authority and the consolidation fund, all of his other statements that evening were legislatively correct. Council is a body corporate. The 1972 local Authority Act asserts that they must be so, and in this respect, Council is no different from Tesco, or indeed any other body corporate. He asserted that Council demanded money. This is equally true legislatively. Council Tax is a demand notice, as a bill would require a contract under the Bills of Exchange Act of 1882.

Lastly the Localism Act of 2011 clearly states that Council has the power to do anything that individuals generally may do. Consequently, given that I may not demand money with menaces, then neither may Council. The gentleman was correct in his assertion, though he chose to rely upon the 1688 Bill of Rights which, albeit substantially older, is both a perfectly legitimate and current legislative item upon which he may rely, as did Boris Johnson in 2019 in the Miller Cherry case, which he also correctly stated.

At this point he had his microphone turned off, and worse still an unlawful attempt to eject him from the public gallery was made. Fortunately the police were mindful of their obligation to keep the peace. Now, given the Council's obligation to act with transparency, the public need to know precisely why, and under what authority, the Deputy Mayor acted as she did last Thursday? Who she received that advice from, and the basis of that advice?

The relationship between the people and those who seek to govern has become inverted, abusive even. When the public speak truth to power, it should be listened to and encouraged. How else are we to otherwise correct the problem that exists between us?"

Brian then had his turn and always to the point said, "I was also present at Thursday's meeting and to be honest I couldn't believe what I witnessed. A public office holder told a gentleman, having his say, that he was vexatious, basically annoying, and then shut him down.

So my question tonight is what is the relationship between the Council and the public? Exactly what authority does the Council, or any public office holder, have over the members of the public? If you can't answer now, please provide a full, accurate and complete answer in writing to me."

There was a lot of blathering from the Scrutiny Chairman at this point, but he did end with the comment that he'd also like to know, and would write to the Chief Executive to find out.

Lance responded thoughtfully with, "I think where we really need to understand, because obviously the Constitution is very clear on what the requirements of the public are, and in fairness we aren't bound by that Constitution, unless I'm very much mistaken. I think the standard rules of the game are respectful. I think everyone knows how we are meant to communicate with one another as adults.

Where I'd really like to get drilled down to, is that we understand the rules of the game, and I think we do. What happened last Thursday were new rules of the game, and that's something, and it's arbitrary, and I can't condone anything I see arbitrarily being imposed.

I have full respect for the position of the Deputy Mayor. I understood that she's got a serious issue with her hearing and it was her first time. I believe she was probably advised. Who was doing the advising? On what authority were they doing it? I think they need to be taking a bit of a back seat to, let's call it a mandated process, as opposed to new rules. Because we can't play in a playground where we don't know what the rules are."

Carinna also went along to follow up on still not having had the legal opinion regarding what she viewed as unlawful searches, and that Cheryl still hadn't had a response to her complaint about the unwelcome intimate nature of her search. I was there for moral support, and camera crew duties.

It was at this point it became clear, Council Watch was being noticed…

# 22

# Farming Fatalities

Up until November, I had been turning down all interview requests. I was still of the opinion that they'd got the Council videos, and I couldn't see why anyone needed to speak to me. I said what I needed to say in the those videos and that was sufficient.

When the Colchester Council Watch YouTube Channel started, I changed my tune drastically when I realised how hard it is to get traffic to a new channel. Suddenly I was willing to speak to whoever wanted me!

My dislike of interviews had to be got over, otherwise the Channel, and all the hours spent making videos, would be wasted as they'd never get any views. Suck it up Princess and do the interviews. So I did. Lots of them.

I went on Former Elite Forces & Veteran of the Year, author, endurance adventurer, Chris Thrall's podcast. Then Carinna and I were back on with Richard Vobes. Independent news broadcasters TNT got in touch, would I do a breakfast interview with comedian and presenter Abi Roberts? It was a bit daunting going on something so professional, but I said yes.

Various members of the TNT team tested out sound checks and camera position and lighting. You're put in a virtual green room while you wait to go live. A very new experience for me. Abi was lovely and made it easy to relax into this very bizarre world I now found myself in of semi-TV. She's another person I admire hugely, fearlessly speaking out and telling it like it is in no uncertain terms.

The first question she asked was could she call me an activist? I baulked at that suggestion. I said I didn't consider myself an activist because I wasn't very active! I just sit at home on my sofa making videos commenting about my local council. In the moment, I'd forgotten that I was also going in to speak at council meetings - it was just so unimaginable for me to be thought of as an activist. Abi was the first of many to do so, despite never having threatened to glue myself to anything inconvenient. Nor had I hurled paint at priceless works of art, nor would I ever even contemplate doing so. Though I suppose our efforts are more active than most manage. At least it's provided an entertaining book title, if nothing else!

On the same day as Abi interviewed me, I had my first UK Column interview. They are an independent multimedia news organisation focusing on delivering alternative perspectives on current affairs and challenging mainstream media narratives. They always like to test people in the Extra's segment before they put you on the main live lunchtime show.

Similar set up to TNT with the sound and vision checks.

## Zooming Here, There and Everywhere!

By this point I was in so many groups there were Zoom calls nearly every evening. My life just wasn't my own any more. I was spending thirty to fifty hours a week on Council stuff, in one form or another. One of the groups had someone who regularly spoke with Neil Oliver. Would I like him to see if he could get me on GB News?

No! I draw the line at TV. I refuse to have one in the house, so the last thing I wanted to do is be on it! And whilst Neil is one of only a handful of well-known people who have bravely spoken up about what is happening in the world, as much admiration as I have for him, I do not trust mainstream media networks as far as I can throw them, and yes, that includes the so called alternative ones.

A few days after that I was on with Geoff Buys Cars. That was fun. I knew from our text and voice messages we'd get on well. He christened me 'Rachel of Colchester' a nickname which has stuck, especially with Ralph Ellis who nearly always addresses me with my now formal title! With over seventy-five thousand views, his channel sent us more viewers than all the others combined.

For a few months I'd been getting emails from people up and down the country wanting to do what we were doing in Colchester. I created a Dropbox folder with all our speeches and research, so people could adapt them, or just read them out as they were. I then made some videos with tips on how people could start their own Council Watch groups.

Before long, these new Council Watch groups started going into their local councils. They were set up in Stockport, Ipswich, Eastbourne, Richmond, Liverpool, North Yorkshire, Lowestoft and Glastonbury. The Thetford group changed their name to Council Watch too. There were also people up and down the country going in to their local councils with our speeches. Many of the Zoom calls I was doing with groups were focused around getting Council Watch set up nationwide. People in Canada, New Zealand, South Africa and Germany wrote to me saying they were doing Council Watch in their countries too.

## Farming Focus

Sandi Adams was in a couple of the Zoom groups I was in, and she was very worried about the state of farming. I suggested we do a video together for Council Watch to raise awareness. She jumped at the idea. Farming protests were kicking off all over Europe, and there was talk of them happening in the UK. Sandi wanted to get the farmers to understand the bigger picture so they could see why the Government were doing all these detrimental things to the industry.

I was keen to help because she had been so instrumental in enabling me to see the bigger picture. Once you know what the end-game is, it makes everything much easier to understand. There's no more head scratching trying to figure out why all these insane things are being done. Nothing which is being done is as insane as it appears, it's all calculated and orchestrated.

In the interview, she talked about how farmers were going to lose their subsidies unless they diversify away from farming into things like re-wilding. The profit margins on many aspects of farming are so low that farmers earn more from turning their fields over to wild-flowers and trees than they do by growing food for us to eat.

Sandi showed reports that detailed the direction farming was being pushed into. Namely agri-tech farming. This would move us away from traditional family-run farms, into huge corporate super-farms. The focus would be on robotics, and replacing meat with insect biomass. Which ties in with the Absolute Zero report. Sandi discussed the corporate takeover of all our land and resources that was under way.

She explained something called NACs, which stands for Natural Asset Companies or Corporations. If approved by the SEC, they plan to launch this new type of investment strategy on the New York Stock Exchange. These companies would hold rights to the ecological performance produced by nature or farms, forests, and even marine ecosystems.

Their aim is to have complete control over the natural landscape, turning it into profitable assets. Financial returns would be made from biodiversity, carbon sequestration, conservation and anything else they can think of. The billionaires aren't content with all the land and billions they already have. They want everything, and the Net Zero Agenda 2030 is the mechanism by which they plan to get it.

In the interview, Sandi, also discussed the delights which Sainsbury's have suggested in their <u>Future of Food report</u>. Their report outlines how they see things changing from 2025 up to 2169. It's a joy to read, if you're plant based and no longer wish to eat meat. And don't worry, for those meat eaters out there, replacements are available. Cultured lab-grown meat, insect biomass, algae, and extending our oceanic diet to include jellyfish, which used to be considered a food of last resort. Not any more. Now jellyfish are seen as nutritional and sustainable.

They also suggest personalised food plans and something called 'patch dinners', with all your nutritional and medication needs drip fed into you via your patch. They do acknowledge traditional meals with other people are important socially. Food that you are allowed to put in your mouth will be hydroponically or lab grown. And best of all, we won't need all that soil based, dirty old-fashioned agriculture. All our food will be grown using robotics in big warehouses. Something to look forward to.

I've family who are farmers, and for years I'd listened to them complain about all the rules, regulations and ridiculous hoops they had to jump through, imposed upon them by the Government, and back then, the EU. So I already knew how hard farmers were being squeezed and how little money the supermarkets paid them for their produce. Having experienced how ruthless supermarkets are in my parents' wholesale plant nursery business, I knew farmers were being pushed in all directions.

This new set up would enable supermarkets to replace the farmers. All that is needed would be the land to build these agritech farms on.

Fast-forward to the end of the 2024, when the new Labour government announced they will be imposing inheritance tax on farmers which will be the literal nail in the coffin for family run farms.

The government said Inheritance Tax (IHT) will only affect around five hundred farms a year, whereas the farming community say it's more like three-quarters of farms. Farmers are asset-rich because the price of land has been driven up, but they are cash poor. A decent combine harvester can cost half a million pounds, so if they are taxed on assets over a million, it doesn't take long to reach that figure. Few farmers have spare cash, so in order to pay the IHT they will be forced to sell land. With so little profit in farming, selling the thing that earns them a living is like a carpenter having to sell their saws and chisels. Farmers need their land.

Many in the farming community are scratching their heads wondering why the Government, who give around twelve billion of taxpayers' money overseas, would bite the hands that feed us, instead of reducing overseas donations. Farmers think it must be a mistake. Much time is spent showing the Government that they have their figures wrong. Pundits tell the population the Government say it's only a few farmers who will be affected, or that they are being greedy and should pay inheritance tax like the rest of us, completely missing the point that farmers are not cash rich and need their land. And so the circus goes on. All the while those of us who understand what Agenda 2030 really is, the biggest transfer of land and wealth in history, know there is no mistake. The Government are doing an excellent job at making family farming impossible.

In the first video I saw with Sandi, back in 2020, she showed us a colour-coded map of the United States, which showed the areas where human settlement zones were going to be. The map also showed which parts would be for military use and the rest over to re-wilding and wildlife corridors. What shocked me seeing this map, was how small the intended human settlement zones would be. The population would have to be rounded up and put into Smart Cities, there wouldn't be rural living allowed. That chilled me to the core.

Sandi has said there has been a lot of pushback against this idea since she did that video, but even if it's been taken off the table for now, the intention is clear - doing everything possible to reduce our freedom is on the cards, it's just a matter of when. Everything we're seeing politicians do around the globe is to enable the transfer of wealth and freedom away from us all.

Make no mistake, once they've crushed the farming industry, we'll be next. If you think the cost of living is high now, it's nothing compared to what is likely coming. When people can no longer afford their mortgages, that's when the Government and corporations will swoop in and buy their houses at bargain prices, and then rent them back to people. All this is inline with the World Economic Forum's agenda. They published a thought-experiment by Danish politician Ida Auken, which they summed up as "You'll own nothing and be happy."

This 'happy' vision for our future is envisioned to be in place by 2030, when private ownership will be largely replaced with shared access to resources. In Ida Auken's vision, people wont own cars, homes, or even clothes outright. Instead, they will lease or borrow them as needed from a collective pool, managed by corporations or governments. Everything in life will be on a subscription service basis. No need to own a car if an autonomous vehicle could be delivered to your door whenever you desired, or a virtual reality headset that can take you to a beach.

If whoever controls the food and money supply, controls the people, can you imagine how much control there would be in a world where you owned nothing and had to lease everything, which was run by AI, controlled by governments and corporations? If you were to say something which doesn't align to government dictates, AI would automatically put you on the digital naughty step, and you could find your Central Bank Digital Currency no longer functions, or you weren't allowed to go anywhere. Just ask those living in communist China with their social credit score system how happy they are. Obviously, they dare not respond truthfully or it would affect their social credit score.

A self-sufficient population who own their own home, with ample food, is a lot harder to control than a completely reliant one. Just a few more puzzle pieces moved into position with Digital IDs and Central Bank Digital Currencies, and they will have us. Few people fully comprehend how every single aspect of our lives will be controlled if all these plans go ahead. If your electric Smart car and Central Bank Digital Currency stop working should you try to stray outside of your permitted zone, how far will you realistically get?

A system of complete control is being rolled out. Governments and councils are blindly helping to build a Smart City digital prison infrastructure, and most don't even know it. Nor do they realise that they and their families will be stuck in it with the rest of us.

I suspect AI has been created to help the powers that shouldn't be, replace and control humans as much as possible. There are many human tasks which can be automated and replaced by thorough AI which completes them perfectly, at lightening speed. A technology which is equal parts fascinating and terrifying with what it can do. I will admit to getting a perverse joy in using it against those who wish to replace us with it. It's been wonderfully helpful dealing with the council. Stuffing longwinded government and IPCC reports, as well as legal documents into it, and asking questions, has saved us weeks of research.

Having cautiously used AI over the past year, I can see how easily it could be utilised in the

Dystopian scenarios Sandi has detailed in her interviews, especially when combined with robotics.

It's an impossible conversation to have in 'normal' circles. Those with predominately dormant brain cells say, "Oh that's a conspiracy theory!" And to be fair to those deeply asleep, it does sound unbelievable - I can see why people roll their eyes and go back to their busy lives. They don't think it will ever happen. These are also the people who have either never researched any of these topics, or have read an article saying that none of it is true, without checking to see who pays the 'fact checker'. This only goes ahead if we allow it to. That's why it's so vital more people wake up to the Dystopian nightmare that's being rolled out, and say no.

Backing our farmers, incidentally, the only ones with equipment large enough to be unstoppable, is essential. If we lose our farmers, we'll be next.

On the 13th February, Carinna, Cheryl and I went to the Scrutiny Panel meeting to have our say. The keen-eyed amongst you might recognise part of this speech! I had some questions for them...

> *"Good evening!*
>
> *I have three questions tonight.*
>
> *Firstly, has this panel scrutinised the decision this Council took in declaring a climate emergency? If not, it needs to examine the basis upon which that decision was made.*
>
> *Declaring an emergency is a serious matter. Especially considering the millions of tax payers' money being spent on implementing measures, many of which are highly detrimental to society.*

*9 months of emails back and forth with Council Officers, requesting evidence of a human caused climate emergency, and no one has even been able to precisely define the alleged emergency, let alone provide the evidence for it.*

*Officers direct us to the IPCC, an organisation that uses cherry picked start-dates for their charts and inaccurate computer generated climate models, which have been shown to be up to three times higher than actual temperatures. Incidentally, the IPCC have themselves **never** declared a climate emergency.*

*It was left to councillors to research if there was a genuine man-made emergency. How many had either the time or inclination to do so properly?*

*No one denies the climate is changing - it has done for millennia, but evidence must be provided that warming is occurring because of $CO_2$, **rather than solar cycles etc.** And specifically the minuscule amount of $CO_2$ that human activity produces.*

*Since virtually no one was listening when I spoke about $CO_2$ at full council, I will reiterate - working independently Dr William Happer and Dr John Christy clearly demonstrates that even if $CO_2$ levels double to 800 parts per million, the resultant warming would only be around 1%.*

*Produce the scientific evidence that disproves Dr Happer and Dr Christy, and categorically shows the tiny levels of $CO_2$ that human activity produces can cause significant warming.*

*The people have had enough of baseless propaganda from weapons of mass destruction to stay inside or you'll kill granny! Net Zero is a crusade that is being waged against the people, and our farming industry will be the first causality if we're not careful.*

*The Net Zero devotees want us to believe we're all going to die because of fossil fuel and flatulent farm animals. This is very questionable. Unquestionable however, is that we won't survive without farmers and the food they produce!*

*This brings me onto my 2nd question - do any of the Council's plans or documents include food security? If not, this too must be urgently scrutinised. It would, after all, be prudent to make such provisions for the people who pay for this Council's very existence!*

*Finally, I've been told that councils have a legal obligation to provide land for people to grow food. If that is true, is this being done sufficiently, or are bicycle lanes taking precedent these days?!*

*Thank you."*

I gave the Chairman a cheeky little wink on that last statement, having given him quite a hard time in a recent video for his support for shoving bicycle lanes everywhere in Colchester where there simply isn't room for them.

Something quite unexpected happened next. The Scrutiny Chairman, Councillor Darius Laws, after telling me about his allotment said, "Your fundamental question around have we scrutinised the climate emergency, we haven't have we in this forum in here. I'm going to make you an offer..."

He paused, as if to double check himself and then said, "If I'm re-elected in May, we will scrutinise it in this forum, because I've seen and heard enough of your presentations to intrigue me enough to want to scrutinise it and this is a spoiler. I say that as someone who didn't vote for a climate emergency in the chamber because I wasn't elected when that vote was called. And so the information that you are continually bringing here is such, rather like what we talked about earlier this evening, there are legitimate questions and the best form of disinfectant is sunshine. So I welcome the conversation, and if I'm elected after May, if the Panel are minded, I'm very happy to bring it here as a formal item and have a substantial look at it for you, if that's okay?"

I replied, "That's a brilliant offer. I hope your colleagues are as open as well. And I know Councillor King has agreed to have a debate, and I realise you have got a lot on the plate with the budget etc., but if we can have a date then we can bring those climate scientists in, because it's all very well us turning up, but why should you believe us? You need to ask the climate scientists. So if you can provide us with a date, we will bring them and you'll be able to ask them for yourselves, because we have it in writing from your Climate Officers that no dissenting information was looked at, and that simply isn't acceptable. This Council must consider all the available information."

I'd addressed the Council Leader, Councillor King, as I spoke regarding the date for the climate debate, but because I didn't have my glasses with me, when I sat down I knew he was in the room somewhere, but from the position I was in another councillor obscured him, so in the corner of my eye I could see to one side there was an older smartly dressed gentleman, so I had addressed what I was saying to him. It's not until I got up and could see above the Councillor that I could actually see where

Councillor King was the other side of the room, so it turned out I was addressing Councillor Sunnucks, not Councillor King, which must have confused them both!

Carinna and Lance had created their own interesting questions for the Scrutiny Panel to address…

*"Good evening.*

*We have not received a proper answer to our question of who advised the Deputy Mayor she had the authority to shutdown a member of the public from speaking. Nor have you provided us with the evidence of the legal opinion we've asked for regarding subjecting members of the public to searches.*

*The question is, why are Council and Council Officers specifically, unable or unwilling to produce the answers to the questions that, us, your employers are asking. This is willful prevarication and frankly becoming absurd.*

*We ask for nigh on a year for evidence for climate change. You produce None.*

*We ask for the law upon which you are relying to breach the peace in searching us, you provide nothing.*

*We are asking on what basis you shut down the public, you run for the hills.*

*Councillor Dundas said in the Full Council meeting on the 18th October that Colchester City Council is just a construct created in 1974 which may or may not survive for however long, on the evidential basis that it no longer serves its master, indeed does everything not in its power to avoid us, then perhaps the time has come for us to be rid of it.*

*Finally, an important matter I would like to draw your attention to is that this Council is granting planning permission for fraudulent 5G applications.*

> *Companies are giving councils declarations that they are complying with ICNIRP safety recommendations utlising companies that do not exist. THREE UK Ltd was dissolved on 27th October 2017. The operator H3G was dissolved on 9th December 2014. I have printed out an example of a mast that was given permission at Highwoods under the guise of a dissolved company.*
>
> *Insurance companies won't insure companies for harm caused by EMFs and the telecommunications industry are warning investors they will need to provision for compensation, all the while telling everyone it's safe. There is also now a study which shows 5G to be harmful by oncologist Lennart Hardell.*
>
> *With this in mind how will the public get compensation for safety declarations being made by dissolved companies and dissolved operators? Is the Council putting itself at risk of claims against the Council that are granting these permissions? This is happening up and down the country, not just in Colchester. How can it be that the Council Officers are acting negligently in not performing their due diligence in respect of these fraudulent applications and putting both the public, and the public purse, at risk?*
>
> *Thank you."*

They weren't happy with the last part of Carinna's speech and insisted that they wouldn't do anything negligent and it wasn't a fair suggestion to say the Planning Officer has to do due diligence around the structures of the Applicant! Which begs the question that if it's not down to Council Officers to check the planning applications, then whose job is it?

There was a lot more blathering, but you get the gist, so I'll leave it there. Finally, Cheryl was back to ask the Council why she had not heard back regarding her complaint about the rather invasive search. Councillor King said he was under the impression that she had been responded to and that he would personally look into it.

In between filming interviews, writing speeches, doing umpteen Zoom calls a week, Sandi and I had also agreed to do some webinars for the People's Food and Farming Alliance (PFFA), who were also trying to raise awareness within the farming community. Katherine MacBean, the founder of PFFA, wanted Sandi and I to get across to farmers what was driving many of the issues they faced. The PFFA had been set up to educate people and help them achieve food security and independence. The organisation educates individuals, groups and communities on how to grow their own food, how to build food networks, and how to support their local producers.

If I'd thought January had been a busy month, it was nothing compared to February. To add to the delights, it was the Full Council meeting on the 21st. I had one mission that evening, to make the whole Council, especially those who sit on the Planning Committee, aware of the threats to farming so that they would hopefully consider the information in future planning meetings. Full Council was my only way to reach them all.

*"Good evening.*

*Are you aware of the plight our farmers are facing?*

*It's not just cheap imports and supermarket exploitation that's destroying the farming industry, but UN directives.*

*Instead of helping farmers transition away from chemicals over to natural regenerative agriculture, our Government is being directed to pay farmers to stop farming food to allegedly save the planet.*

*We should be preserving biodiversity in areas like Middlewick, not sacrificing the farmland that feeds us.*

*The ever-increasing Net Zero bureaucracy is driving up the cost of food production which farmers aren't properly compensated for, and they cannot continue.*

*So, the question is, do you know what Net Zero looks like in real terms?*

*Starting from 2030, all flying, shipping, food imports and homegrown beef and lamb is to be phased out. With the majority of UK farmland going over to wind & solar farms.*

*How is covering our beautiful countryside in toxic solar panels, environmentally harmfully mined lithium batteries and wind turbines, - all difficult to recycle, saving the planet?*

*And saving it from what exactly - $CO_2$? The vital gas that keeps plants and us alive, which has been at record lows for centuries.*

*Provably, $CO_2$ simply isn't a strong enough forcing agent for the warming we're told to be so fearful of, and neither is methane.*

*More people die in cold weather than warm. Melting sea ice will not cause a rise in sea level, only land ice is capable of that - which did not happen during the Holocene*

*Maximum, when Artic temperatures were much higher than now.*

*The Net Zero industry is worth trillions - over 4 billion dollars a day in revenue. That kind of money buys an awful lot of 'science' and influence.*

*Ethical scientists easily disprove the nonsense of Net Zero. Those scientists aren't included on mainstream media, but their peer-reviewed research papers are found easily enough online, for those who bother to look.*

*But that's the problem - few bother to look - did you before you voted to declare a climate emergency? Raise your hand if you did!*

*Net Zero will destroy our farming industry.*

*If people are forced to choose between feeding their family and paying Council Tax, which do you think they are going to pick? Assuming of course there's enough food, which will be difficult without farmers.*

*Food is one of the 13 Critical National Infrastructures, as set out by the National Protective Security Authority (NPSA), which councils are supposed to consider. Yet I couldn't see mention of food security in any of the Local Plan documents. It needs to be included. Councillors must have the ability to turn down planning applications that threaten our food security.*

*So will you include it?*
*Thank you!"*

The mayor passed it over to the Council Leader to answer. Councillor King said, "You do bring us stimulating alternative views to the mainstream." He went on to say that he thought it was unlikely the majority of land would be put over to wind and solar. But he was sure the Local Planning Committee would consider food security.

I told him to take a look at the plans for Somerset. There was an image Sandi showed when I'd interviewed her - huge areas of farmland that was considered good for renewables.

Carinna was next with a speech that had a very simple request, something so easy, the Council could have earned themselves some 'Brownie Points'. But no, it ended up turning into an unfathomable saga, and a ten month battle of such levels of ridiculousness that almost sucked the life-force out of us both. It was the point of no-return with Colchester Council, and helped us all see that there was only one real solution. The whole Council needed to be replaced...

# 23

# 5G Fiasco

Up until this point I had given the leader of Colchester Council the benefit of the doubt. He always sounded reasonably sincere and helpful, and I knew he had an impossibly hard task of being Council Leader. Not only did he have the responsibility of the Council and its dreadful finances, he had to deal with politics and mind-numbing levels of bureaucracy, as well as the public, no easy task. Less than generous members of the public, outside of our group, had nicknamed him 'Dodgy Dave' on social media, and by the time we got into this saga, I could begin to see why.

When I first started making Council Watch videos, they were polite and respectful, with a little bit of humour thrown in for good measure. Over the months, reporting on so many nonsensical attitudes and idealism got to me, and more and more sarcasm seeped its way into the videos. The 5G Fiasco pushed me over the edge and the videos were supremely sarcastic. Yes, I know it's the lowest form of wit, but frankly, they didn't deserve a higher form. The sarcasm was about the only thing that got me through the videos. It wasn't for the audiences' benefit, it was to keep myself from screaming!

I'm not going to recount the full saga because it's been so well documented on the Council Watch YouTube Channel, and I lost the will to live then, so I've no desire to regurgitate any more than is strictly necessary here. It was unbelievable.

It started in December with Ian. At that time, he felt we weren't going in forcefully enough. And the episode with Gordon at full Council, shaking things up, had also spurred many people to want to do similar.

It's funny, Ian has since messaged me a few times saying how well he thinks we've done, and that he can see our softer methods got some good results. Whereas now I feel the opposite, and think he was right, we should have gone in harder, sooner.

But anyway, at that point in time, I was mistakenly optimistic that if we went in gently giving a bit of information at a time, we could gradually educate the Councillors. Ian had more of a tell-them-everything-at-once approach. I tried to put across to everyone in the groups that we didn't learn everything in a day, and too much information at once isn't always wise.

I could also see things from the Councillors' perspectives. Aligning with anything we said would put them at odds with their peers and the Council, so we had to make it easy for them. Slowly opening the Overton Window. And also, categorically, we must not go in with anything that sounded like 'Conspiracy Cranks R-Us'.

Carinna had wanted to go in about 5G for quite some time, but we'd been busy on other topics. As a physio who's worked with pulsed electromagnetic frequency devices, she had first hand experience of the healing effects of EMFs, but also knew the harms.

I'd had a meeting with one of the councillors who'd attended the Environment and Sustainability Panel after the night I first talked about EVs and renewables not being as green as advertised. She wanted to know more about us, and so we met for a coffee, discussed many things and ended up spending three hours chatting. I'd told her 5G was on our list and she warned me it would be an eye-roller from the Councillors. I assured her it wouldn't be with the way we'd do it.

I knew with Carinna we'd all work on her speech and hone it so that it was framed in a way that would be thought-provoking, rather than on the nutter spectrum, at least I hoped we could. Most of the subjects we've found ourselves covering on Council Watch are controversial. It is almost impossible to raise a concern about anything these days, even if you can evidence the reasons for your concern. The label 'Conspiracy Theorist' is a fantastic tool for enabling people to switch off and dismiss things without ever thinking or researching for themselves.

I'd offered Ian to have the team work on his speech, but he said he was fine and didn't need our help. I knew he didn't like how we were handling things and prayed he wouldn't mention energy weapons. 5G technology uses millimeter waves (typically 24–100 GHz), which were originally developed by the U.S. military in something called ADS, which stands for Active Denial System. It is a non-lethal weapon which uses 95 GHz millimeter waves to heat the skin's surface, creating a burning sensation to disperse crowds.

The ADS operates at a much higher power level, around 100 kilowatts, focused in a directed beam, whereas 5G base stations emit low-power signals (often under 1 watt per antenna). The frequencies overlap, but the power levels and dispersion are different. So I felt it wasn't a good idea to mention it because there's more than enough concerning aspects to 5G without going into something which sounds like a conspiracy theory. I also prayed he didn't say anything which couldn't be proven, or mention Covid, and I hoped that he would keep to the subject at hand.

Ian started off by telling them he was there representing a new group called the Essex Residents Association. He said they wanted to highlight the many issues facing today's troubled world. He listed everything from the climate change, lockdowns, vaccines, cost of living, child sexualisation and more. He said they were part of a national organisation campaigning against 5G and that it was a blight on the countryside, and a danger to humanity.

He told them it was clear from Covid that all these issues had been on the Government's agenda for many years. He added that the lockdowns were used as a cover to speed up the roll out of the infrastructure for the 'Internet of Things', which would bring in a comprehensive surveillance state to keep all citizens under control, round the clock, in smart cities.

Watching the livestream from home, a small squeal escaped me at this point. Nothing he said was untrue, it was how he'd said it which had made me twitchy. Though I felt a bit better when he started evidencing his claims, something we feel is essential with our Council Watch work. If we can't evidence something, we don't say it. Our opinions and beliefs are irrelevant, evidence is what counts. He referred them to a planning document within their own planning portal which said 5G would be used for Smart City infrastructure for things like autonomous vehicles and interconnected technologies.

He talked about the effects of electrosmog, which we're all bathed in 24/7. He said 5G is a focused beam which is one hundred times higher than current levels in the same way as directed energy weapons. He said his group had been taking radiation readings round Colchester and they were well in excess of the International Commission for Non-Ionizing Protection guidelines (ICNIRP). He finished, having pushed his luck going well over the allotted three minutes, much to the annoyance of the Council Leader, with reminding the Council they have a duty of care to the public.

The Council Leader said to Ian, "Well that's a very interesting set of remarks" and immediately passed over to his colleague, Councillor Andrea Luxford Vaughan to answer.

She addressed his concerns admirably saying was very sympathetic and shared some of his concerns over 5G. She said she'd campaigned very strongly to object to one going up near the school her daughter attends. She said the reason for that is that there is no evidence to say they don't cause harm. She added that physicists had done research with young people to show it fries their internal organs and reproductive systems. She said there's no proof because we haven't been doing it long enough, but that she was deeply sympathetic to his concerns.

She told Ian that masts rarely need planning permission, just a public consultation. When you ask the telecoms companies questions, they won't tell you anything. They won't send you the mapping diagrams of the radiation, nothing. She said in her personal experience the only way you get them stopped is because of the disruption to the landscape or wildlife. She said their hands are tied and that she'd spoken to officers who told her they can't stop it happening.

I sat back amazed she had been so supportive, considering all the other things Ian had thrown into the already difficult pot with 5G. Unfortunately for her, she paid the price with her poor word choice about internal organs being 'fried'.

That evening, our favourite gobby Councillor was back on Twitter bad-mouthing Councillor Luxford Vaughan and Ian. He wasted no time, and tweeted from the meeting that he was 'in a Colchester Cabinet meeting where a conspiracy theorist is spreading nonsense about 5G'.

He then proceeded to have an absolute field day on the sympathetic Councillor, which in turn got picked up by the newspapers. The newspapers asked a professor from Edinburgh University, who said there is no evidence to support the Councillor's claims about 5G masts affecting people's internal organs, and that it's not going to fry people's organs, that, he said, was ridiculous.

## Damage Control

After Christmas, Carinna and I interviewed the knowledgable 5G expert called Ian Jarvis, who we'd met at Sandi's event in Glastonbury, to try and do some damage limitation. We knew if we didn't turn things around ASAP, no councillor would ever stand up against 5G again. We needed to do everything we could to get a more scientific word usage than 'frying' to describe the mitochondrial DNA damage that occurs 69% of the time when cells are exposed to non-ionizing radiation.

3G and 4G towers pump out radiation at a similar frequency to a microwave oven, so whilst the Councillor shouldn't have used the word 'frying', we asked Ian Jarvis how far off was she with her description. He said that microwaves work by jiggling the water molecules around to create heat, and our bodies have a lot of water in them. The difference of course is the power and proximity. He and Carinna discussed the body being electromagnetic, he said, how could frequencies like that not effect the body?

Carinna decided the interview wasn't enough, even though Ian Jarvis had done a great job with analysing the other Ian's speech and correcting the language the Councillor had used. We'd have to tread very carefully with what she said. 5G was hugely controversial before the newspapers' had had their field day, her task had now turned into Mission Impossible.

Here's how she framed it to the full Council on the 21st February 2024

*"Good evening.*

*The Post Office scandal offers insightful learnings. Those in top positions of influence, both government and corporate, absent moral compass are free to mete out harm to large numbers of innocent people. Having fine-tuned the art of deception, the dishonest use media to fool the public for decades.*

*We have been given countless reasons to mistrust government, media, and my particular area of experience, healthcare establishments; smoking, DDT, asbestos, thalidomide, to name but a few. By this point, government caring, media telling us the truth, and pharmaceutical companies there to help restore health, is not a fantasy I buy into.*

*Before qualifying as a physiotherapist, I was taught the importance of critical thinking when appraising research, to look at empirical data, to recognise that researchers have certain beliefs and biases, will have financial incentives, and that conclusions drawn will be influenced by these factors.*

*When a group attended cabinet in December, wishing to present evidence regarding 5G affecting health, I was very interested as I share their concerns, and logical rationale dictates to not abandon the precautionary principle.*

*Thank you Councillor Luxford Vaughan for recognising legitimate concerns with regard to 5G, and, as the role obligates, for considering matters brought before Council.*

*What is unacceptable conduct, however, is the mocking of both the member of the public and Councillor Luxford Vaughan. The Councillor in question is operating under a belief that 5G is safe, and that any claim to the contrary is nonsense. This ill-informed opinion was subsequently tweeted.*

*If evidence contrary to the current political science is presented, let us not partake in misgendering that as conspiracy theory. Is it not long past time that we approach questions on a rational and evidential basis?*

*A study by oncologist Lennart Hardell evidences microwave syndrome caused by 5G radiation, symptoms generally subsided when the exposure ceased; children and unborn babies are particularly susceptible. Having now been informed of harm, the government instruction to not refuse masts on health grounds does not absolve Council or Councillors from liability.*

*It is evidentially true that companies installing the masts are using dissolved companies to obtain planning permission and claim compliance with ICNIRP safety recommendations. Council has been given evidence of this. You are complicit if you do not take action on the companies who have gained approval fraudulently. 5G may be effective, but it certainly isn't safe. Council needs to consider its obligations to properly examine the evidence before approving any more 5G masts.*

*Thank you."*

The Council Leader completely dismissed Carinna's concerns citing, " I spent some time on this and I know other members have. I've looked at in my lay way, at the evidence positions published by the Government and Ofcom, the World Health Organization, ICNIRP with their responsibilities for 5G and its health effects. They all say 5G, like earlier mobile standards, is safe for the public on the evidence as published and that tested rigorously, internationally, that's the position that we responsibly should take."

Bearing in mind Carinna had already corresponded with him explaining that nowhere in the ICNIRP guidelines do they say it's safe. The well-known scientific term, 'unlikely' was their word of choice regarding harm. Nor do their guidelines protect anyone with metal in their body. So, if you have any kind of implant or even dental work which contains metal, their guidelines exclude you. 5G masts usually need a fifty metre exclusion zone as well. How many really safe things can you think of that you can't go within fifty meters of, or anywhere near at all, if you have metal in your body?

To brazenly tell full Council that 5G was safe, listing all those organisations, and that it had been rigorously tested, was completely false. There has been no long-term safety testing done on 5G exposure. How could there be, it's a new technology. The lab rats will be us.

There was already a newspaper article about thirty calves being born blind in a field with a new 5G mast. The farmer had never had blind calves before the antenna. I've just tried searching for the article to find out if it was in Switzerland or Sweden, but it's been scrubbed from the internet. After my third attempt at searching, I was asked by my browser to verify I was human. Touchy subject, it would appear. There is a screen shot of the article in some of the Council Watch 5G videos.

## Misleading Complaint

Carinna put in a formal complaint about the Council Leader misleading the Council and the public with false information. We knew it wouldn't go anywhere, but it would mean they'd have to review everything and it was a chance to show on video how it would be wriggled out of. We weren't disappointed. The emails, which are in the Dropbox resources folder, take some reading to believe.

From then on out, Carinna's main line of attack was getting the Council not to accept safety declarations using names of companies which have been dissolved. For some reason, telecommunications companies seemingly change their name and company structure more often than most of us do laundry. Companies are dissolved and restarted more times than you can shake a stick at. For years, countrywide, the names of dissolved companies have been put on safety declarations. Apparently, it was an innocent error.

The innocent error continued after it had been discovered, begging the question over the innocence. If the company on the safety declaration doesn't exist, who is liable in the event of harm? We also presented the Council with an email from the Planning Inspectorate stating it was the Local Planning Authorities job to check the documents submitted in the application, shocker, I know. Still the Council denied it was their responsibility, and on and on the games went.

Carinna and I interviewed Karen Churchill, who is one of the litigants in person protecting public health alongside Neil McDougall against the UK Government for failing to protect public health with the 5G rollout. She told us there are 39K papers written on the effects of EMFs. It has been shown to cause mitochondria DNA damage and cancer. Neil wasn't in the interview, but Steven Thomas, who had managed to have some success challenging his council in Gloucester, was with Karen. He told us of his legal battles, which are still on-going at the time of writing this.

All the 5G experts we interviewed had told us that insurance companies have stated that they will not cover liability for harms caused from EMFs. They've clearly learned their lesson from asbestos. Investors have been warned that there could be liabilities from harm caused.

International Commission for Non-Ionizing Protection Guidelines (ICNIRP) standards, which are pretty low, aren't being met in some installations. The organisation was set up by people who have connections with the telecommunications industry. The industry safety tests are done on a pure signal, ie. one that isn't carrying data. Those empty signals don't appear to be that harmful from the short-term tests which were done. However, when radiation expert Victor Leach, a retired radiation physicist with forty-eight years experience working in the field of radiation protection, and his team tested a real-world signal containing the data, they found detriment 69% of the time. I've included his video on the Resources page.

When Carinna sent the Council evidence of the error on the safety certificates on the Council's own approved mast applications, they spent months denying there was anything wrong. I've lost count of the number of times she physically went into the Council, as well as wrote extensive emails showing the fraudulent certificates and the risk of harm to the public. Anyone would think she was trying to get the masts taken down, but all she'd asked was that the Council didn't accept any further safety declarations using the names of dissolved companies. It couldn't have been more straightforward.

I did goodness-only-knows how many videos tracking her progress and highlighting the evidence. The last video was called 'Pants on Fire, Farcical 5G Fiasco Continues'… It took ten months of constant battling for them to finally admit they had accepted certificates with the names of dissolved companies on, the declarations of conformity, and that Councillor King may not have worded things correctly. They would look into it further and make a public correction if necessary.

Spoiler alert. Carinna went back to the Council on 28th January 2025 to mention it again!

Almost a year after she first raised the topic of 5G. As luck would have it, Councillor King happened to be at the Scrutiny Panel meeting and said he was "prepared to accept his phrasing could have been different and he puts his hand up to that!" How very generous of him.

Carinna had quite a reply to that…

# 24

# From Colchester to Countrywide

The crux of Carinna's speech at the end of January 2025 had been to ask where is the accountability that we hear Councillor King speak of so often because we haven't seen any signs of it.

She had a long list of grievances, the council hadn't answered from the lack of legal opinion on the searches to officers making decisions and steering councillors with no accountability. By now it was our two year anniversary of going into the council.

Councillor King responded, as we guessed he or one of the others would, that he had retracted something he'd said in error to Lance at full council. Unbeknownst to him, we'd read the email exchange between them and knew he had no intention of retracting what he said about Lance until legal action was threatened. Carinna duly pointed this out to the whole room.

With regards to councillor King's phrasing, Carinna said, "I had provided evidence that 5G was unsafe and suggested to councillor King he could retract that in the previous full council. He chose not to. So I am suggesting that your phrasing was inaccurate and by not retracting that the first time it was requested you are being deliberately misleading."

Boom. Great work, Carinna! She just gets better and better every time she goes in. That wasn't the end of verbal punches swung in councillor King's direction. The next member of the public who goes by the name 'Colchester Mum' on Twitter, got up and immediately said, "Before I start, can I just say that it's very off-putting to see the leader of the council rolling his eyes when a member of the public is speaking. I hope you're going to treat me with more respect." It really wasn't his evening.

But that's jumping ahead, let's get back to where we were, in February 2024. It was a ridiculously busy month with council speeches, farming videos and webinars, group Zoom calls and helping Carinna respond to all the nonsense she was getting from the council. March was going to be just as busy and I was trying to flee the country. My parents had finally sold their house in Spain and I was going to drive out there and start packing up the house before they joined me in April.

Before I left, I just had a few commitments to take care of. The big one for me was ending up on stage in London with Clive de Carle, Matt Le Tissier, Richard Vobes and Janey Lee Grace. I'd got to know Clive because he was one of the expert guests who'd been interviewed on the Crrow777 podcast. I'd contacted him because I'd used a clip of his interview with Dr Andrew Kaufman in one of my anonymous Covid videos and I had been interested in buying one of his restored Tesla devices.

Alongside the Tesla Violet Ray and other medical devices Clive sells exceptionally good vitamin and mineral supplements. We'd met upon my return to England.

Clive's invitation to speak at his London event came as quite a surprise. I have no idea why on earth he decided to invite some woman from Colchester few had ever heard of to talk about going in to speak at the council but he did, so I did!

Tim from Fairplay Now YouTube Channel, recorded Clive's Leicester Square event and very kindly gave me a copy to put on my YouTube channel. As you know, it was a bit of a winging it speech but it was my first time public speaking so I wasn't too hard on myself over it being a bit waffly.

I've had no media training or public speaking experience and I have a lot to learn. I didn't mind it going on the Council Watch channel because the audience already knows me and they knew it was my first go. Tim's channel wasn't big and his videos usually got under five thousand views so I was happy in the fact that hardly anyone would watch it. I wasn't going to be precious over it not being the perfect public speech.

Besides, how many people have to make their public speaking debut to an audience in a London theatre alongside well-known professionals? The last thing you'd want, having completely winged it, is for thousands of people to watch said debut and then start critiquing you like you're a professional speaker or something...

That is exactly what happened. The video took off on Tim's channel and ended up being his second most viewed video with over fifty thousand views. So much for my self-assurances that hardly anyone would see it!

## Council Watching Everywhere

Our Council Watching intensified when I was invited to go to the neighbouring market town of Sudbury just across the border in Suffolk. Local residents wanted me to witness the battle they were up against with Babergh District Council imposing car parking charges on their town's free car parks. Everyone knew it would likely be the death blow for the struggling town and were fighting hard against it. They had the added battle of their town council wanting to take away the parking on Market Hill and turn it into what was billed as a cosmopolitan pedestrianised area.

An evening of insanity ensued which I filmed and documented. It unexpectedly became our most viewed Council Watch video at the time, with over a hundred and thirty thousand views. Of all the really important issues we'd covered, the thing the general public were most irate about was parking charges. People up and down the country reporting how their towns and villages had died as soon as parking charges came in.

While I was in Sudbury, Carinna and Cheryl had gone along to support Brian and Terry who were pushing for the council to have a climate debate so that councillors could hear both sides of the argument. We'd got lined up the same speakers Sandi Adams had for the Net Zero debate in Glastonbury. We were determined to have a proper debate.

The following evening we were all back at Colchester to support Carinna following up on all the falsehoods which had been emailed to her regarding 5G. The next night we all tootled off to Needham Market where The Bowler Hat Farmer, Mark Byford was giving a talk on the state of farming. I'd got to know Mark working with the PFFA with Sandi Adams on their farming Agenda 2030 awareness videos.

Unfortunately for me, he'd spied my name on the list of people coming and dragged me up to speak about man-made climate change and what I'd learned regarding $CO_2$ not being quite as evil and lethal as advertised. Man-made $CO_2$ only causes anthropogenic global warming on flawed computer models, real world observed data does not support it, as shown in Dr Happer from Princeton University's work.

I was still intensely uncomfortable talking about a subject I'd no real expertise in. Climate is an enormous subject and no one really truly understands exactly how every aspect works. So I merely relayed what I'd learned to date. The room was packed full of farmers and Mark wanted to get across to them a lot of the measures they were being put through from the government were unnecessary.

It's very hard to get across to people who have deeply held beliefs that there is another argument. When virtually every television programme these days mentions man-made climate change, people simply do not accept a different point of view. It is also impossible to change people's opinions with graphs, charts and data if they have made up their minds without using such things. Belief, as Crrow likes to say in his podcasts, is the enemy of knowing.

Most people don't even know why they believe in man-made climate change, they just do. I often ask people who are adamant it's all our fault, which climate papers have they read that convinced them? No one has been able to reference a single paper yet. The computer models which people seem to trust so much haven't managed to make accurate predictions in the last three decades, so why trust something which has been up to three times higher than reality? Fourth decade lucky?

Despite it being challenging for me, it was a good evening and I think Mark did win a few people round with what he said.

## One Year Anniversary

The following week Carinna informed me she wanted to go along to the Environment and Sustainability Panel meeting as it was a year on from my first proper speech and she wanted to follow-up on all the outstanding queries. It was just before I was about to leave for Spain so I was unable to accompany her, I had too much to do, so her daughter, Rebecca, went as camera crew and moral support instead.

I like to have speeches written well in advance of meetings. Carinna, however, is a bit of a last minute Lara. She was still writing her speech that night walking up the hill to the Town Hall. She was leaving me voice messages, reading out what she wanted to say as she headed to the meeting. Did I think it was alright?

I gave her some feedback on a couple of bits I thought needed changing which she listened to once she was seated waiting for the meeting to start. Unfortunately, she'd still got her phone volume set to the full blast she'd needed to hear me through the traffic of Colchester's High Street in the previous messages. My voice came booming out filling the room with suggestions.

When it was her official time to speak once the meeting started, she asked them why they were ignoring the public's safety concerns over eBikes and eScooter fire hazards? And why they were continuing to increase the number of them on our streets when their production is polluting and devastating to the environment, not to mention goes against the council's anti-slavery policy.

She also asked what evidence the council have that they are saving the planet by introducing these measures? And finished with asking who is the decision maker responsible for putting these potentially explosive bikes everywhere?

They said they were getting training on the recycling side of EVs and would get back to her afterwards. Then a very patronising officer said her colleagues had already given comprehensive responses to those questions on previous occasions which she could send again, but they didn't have anything further to add because it felt like they were in a continuous cycle of us asking the same questions and them responding.

If you've never dealt with a council, a 'comprehensive response' is basically a lot of word-salad-waffle that gets you nowhere, going round and round in circles and makes you lose the will to live without actually answering anything you've asked. Which is why Carinna had gone back.

Councillor Lissimore, who'd requested the previous year for a full-lifecycle report on purchasing decisions asked if they were any further forward in delivering that? This took them twenty minutes to discuss whilst Carinna sat there.

An officer called Simon, the one who I had a nine month email conversation with trying to get an answer to precisely what was their climate emergency and what evidence did the council have for it, told her it was a lot of work. It was the same guy who had told the council in the last meeting he didn't feel the need to respond to my email because there were no questions in it. I then did a video showing him seven or eight questions, pointing out that questions have the little question mark on the end of sentences. Yes, that Simon.

Anyway, Councillor Lissimore was not happy to be given the brush off and persisted. She felt Cabinet members should know the impact of what they are buying from production to end of life and recycling. Simple Simon said, everything has lithium in it from laptops to mobile phones including regular car batteries and all mining is bad and shrugged his shoulders.

Simple Simon is incorrect, regular car batteries do not have lithium in. I was fairly sure of this but double-checked and asked Geoff Buys Cars who said some high-end luxury vehicles might have an additional lithium battery under their seat, but not a regular car battery.

The meeting Chair, who Carinna and I had locked horns with in our first encounter with her, had come round to the fact we weren't troublemakers, as I suspect she'd been told before her first meeting. She had actually been very helpful and polite from that bumpy start onwards. She had a bit of a glint in her eye as she said to Carinna she'd give her extra time to respond to so much information. It was her last meeting as Chair, elections were coming, so she had nothing to lose by letting Carinna go for it.

Carinna did not waste the opportunity and responded to all the nonsense she'd sat through for twenty-two minutes. "First of all, it's quite concerning with the obligation that Council has to look at all evidence impartially how we can get to the stage where no one knows about this until a member of public brings it forward. Whatever you've been exposed to sounds like an echo chamber of people who support this and obviously in certain job titles you're going to have to believe in that and it's concerning that information wasn't there already.

If you are genuinely trying to save the planet it's all about environment sustainability then why isn't this one of the primary considerations you know the the toxicity of procuring these minerals etc? It does seem quite hypocritical of the virtue-signalling of the green agenda to not even have looked at the toxicity in the manufacturing and the recycling which is all very difficult.

The mobile phones is really deflecting from the issue we have, which was the EV procurement the eBikes and the eScooters, obviously scale is the issue and if you're going to be buying lots more then this is all going to continue. There's been a hundred more eBikes and rScooters added so if you are here serving the public then why are you not listening to the public and acting on that?

Can you recognise the disparity between a climate emergency and the speed in which things are addressed through this Council? We've had a lack of responses, we don't get questions answered and the lady who suggested that we've had lengthy answers as I've said before, there's not a lot of substance in there. We would like to have robust evidence.

It's shocking how council is allowed to procure this without this information available and it seems very much there's only one line of thinking that's allowed and anything that doesn't agree with that is silenced. So I would just like to say you are obligated to look at all the evidence. Council admitted to not doing that. Council is now admitting to being ill-informed on the mining and the EV batteries and the recycling etc. until the public brings it here.

So if you truly are about environment sustainability can we have less polluting technologies moving forward and recognise the assumptions that you are basing your climate emergency on the $CO_2$ levels is false. We've asked for a discussion around this to bring both sides of the argument, again there is deflection.

We're after just finding the truth. I'm not about winning with whether there is, or whether there isn't there is climate change. Of course there is, but what I'm finding is evidence being hidden and ignored in preference to serving the agenda and all the grants and money that comes in from following what is being pushed down not serving the people."

The next day, the Green councillor was complaining on Twitter about what was said at the meeting. He said he's fed up with hearing about the mining of lithium batteries and feels we should be focusing on all aspects. Specifically he's concerned about car tyres made by children in sweat shops. I must admit I didn't know about this dreadful occurrence. There was me thinking Michelin made their car tyres in precision factories with machinery. I didn't for one minute think it was children in sweat shops, but there we go. We can all learn something new each day from these knowledgable councillors!

## Glorious in Gloucester

Before I left for Spain, I had an urgent video to film with a gentleman from Gloucester called Matthew Randolph and his friend Johnny. We'd already featured Matthew going into the council and serving Notice on the councillors for accepting fraudulent 5G safety declarations. Matthew had been in a few times to Gloucester Council, they'd tried calling the police to have him removed, but of course they couldn't. Nine councillors ended up resigning.

Matthew had now decided to run for the Police and Crimes Commissioner post so he could really get in there and sort out the fraud. In order to run you have to put down a five thousand pound deposit. If you get five percent of the votes, I think it is, you get the five thousand pounds returned to you. I'd agreed to interview him and see if people would support his fund raiser.

Matthew and his friend Johnny are quite a pair of characters. We spoke on a Friday night when they'd normally both be down the pub. So it was very much like an evening in your local. They both drank and smoked through the entire interview, which some of the Council Watch viewers didn't approve of in the comments, whilst regaling what they'd got up to at the council. It was a very entertaining chat and quite a lot of it edited out as it wasn't suitable for YouTube because of censorship rules.

The only slight glitch was how on earth I was going to get it edited and out on the Council Watch channel. At this point I still hadn't finished the Sudbury video and I was about to catch the ferry to France and drive to southern Spain.

I had a cunning plan, which needless to say, didn't go well.

# 25

# A Spanish Farewell

It was Monday 25th March 2024. I took my laptop onboard the P & O ferry from Dover to Calais with the intention of editing during the two-hour crossing. I thought I would be able to get a bit done at least. I was sitting with the dog in the allocated area in the pet deck. I was exhausted. It had been non-stop for over a year.

It was lovely and warm in the sunny area by the window. We'd got a cubicle at the front of the boat. I decided to just rest my head for a few minutes on the bench seat before I started working on the video. The next thing I knew the horn was sounding... we'd arrived in Calais.

I hadn't even eaten. I rushed to the café, which was adjacent to the pet area and asked if they could do me a takeaway meal. Thankfully they could, and I was able to eat in the car prior to disembarking. I don't even remember how far I drove that night, or where we ended up, other than in a cabin in a campsite somewhere near Rouen. I cooked myself supper, and managed to get a bit of editing done, but I was too tired to do much.

The next night we'd made it to the other side of Bordeaux. Campsite options weren't great. I eventually managed to get the last spot on one that was so cramped that we ended up sleeping in the car. There wasn't room to have a car and a tent. It was tipping it down with rain, so my dinner was egg and beans on soggy toast.

The weather the next day was even worse. Driving conditions were awful. I'd had a text from Johnny before I set off. Was the video done yet? When would it be uploaded? Good question. Even if I had been able to get it done, I didn't have enough mobile data to upload a forty minute video, so it would have to wait until I reached the house in Spain, which would take another couple of days. I don't like driving more than six hours. Boredom, and it's not great for the dog to go longer. Famous last words...

I filled up with fuel the moment I got over the Spanish border, having done so on fumes. Spain is considerably cheaper than France, sometimes as much as fifty cents a litre. The further south I drove, the worse the weather got. I wasn't going to be messing around with sightseeing, and programmed in the quickest route and prayed I didn't end up in the centre of Madrid like last time.

The one advantage of such awful weather was that the roads were relatively empty, with gusts of over 50mph and rain sheeting it down so you could barely see. No one in their right mind was out driving unless they had to be.

I was listening to a good Jacqueline Winspear, Maisie Dobbs' audiobook my mother had recommended. Thank goodness, or I would have gone completely crazy. I have a very low boredom threshold, although the weather conditions were certainly keeping me on my toes.

I'd hoped after eight hours of driving we would clear the storm, especially the other side of Madrid. No. Still bad. I carried on driving another couple of hours and stopped for a bite to eat. No idea where we were at this point, certainly nowhere memorable. Just as I was about to start driving again, my mother phoned wanting to know where I'd stopped for the night. I explained my predicament.

There was no way I could get a tent erected in this weather, let alone sleep in it. We weren't a million miles from Granada, which was only an hour away from their house. I was in half a mind to see if I could drive the rest. My mother was concerned at this idea and said she'd pay for a hotel, not to try to drive it if I was too tired. Finding a dog friendly hotel might be more challenging than driving, which is why I prefer campsites. I said I'd see how we got on.

On we drove. The dog was incredibly well-behaved, but did start to squawk when we reached Granada. I stopped to let her out to pee and assured her it would be just one more hour in the car. The worst of the weather had subsided, but it was still fairly windy and rainy.

When we finally reached La Herradura (which is the village nearest to my parent's place), I stopped the car and let her out to go for a run along the windswept pebble beach. She charged towards the water and then suddenly stopped and sniffed the air.

She whipped around to look at me with her head tilted to one side, a look akin to disbelief on her furry little face. She knew where she was. Back to the place of her birth, her motherland. She barked and started chasing her tail round and round in excited circles, clearly overjoyed at being home. Then she pelted full-speed towards the sea.

Oh no! That would mean a very wet dog in the car and then my parents' house. Oh well, my little water lover had been stuck in a car for an unimaginable length of time, not surprising she wanted to go for a swim. Which she did until she got in to halfway up her legs and saw the size of the waves heading towards her. She immediately about turned and ran out barking. I bundled her back in the car, relieved she hadn't immersed herself any further. We made our way up the winding mountain road to Marina del Este. Finally, we'd made it. It was 11pm Wednesday 27th, we'd been in the car thirteen and a half hours.

The weather was still pretty awful for the next few days. It was nearly Easter, when so often it's not great in Spain. I've lost count of the number of wet Spanish Easters I've endured. I couldn't stay in as I needed food and to get the 'pay as you go' internet up and running. I just hoped it would still work. Satellite internet can be temperamental. Thankfully the shop was still there and knew which house I wanted re-connected for a month.

It was really annoying the weather was so awful as I desperately wanted a few days lying on a sun-lounger doing nothing before my parents flew out and it would be weeks on end of packing up twenty year's worth of stuff. It did mean I got Matt and Johnny's video done though. I uploaded their video in the evening of the 28th, the day before Good Friday. I hoped the Easter weekend would bring a good number of views.

One of the best parts of Council Watch is definitely the viewers. Their witty comments and support has meant the world to us, but none more so than that Easter weekend. Considering the channel only had about five thousand subscribers it was incredible to watch Matthew's fundraiser reach his target in under two days. The guys were over the moon. What I hadn't known at the time was that the deadline for Matthew to register his application form was the Tuesday after Easter.

It was a close-run thing. On the bank holiday Monday, Matthew had to go around his community collecting signatures of people wanting him to run to show he had support. Then there was the endless paperwork which needed to be filled in and delivered to the right department. They wanted proof of his funds, so they showed the fundraiser page. With just a few minutes to spare before the deadline, they got Matthew's name on the list of applicants for Police Commissioner.

This really put the wind up the Council, and the police. No one wanted him to win. The local BBC tried to do a less than favourable interview, and other times pretend like he didn't exist with their meagre coverage. I put a video of it up on YouTube, but it got removed and a strike to the channel because the

BBC reporter mentioned vaccines. Matthew had wanted an investigation into why these experimental shots were recommended to the public without adequate safety warnings.

There were all sorts of other shenanigans with Matthew not being invited to attend public meetings and interviews. The press then reported that he hadn't turned up. Every trick you can think of, including trying to have him arrested for fraudulently filling in his application form to run for the position of Police and Crimes Commissioner. They accused him of lying on his application about a criminal record.

When Matthew was seventeen, he'd worked at a local printer who'd been responsible for printing tickets for a black-tie ball. Matthew's co-worker had thought it a good idea to print a couple of extra tickets so they could go along! That was his criminal record. Being stupid at seventeen. Because he wasn't eighteen, he didn't think he had to mention it, and didn't.

Matthew told me that the police didn't follow due process and had to drop the case against him. Plenty more has happened since then with the police, the Council and now the courts. It would be a book in itself, but suffice to say, Matthew is in the process of taking the lot of them to court for not correctly following due process. It just shows how much power you have when you know the law.

The rain-soaked Easter meant I finally had time to finish editing the Sudbury video. The video caused quite a stir with the public, and particularly with the leader of Babergh District Council. He wasn't at all happy with a derogatory comment I'd made about one of his Green councillor colleagues. The councillor in question had turned up late to the meeting, swanning in as if it was nothing. When questioned about why she had voted in favour of the parking charges, which everyone felt would destroy the local economy, she came out with the biggest load of drivel I'd ever heard. It seemed she hadn't really understood what she'd voted for. I made a quip that perhaps she'd had one of her dreadlocks stuck in her ear, which is why she hadn't understood.

The next day, one of our loyal Council Watch viewers gently pulled me up on the comment, saying, "Rachel, you don't normally make comments about councillors' hair, why this time?" She was right. I'd made a point of asking people in the comments not to make personal remarks about councillors, and yet I'd broken my own rule. I usually take comments like that out in the final edit. I get things off my chest and then delete them. On this occasion, I was so incensed with the clueless councillor, I left it in. After the viewer's comment, I edited it out. The video had only been up for 12 hours and didn't have many views, so no harm done. Or so I thought...

The Leader of Babergh District Council had seen it prior to my edit and wrote in the community Facebook group under the video: "Who is this stupid, offensive woman? She clearly knows nothing. Perhaps an engagement with the debate rather than making supercilious insults would be more mature." His comment enraged the group, and quite a heated debate followed.

I owned up to my inappropriate comment in the next video and explained to viewers that my remark had provoked the Council Leader's outburst. I acknowledged that we'd both said things that weren't ideal, so there we go, let's move on. While I could have easily said considerably worse about the clueless councillor, the damage had already been done behind the scenes with the Council Leader. His outburst at me, and the subsequent public outrage, turned out to be the nail in his leadership coffin.

I was contacted by another councillor who apologised to me and told me they were going to get rid of him because his behaviour was unacceptable. Apparently, he had quite a history of offending people. Ironically, I wasn't remotely bothered by his comment. By this point in Council Watch, I was way past being offended by things like that. I explained that my inappropriate comment had provoked his response, but they'd already decided they wanted him gone. Sure enough, a few weeks later, he stepped down as Council Leader with no real explanation given.

This may surprise people, but I didn't actually like that outcome. Although I felt his decision-making and constant push for parking charges would be highly detrimental, it didn't seem fair to force him out over expressing a personal opinion. His comment was nowhere near as offensive as the Colchester councillor who made libellous statements, claiming we were "dangerous far-right extremists who prey on vulnerable people" who got away scot-free. I don't want two-tier justice in any form. I know he had a history of upsetting people, so it was just a matter of time, but even so, it didn't sit well with me.

The clueless councillor did eventually get her act together and was the only one in the Cabinet who voted against the parking charges in the final vote. But alas, it was too little, too late, and the scheme went ahead. There was a small win, though. Being in the spotlight, with over 130,000 views and so many outraged comments caused them to rethink closing off Market Hill. So, at least something was achieved.

There ended up being several Sudbury videos when a para-legal called Damian got in touch to interview me for his friend's YouTube channel and said he thought he might be able to help the people of Sudbury start a legal battle to stop the Council proceeding. He very generously offered his time free of charge and spent a lot of hours working tremendously hard to do everything he could to help. As it turned out, he was unable to because the Ombudsman who'd been very helpful on the phone, turned out not to be when it came down to it. Without the Ombudsman's agreeing that there had been a breach of Council process, we had no grounds for a Judicial Review.

## Hello Sunshine!

Thankfully, by the time my parents arrived, so had the sunshine. The next few weeks were ridiculously busy. Mornings were spent packing and sorting. Siesta time was spent making video after video. Although the Council had more or less stopped because of the upcoming elections, there were so many things going on elsewhere that the video making never stopped.

It was at this point I changed the channel name from Colchester Council Watch to Council Watch (Colchester & Countrywide). I'd also got a load of interviews lined up. Although we'd sold the house, the new owners were incredibly kind and were happy for me to stay on in the house while they were in England waiting for the birth of their first grandchild.

My parents had rented an apartment further down the Marina for a week so they could tie up loose ends and hopefully have a few days break. We were all worn out. The new owners were due back on the 25th April, so on the 24th, my last day with decent internet, I spent the whole day doing interviews.

The first was with Damian, the para legal, regarding the question of what we could do about the Sudbury car parking charges situation. Lunchtime it was with TNT again, this time with David Kurten interviewing me. And in the afternoon, it was my friend Eli, who'd given Carinna and I the tickets to the Shine Seminars. It was lovely speaking to Eli, probably my most relaxed interview because it was with someone I knew, it's also my least viewed. Clearly the more stressful ones are more popular!

As much as I don't like interviews, being the interviewer is worse. It's such a skill to be a good interviewer. Done well, it looks effortless, but it's anything but. I've discovered the hard way that in order to be a good interviewer, it helps to know the subject almost as much as the person you're interviewing. There's an art to asking questions in a way which allows people to shine and also to express their knowledge in a way people can easily comprehend. I don't have those skills, though I try my best.

Two days before my parents flew home, I had another airport run to do. This time collecting Tom and Carinna from Malaga. Tom was buying my parents car and I'd persuaded Carinna to come over for a holiday – it didn't take much persuading once she'd found her passport was in date. Although I was exhausted from the house moving and my non-stop video making, I knew it would be good to have them both over.

We only had one day to sort the car transfer as my parents had to leave early on the last day for their flight. Buying a car in Spain is more complicated than you can ever imagine. I won't bore you with the details, but it was touch and go getting all the necessary paperwork done so it could happen. We got there eventually, but it was a headache inducing process.

Carinna had stayed at the apartment to relax as well as dog sit. She definitely picked the better option. We were so long, by the time we did get back to the house she was lobster red, despite spending the majority of the time in the shade. It's easy to underestimate the strength of the Spanish sun compared to our meagre English fleeting glimpses of sunshine.

We did manage to get a glorious afternoon walk in one of my favourite areas, the Cerro Gordo, which has a little mountain restaurant called the Mirador, with stunning views overlooking the bay of La Herradura on one side and the bay towards Cantarriján on the other.

Tom departed for his house in Jimena the following day. Carinna and I were going to spend a few days with friends of mine in the mountains. My mother had suggested we spend a night in Nerja first so Carinna got to see the sea and a lively part of Spain, otherwise her trip would be nothing but mountains as we were going to join Tom after my Otivar friends.

My parents left early Friday morning, leaving Carinna and I to clear the last of the stuff out of the rental apartment before heading to the hotel in Nerja. It was odd to still be in the area but no longer at their old house which had been such a huge part of my life for twenty years. It was like leaving behind an old friend but at the same time it was a relationship which needed to end, it had become a burden to us all now that I had returned to live in England. We drove past it one last time, I dropped my set of keys in to the new owners. I bid the house, and the garden I'd filmed so many videos in, a fond farewell and that was that. The end of quite an era.

We celebrated my birthday at Scarletta's restaurant in Nerja and then the following day had a much needed beach day. I'd been in Spain five weeks and I'd hardly seen the beach, other than to briskly walk the dog past it first thing in the morning. We had a lovely few days up in the mountains with my friends at their off-grid finca. Views were stunning but with good views there comes a price.

Before we'd headed up there from the coast, I said to Carinna that I hoped she was OK with heights. She eyed me suspiciously and said, "Usually, why?"

"Oh you'll find out soon enough." I replied with a grin.

We wound our way up the mountain road to Otivar and then had to take an incredibly sharp right up a small mountain road. Carinna commented that she could see why I'd mentioned heights. It is a bit of a heart-stopping road. It was then I had to inform her that wasn't the bit I was referring to. She started to look a little pale.

"There's worse than this?" She tentatively enquired.

"You'll see!"

After a few minutes of snaking round the very narrow mountain road, we pulled off onto a single track concrete road which was even smaller than the mountain road. Carinna muttered that at least it looked like it was a good road, even though it was rather steep and narrow. Being a newcomer to this part of Spain, Carinna did not know the golden rule on Spanish mountain roads. Just because they start out good, doesn't mean to say they are going to stay that way...

Eight minutes of steep hairpin bends on the concrete road, followed by another few minutes on a stone chippings road. To her credit she didn't scream or throw up. Though I think she may have had her eyes closed for most of it.

The very worst part is my friend's actual drive. It's so steep and rutted, it feels you're going to drive off the edge with every corner. I did offer for Carinna to get out at this point and walk down, which she duly did. My friends drive this hazardous road all the time without batting an eyelid, but for those of us not used to it, it's a fairly heart-stopping experience.

They had bought the land and had the house built over the last few years. It was lovely seeing all the progress they had made. It's such a lovely home. Carinna and I would be staying on the lower level in the Cortijo made from a shipping container. We decided to walk down to the next level rather than drive as the road had deteriorated with all the recent storms.

My friend's son had grown tremendously and was now walking and talking. They also had a dog called Sam. Lena took to him instantly and they started chasing each other all over the property. This upset my friend's son as he thought they were attacking each other. We tried to explain they were playing, but he was convinced his dog was in danger. We spent a lovely few days there. It was great to catch up with my friends. They had been one of the first to reach out to me once I started muttering on Facebook. At that time, we had just been acquaintances, but an awareness of all not being well in the world had created a tight bond of friendship.

As they both led busy lives, I took Carinna to one of my favourite walks. The spectacular Hidden Valley hike near Lentegi. I was desperate to see it again, hoping the lavender might still be in flower. I should have put a bit more thought into that choice. The Hidden Valley hike is fairly demanding. Although I certainly wasn't mountain hiking fit any more after two years back in England, I did have some residual conditioning from years of clambering up steep mountains in hot weather. Carinna did not.

Carinna also doesn't do heat any better than she manages with cold. She's like my friend Cathy, who always used to say she liked temperatures between 19-24 degrees, no colder and no hotter. What on earth she was doing living in Spain, I've no idea. It doesn't stay those temperatures for much of the year.

The first part down into the valley is very steep, we could have done with my walking poles, but they were on their way back to England with the removals company. We made it down to the waterfall OK, but Carinna was very conscious the only way out was to walk back up the very steep section. We probably should have just done the waterfalls and called it enough, but I really wanted to show her the spectacular lavender hillside. About halfway up the other side of the mountain, I realised what a bad idea that had been.

Carinna was not looking good. She said she needed a sit down. I agreed that would be a good idea and I'd just go on ahead to see how far we were from where I'd wanted to take her. I thought it was just around the next corner. Turns out I was very wrong about that. There were probably about another ten corners to get up the mountain and I couldn't see any lavender, so I headed back to where I'd left her.

She wasn't there! Uh oh! I hurried to where she had been, praying she hadn't passed out and toppled off the side of the mountain. Thankfully I found her around the next corner in the shade. We decided the best option was to head back. I knew it was serious because it's the only time I've ever witnessed a sense of humour failure in Carinna. We took it slowly and eventually dragged ourselves back up and out of the valley and to the car. By the end of it Carinna, understandably, looked like she'd quite like to throttle me, but thankfully didn't have the strength left. I drove the rest of the route on the dirt track so she'd get to see the stunning scenery without any further walking. We drove further up the mountains for lunch at a packed restaurant.

We spent our last day hanging out with my friends and helping them plant some avocado trees on the mountainside of their property. The next day we were off to Malaga, and then on to join Tom in Jimena. By the time we got to Tom's, I was completely done in. Weeks of non-stop work had caught up with me. It was all I could do to drag myself on to his terrace and flake out listening to another Maisie Dobbs audiobook.

We did do a few mountain walks, but not as steep as the one we'd done near Lentegi. Carinna was fine, it was me who was flagging now. I had no energy and had developed a rather bad cough. When I'd helped plant the avocado trees, I'd got the dog to help as she loves digging and the ground was rock solid. It was more like rock dust than soil, and clouds of it had wafted up into the atmosphere as she frantically dug, and I'd been breathing it in whilst planting. Carinna had been on the lower level keeping my friend's son entertained.

When it was time for Carinna's flight back from Gibraltar, I was still quite poorly so Tom drove her. That night my cough got considerably worse. My lungs felt awful. When I got up in the night, I was coughing up blood. An alarming sight.

# 26

# On The Road Again

It was about 3am and at the sight of blood, Hypochondriac Me was in full swing, having never coughed up blood before. A full-scale drama was playing out in my mind, it must be all that rock dust. What was in it? Some alien lung-eating bacteria? Or was it silica from quartz rock dust, had I got silicosis? Sensible Me immediately stepped in at this point. "You haven't got silicosis and you're not dying!"

"How do you know? You're not a doctor."

"Likewise, so go to sleep and see how you are in the morning."

There was a small internal debate whether to go downstairs and get Tom, but the thought of being driven to La Linea, the nearest hospital, then waiting all night to be seen, did not appeal.

My hand reached for my phone. Sensible Me barked, "Do not go near Google! Do it in the morning."

I reasoned that whatever I'd breathed in needed to come out and if there were micro-particles of granite, it would be like sandblasting every time I coughed, therefore it wasn't entirely surprising there was blood. I hoped that's all it was.

By the morning my lungs still felt awful, but there wasn't any more blood. I also still had my appetite. So therefore the 'I'm not eating, call an ambulance.' scenario wasn't the case. I knew if I went to a doctor, the most likely course of action would be antibiotics, which I didn't particularly want. It was possible I was fighting a bit of an infection, it would explain why I'd been so exhausted all the time despite resting.

It's a shame I didn't have a nebuliser. I knew from my time spent researching during the Covid era that nebulising a small amount of hydrogen peroxide in a saline solution is great for chest infections. I'd purchased one in case my parents got ill. I wanted to do everything I could to keep them out of hospital. The protocol during Covid was to put patients on high doses of Midazolam, which has a side effect of causing breathing difficulties. When those difficulties arose, the next part of the protocol was a ventilator.

I'll let you research the rest for yourself. Journalist Jacqui Devoy has done a lot of research into this. She has collected hundreds of testimonials on the deaths this protocol caused, especially in the elderly. She plans to publish a book called 'Murdered by the State', which documents the claims made by families and medical staff on inappropriate life-ending protocols.

This is why I made sure I had a means to treat my parents and do my best to keep them out of hospital. As it happens, they both got chest infections and I used the nebuliser solution on them and they both said how much it helped. Trouble is, my nebuliser was in England. I did want another as it wasn't a particularly good one so I looked on Amazon, but it would be a few days before it would arrive. I didn't hold out much hope of buying one in the small town of Jimena, but Tom drove me to the chemist to see if they could get one any quicker.

Tom asked for a 'nebulizador' and the chemist checked the computer. It said they had one in stock, but when he looked he couldn't see it. He didn't know when they'd next get one. Fortunately for me, his female colleague overheard the conversation and knew where to look. She found it. What a result. I asked if they had any saline and hydrogen peroxide. They did. Forty Euros later and off we trotted back to Tom's for me to try out my hopeful cure.

I carefully measured out the mixture, as per the online doctor's instructions, and sat breathing it in for ten minutes. My lungs did feel a bit better afterwards, but I wasn't sure if it was the solution or the moisture.

I used the nebuliser three times that day and did start to feel considerably better. I had been planning to set off to Portugal, but Tom suggested I stayed a few more days and rest. There was always something that made it hard to leave Jimena. It's like being snared by the place every time I visited. I did love it there, so it was by no means a bad place to be, other than it was rather dusty, which I knew wasn't helping my lungs. There were a lot of dirt tracks near Tom's house.

The next day I decided I was well enough to leave. I knew he had guests coming for lunch who were likely to stay a long time and I really wasn't in the frame of mind to be sociable. I just wanted to be quiet and rest, so heading off felt like the lesser of two evils. I could always head back if I felt unwell again.

It turned out to be the right decision. Tom's lunch guests arrived at 2pm and didn't leave until gone midnight. They worked their way through a large bottle of whiskey I'd given him from my parents. As a non-drinker, I wouldn't have enjoyed that 'lunch' and people who drink tend to always insist you join them and get tetchy if you don't. As I was staying in the bedroom upstairs next to the living room, there would have been no escape, so I was very glad I was in a quiet tent in the middle of nowhere, in peace and quiet.

I drove up through Portugal to a wonderful campsite I'd stayed at many years before, near Gouveia. It was run by a Dutch couple. When I'd first been there, the owner's sister had been running a sculpture workshop. I'd asked if she did them every year and could I come and join them sometime. In that very direct Dutch way, she said, "Why not now?"

I had no reason why not, other than I was on my way to the beach because I wanted to learn how to surf and had only intended on staying one night on route. I ended up staying all week with the bus load of Dutch tourists she was teaching. I joined in with their excursions and meals. Some of the Dutch I'd learned when I was seventeen and had lived in

Holland for a few months started to come back to me. I had a great time learning to sculpt soapstone.

I was really pleased to see the same couple still running Quinta das Cegonhas campsite. It had developed with a rental apartment at the top and some cabins, but other than that it was how I remembered it. Luckily, they allowed dogs. After I checked in with the receptionist, I saw the owner and said I had been there many years ago and told her about the sculpture course. She remembered me! She gave me a big smile and we chatted a while. She asked how long I was planning on staying. I replied, like last time, just a day or two. She smiled and said, "We'll see!"

I did end up staying longer. I was still tired and needing the nebuliser at night. And I realised I didn't want to go home. So, I stayed. It wasn't the best weather, but I just didn't want to come back to England and pick up with all the council stuff again.

It's funny that on the way out I hadn't wanted to leave England as it felt like a wrench, and now I was away I was not wanting to return. I knew something needed to change, I couldn't keep doing this. I'd have to find a suitable point to stop. Financially it was crippling. I had been spending all my time either making council videos, writing speeches or helping other Council Watch groups. My life just wasn't my own any more.

I certainly wasn't bored anymore, but I wasn't happy either. I was being consumed by it all. Speaking of the devil, my phone was going. Videos of the latest full Council meeting were pinging into it. By this time the elections had come and gone. Sadly, no change in Colchester, except for the 'Have Your Say' rules.

The Council were tightening up their rules to limit the number of speakers. A subject was not allowed to be raised more than once in a six-month period by the same person. Only one person per group was allowed to speak. They wanted to do away with the right of reply, but thought better of it and amended that. All questions would now have to be put in writing before the meeting, and the Council would decide if those questions were to be allowed. Who pays their wages again? Anyway, several had gone along to have their say before the rules changed. I was glad I was in Portugal.

Peace Keepers were also there pushing for the climate debate to happen. It had been their idea to push for a proper debate. By this point, if I'm completely honest, I rather hoped it wouldn't happen, purely for selfish reasons. I knew how much work would be involved. Plus, I knew it wouldn't change a thing. I'm all for doing things if it will make a difference, but when it won't, there seems little point.

But anyway, it's what everyone else wanted, so I made sure it went in all our speeches, regardless of my own personal preferences. And if it did happen, I would of course put a hundred percent commitment in to make sure it went smoothly.

With my time in Portugal coming to an end, I reluctantly left my lovely campsite and headed back to the place I didn't want to be. I made it as far as Donostia-San Sebastian on the Spanish border with

France. With my limited language skills, I wanted get the dreaded vet trip out of the way in Spain. The vet's website said booking only, so I booked the earliest slot I could, which was 11am.

The vet wanted the dog weighed so she could give her the right dose of worm pills which I wouldn't be allowed back in the UK without doing. I took one look at the dog and said 25KG. She put her on the scales and sure enough, 25KG. She asked if I had food for the dog so she could hide the pills. I told her just to throw them in the air, no need to disguise them in food for my little piggy. The vet looked at me disbelievingly, but did as instructed and sure enough Lena crunched them down like sweeties. I just hoped they wouldn't make her sick like last time.

My wish was heard, in a careful what you wish for kind of way, they didn't make her sick. No, this time they gave her explosive diarrhoea. She started squawking on a section of motorway halfway up France. I told her I'd pull off as soon as I could. It wasn't soon enough.

Diarrhoea all over the back seat. I pulled everything out and washed it while she ate grass and got rid of the rest. Thankfully French Aires (service stations) are well equipped with outside sinks which enabled me to do all I needed. Poor dog was in a bad way, foaming at the mouth, little legs shaking. I'd got a pet homeopathic first aid kit in the car, so I grabbed it and instinctively gave her some Nux Vomica. Within a few minutes she looked a lot calmer and the frothing at the mouth stopped. I gave her water and sat a while with her on the grass to give her plenty of time to recover and evacuate her bowels again if needed. She didn't, so I gave her a second dose of Nux so we could get back on the road.

Needless to say, the car stank, despite my best efforts at clean up. The dog took one whiff when I opened the back door and point blank refused to get back in. I had to pick her up and hurl her in or we would never have got anywhere. She wasn't impressed, and neither was I. Bloody pills. At home she's wormed monthly, but with a natural mixture made from oregano, wormwood and a host of other things. I'm glad the natural one doesn't have this effect on her. At least it would be a couple of days before she'd have to face the boat, hopefully she'd be alright by then.

I managed to get us to a rustic campsite near Poitiers. That evening, I had a Zoom call with David Charalambous and the other Council Watch Groups. He was going to talk to them about communication techniques, which he thought might help us with the Council. We just about got through the call before sunset. The rustic campsite proved a bit too rustic for my car and it got a puncture. The warning light came on as we pulled off. I stopped to check the tyres, but couldn't see anything. When I stopped for lunch, there was a free air pump so I topped up all the tyres, but none of them looked low and the warning light was still on.

Since there was nothing obvious, I decided not to worry about it. Getting to Calais was going to be a seven hour drive. Considering I didn't want to go home, I was certainly putting the effort in now that I was on the home stretch. I'd left on the 25th March and it was now 25th May...the time had come to return. I'd stretched it out as long as I could and now I just wanted to be home, in my own bed. The constant tyre warning light was concerning, would I make it to the late afternoon boat I'd booked with a dodgy tyre? It was a Saturday and garages weren't open...

# 27

# A New Career?

On the drive though France I'd been listening to Celia Imrie's 'Not Quite Nice' audiobook. It had been light-hearted and fun to listen to, especially considering I was driving through France, even though I hadn't made it anywhere near Nice. I found myself thinking what a lovely job it must be to write a fun book and then record the audiobook version, with all the different character voices.

Despite the constant threat the tyre warning light issued, we eventually arrived back at Calais. We got through Customs without bother, which was nothing short of a miracle considering how loaded up the car was with the things my parents decided they didn't want to risk shipping back with the couriers. We'd been so overloaded that poor Carinna had to do the journey to Tom's with all her belongings and a saucepan or two crammed in by her feet. The passenger wells by the dog were also full. It was a great relief we weren't searched. Not because there was anything dodgy, it was the re-packing I dreaded, and explanations for all the junk my car was filled with.

I finally got home about nine or ten pm. On waking the next morning after a lovely night's sleep, not in a tent, the idea that I ought to do audiobook narration popped into my head. It had occurred to me before as I'd done a small amount of voice-over work for a friend's husband when he needed an English accent for an advert. Audiobooks would be a lot more fun, especially if they were jolly like Celia Imrie's book.

I decided I'd have a go at trying it. The perfect book to practice on, of course, would be my Misadventures book. That would give me a good taste of doing it, and I'd soon know if it was something I was suited for. It certainly appealed to my introvert self. I could sit all day in my tiny homemade studio, where no one could bother me. The phone would have to be off. The more I thought about it, the more I liked the idea.

I ordered the sound proofing foam, which arrived as flat as a pancake and had to be soaked in a bathtub of hot water, wrung out and dried to re-inflate it before I could put it up. But by the first week of June, I'd converted my airing cupboard into a miniature recording studio. I didn't get a chance to start recording until July as there was so much work to do with Council videos and meetings. Just as I got going, we had a family holiday on the Isle of Wight, so recording had to pause. Recording an audiobook is a laborious process, but I enjoyed it. Reading about my epic 2013 road-trip in a campervan brought back a lot of nostalgia for a more innocent and happy time.

I was glad I'd been clueless about how the world was really run.

## A Green Invitation

June and July were a flurry of videos around the never ending 5G fiasco, the general election, and we were still heavily pushing for a climate discussion. I asked a friendly Green councillor in the next county if he would help find experts to speak on behalf of man-made climate change. He said he couldn't provide anyone because the condition about no computer modelling is like asking a brick layer to build a wall without in any mortar.

He said he was glad I wished to have a sensible discussion but that he wouldn't want to go anywhere near it if he'd been in our local Green Party. I thanked him and said, in that case, could they provide the information that's behind the computer models, or someone explaining how they worked? I told him we were looking for more than just predictions, we wanted the information behind them. I asked him to tell me what would make him go near it as a Green Party Councillor?

I got a rather astounding response to that question. He said, "The real issue for me is that this is becoming a trial of those that agreed a policy. If you wanted my take, if it were going to allow both views on this to come together you should allow the balance of scientists to be representative of the scientific community as a whole therefore if you fielded two scientists that believed that man-made $CO_2$ emissions have little or no effect on climate then you would need 16 to argue for. Anything less would give the wrong impression on those witnessing or viewing the debate."

He went on to add, "Given the country seems to be rioting at the drop of a hat on the basis of misinformation, quality information is a sometimes rare, but precious commodity. I share some of your frustrations and wish you well."

I replied, "You'd be most welcome to bring as many expert speakers as you like. However, we would have to divide the time for and against equally. The scientists we have lined up are actually part of the 97% consensus, as they both believe in climate change, they just don't think it's entirely man-made. In fact less than 1% of climate scientists agree with the IPCC (as you, dear reader, can see in the research paper breakdown here: https://co2coalition.org/2021/10/31/97-consensus-what-consensus/).

Though it's not the quantity of people, but the quality of the argument that counts. Science is not consensus. This is a simple presentation of facts, and then the audience can ask questions and make up their own mind. I thought you would jump at the chance to have experts put your views across in a constructive way. It's going to be critical moving forward that the population are on board with Net Zero, especially considering the financial implications of making it happen. You mention riots, how happy do you think the population is going to be when the cost of electricity goes up massively because of

Renewables, and they can't afford to heat their homes, or buy food?

You can't force Net Zero onto people, you have to show them it's necessary, and now is your chance. If no one is willing to put forward speakers, it does rather prove that the climate emergency is pure propaganda."

I didn't get any further responses from him.

Any expert with any degree of professional pride wants to prove their point. In my industry we get horticulturalists telling us that the only thing you need to make a good garden is plants, and as a garden designer I have a different view. You need good design, as well as plants. If I was called in to give a talk on why design is important in order to have a beautiful garden, I wouldn't need to bring fifteen other garden designers with me to prove that point, I can do it on my own. I do concede that garden design is a slightly less complex topic than climate change, but the point I'm making is that any professional that believes in what they are saying is more than happy to talk to people about it. And that's just on garden design, you are telling us we are destroying the planet. Surely that's worth someone's time to come out and prove it.

Our local Green Party councillor did respond on Twitter along similar lines saying, "I personally do not debate is there a climate emergency. Debating facts just creates a false impression about what is scientific consensus. However, what we should do to tackle the climate emergency would be a legitimate discussion."

My response, "we're not asking you to debate the facts, we're asking you to present them! What's behind the computer models? Why have scientists drawn those conclusions? If you're going to get people to go along with Net Zero, just telling us there's a climate emergency, the end, doesn't cut it."

He responded, "the point is 99% of scientific papers agree with man-made climate change. In that context, there is nothing to debate and doing so just creates a false impression that there are two legitimate views." Interesting word choice, if you dare to disagree, your point of view is not considered legitimate.

I went on to inform him that less than 1% of climate scientists agree with man-made climate change as set out by the IPCC. He then sent me an article from that trusted scientific source, Wikipedia, stating warming is all our fault. Another person chipped in with various name calling, instead of producing actual scientific papers, labelling my questions anti-science. Then a whole host of people showed this person the actual science, showing MODTRAN models, to which he said he was muting the conversation because it was becoming a crank-fest.

So, a typical day on social media, hurling insults and abuse instead of facts. Belief really is the enemy of knowing. It's funny, I tend to always assume I'm wrong about everything, which makes me triple check. After, the insult hurler had sent me a very well put together video by someone who debunked Climate The Movie that Tom Nelson had been the producer of. I sent the video to Paul Burgess and Ralph Ellis.

They both instantly debunked the debunking and showed all the falsehoods and misleading information in the video. Paul left me numerous voice messages with how awful the video had been, and Ralph wrote a long email covering the first ten minutes of the video showing how flawed it had all been. When I next spoke with Paul, we were chatting away about how few people understand climate change. He told me that I was a better scientist than most of the so-called climate experts he's had to debate on TV. I burst out laughing. He told me he was serious. He said, "You think like a scientist. And you're willing to think you're wrong and want to discover the truth."

Paul went on to say that if he's wrong on something, he'd rather someone correct his ignorance so that he can learn, and he said that he could see the same trait in me. He's right, I'd rather know I've got something wrong and correct it than stay stuck in ignorance.

I still hated talking about climate, I was painfully aware I didn't know enough. But the interviews kept coming. TNT were back in touch for the third time. Former MP, Lembit Öpik wanted me on his breakfast show to discuss the warmest June on record. Not a scenario I'd ever imagined. Luckily for me, he was a good interviewer, thoughtful as well as knowledgeable on climate.

In the interview I spoke about my favourite climate paper from the CERES group, headed up by

Dr Willie Soon, Dr Ronan Connelly and Dr Michael Connelly. The CERES team, which comprises of thirty-eight independently funded scientists from all over the world with different views, had compared urban temperatures with rural ones. Surprisingly, urban areas only make up 2-4% of the earth's surface. Only 5% of weather stations are rural.

When they say the hottest June on record since records began, what they aren't taking into consideration is that those early weather stations were on the outskirts of towns. Then as urban areas grew, those once rural stations ended up in urban areas where temperatures are thirty percent higher than the adjustments the IPCC made. At the end of the interview, Lembit invited me back to join him on his Saturday show when we would be able to discuss climate for a whole hour. I said it would be better if he got Dr Connelly on who could give him the science. He insisted he would get scientists on, but he liked the way I explained things as well.

In my conversation with Paul Burgess, he picked me up on it and said, "You explain things in a way that people can understand. The scientists can be too dry and hard to listen to." I explained that all I was able to do was regurgitate the information in a palatable format, but I was very uncomfortable that I did not understand it at a deeper level. It felt dangerous to me to be explaining things without a deep understanding of how the mechanisms worked. Paul said he was happy to explain anything whenever I had a question. He wanted me to continue. I wasn't as keen, but I valued his offer to help me gain a better understanding. He and Ralph had been invaluable with all the help they'd given me.

I decided though that I couldn't keep taking up Paul and Ralph's time. They'd both been so incredibly generous for every speech and video I'd made on climate. I'd run it by one, or both, of them. Paul was trying to make videos to educate the masses, and it wasn't fair for him to have to spend an hour on the phone to me. There was only one thing for it. I'd have to make a concerted effort to learn it for myself. From then on, every morning when I walked the dog, I'd play one or two of Paul's videos, starting from the very first one that he made on climate. I'd spend an hour everyday educating myself. So, when the opportunity to join an advanced climate science class came along, I jumped at it.

Talking of Ralph, I got to see him again when Climate The Movie producer, Tom Nelson came to London and invited us to meet him for what he termed a 'Climate Realists' lunch, along with Tilak Doshi, a contributor at Forbes (until he questioned climate alarmism too much) and Martyn Love, an engineer and a fellow campaigner against EVs.

Tom treated us to a lovely lunch at The Hansom in the iconic St. Pancras Renaissance Hotel. It's situated in what was once the cobbled entrance to the original St. Pancras station. It's a stunning atrium with a wonderful high-vaulted glass ceiling. The cosy seating areas are flooded with natural light, that the floor-to-ceiling windows and atrium ceiling provides. The Marriot-owned venue is a sight to behold. I particularly liked the giant pots filled with plants.

Whilst they were nowhere near the scale of the Atocha station in Madrid, they were still a wonderful addition to the ambience of the amazing venue Tom had chosen.

It was wonderful meeting to discuss the climate so freely with knowledgeable people who really understand the subject, and who are opposed to climate alarmism fearporn, which is constantly spread by the mainstream media. It was an uplifting day, and it was nice to properly catch up with Tom and Ralph again, as well as meeting Tilak and Martyn.

### Laughter Fest 2.0?

In early August, Carinna and I were incredibly lucky to be invited back to the Shine Seminars as Eli's guest again. We jumped at the chance of another fun-filled weekend away in Gloucestershire. Though we did say on the way down that though there was no way it could possibly live up to the year before, we were sure we'd enjoy it nonetheless. We also hoped we'd manage to walk past the composting toilets this time without erupting into fits of laughter. Surely, we couldn't still find the incident with the third party as funny as it had been at the time?

We arrived and picked the same camping spot as the year before, away from everyone else, just in case the giggles started. The event was much busier this time as it was a four-day event and the weather was better than the year before, so we did end up with neighbours and hoped we wouldn't drive them insane if it did turn into the laughter-fest of the year before.

Many of the people we'd met from the previous year were there, along with the familiar faces of Sandi Adams, Richard Vobes and his partner, the lovely Julia, Ian Jarvis, Clive de Carle and many more. As it was close to Gloucester, one evening we met up with Matthew Randolph, who the Channel had done the fundraiser for to run for the Police and Crimes Commissioner, and his friend Saskia. It was great to meet them and catch up on all of Matthew's exploits. Although he'd not been successful, he had certainly put the wind up the establishment and was continuing to do so with much enthusiasm.

It was another wonderful weekend away. Thankfully, we had managed to get over laughing every time we passed the composting toilets, but there was plenty more for us to find amusing. In part, thanks to a particularly tyrannical councillor in Devon.

Before we'd left, I'd recorded a video intro for some footage I'd been sent from a council in Devon, from a district called Teignbridge. It was the most unbelievable meeting I'd ever witnessed, and that's saying something after the hundreds of hours of council meetings I'd sat through in the last eighteen months. This featured various members of the public trying to make sure the Council provided female-only changing facilities at the leisure centre, which was being refurbished.

Every time one of the women raised a concern, the Chair of the meeting would immediately cut them off. Other councillors protested, especially when she misquoted the Equality Act, but she wouldn't accept their points of order. This woman was completely out of control. She was incredibly dismissive about the points they raised and only seemed interested in protecting vulnerable characteristics of a minority group, rather than women and children.

The meeting spiralled out of control, and in the middle, one of the councillors, who suffered from Tourette's, had a bit of an outburst. It was beautifully timed, and he probably articulated what a lot of people were thinking, but couldn't dare voice. The whole meeting was completely surreal. It played out like a sketch that was a cross between Little Britain and The Office.

Because I was going away that weekend, I'd run out of time to edit and upload the video I was working on, so I thought I'd give it one more round of editing when we arrived, and then upload it to the Council Watch channel. On the drive to Gloucester, I started to think about the content. Something was niggling away at me.

Initially, I'd not particularly wanted to tackle the trans debate on the Council Watch channel. We were already fighting so many other battles, it was the last thing I wanted to add to our load. Plus, I'd known trans people a decade earlier who were not a problem to women, and nor would they ever be.

I'd been contacted some months earlier by a lady who goes by the name of 'Colchester Mum' on Twitter. She had some disturbing things to tell me about the Mercury Theatre, which the Council were in-part funding. The Mercury had allowed a band who actively promote violence against women, singing about 'kicking TERFs' (which is an acronym for trans-exclusionary radical feminist) to play to children of all ages as part of their tour. Many of their song lyrics are highly unsuitable for children. They were also allowing men to use the women's toilets.

I met up with Colchester Mum, and she told me about the families she knew whose children had been groomed at school to become trans. In my ignorance, I had assumed it was a trend and kids were jumping on the bandwagon because of influencers on social media and mainstream media. I had no idea they were being preyed upon at school, and other organisations. I've since had what she told me confirmed by several others.

I also hadn't realised how homophobic this push for trans is, doing everything to persuade those questioning their sexuality that they aren't gay, they've just been born in the wrong body.

Colchester Mum told me that adults in schools were targeting the less popular kids, those with learning difficulties or on the spectrum and those questioning their sexuality. The kids would suddenly get loads of attention, everyone telling them how special there were if they assumed the trans identity.

She had said she'd spoken in-depth to people who'd been convinced they were trans, had the surgery and now regretted it and had de-transitioned. The person I had known a decade earlier had been a grown adult when they'd decided to have the surgery. They had to have a full-psych evaluation and counselling before surgery to make sure they knew what they were doing. The thought of vulnerable teens and younger children being preyed on by organisations and individuals, left me horrified.

I'd been a tomboy growing up. My childhood was spent climbing trees, den building and go-carting with the four boys who lived next-door. I had learning difficulties and was not one of the uber-fashionable popular kids, so I would have mostly likely been targeted. I felt sick to my stomach by the time Colchester Mum had finished telling me about the children she knew who'd been brainwashed by what she described as a cult.

When the Olympics came and I saw what was happening in sports like boxing, with biological men thumping the living daylights out of female opponents, I immediately changed my tune. We would definitely be covering the trans debate now. Enough was enough.

I'd had long conversations about the surgery with the trans person I had known, and everything they'd gone through afterwards with discrimination and threats. The person in question was a kind and thoughtful person who was tormented by the belief they'd been born in the wrong body. The amount of surgery and the effects are brutal, it's not a decision which should be taken lightly, nor had things worked as advertised. They just wanted to be left in peace to live their life. This was not someone who was pretending for kicks, or who wanted to dominate women.

So, I wanted to make it clear in the video that many of the so called 'trans' were merely men with fetishes using the trans identity as a way to gain access to women and girls. It had been niggling away at me on the drive down that it wasn't clear enough from the footage that this is what has been happening. So, by the time we arrived in Gloucester, I'd made the decision to add something to the end of the Teignbridge video. The issue now was how to film it. I'd fortunately packed the same shirt I'd worn for the intro. Trouble was, now we were parked in a field with sheep adjacent to us, and the only space to film was inside Carinna's tent, which was blowing around in the wind.

It also meant I'd created a mountain of extra editing to do on top of what already needed to be done. So much for having a weekend break! I suppose I could have waited, but it was a Bank Holiday weekend, and it felt like the perfect time to put it out there. This was a video which needed to be seen. I had to film the ending several times because I just wasn't happy with how it had come out, and I kept thinking of other things that needed to go in. So much for this being a quick, easy video.

I persevered and did the editing every time we had a spare moment. Although meals were included in the camping we'd paid for, one of the evenings the chef was delayed and the queue so long that we'd dashed to the pub to eat instead, as we were both starving and couldn't wait any longer. This meant we were back nice and early so I thought I could probably get the video finished and out.

Carinna was sitting next to me while I was editing and did try to control herself, but when you're doing edits you often end up playing the same bits several times. By the third time she'd heard the meeting Chair indignantly say, "I'm not being sat in this chair for my own glory, I'm not sat here to advance anything in my own life, I could have taken up crocheting!" Carinna couldn't contain herself any longer and roared with laughter, which had us both in convulsions, nearly wetting ourselves laughing.

I immediately had the idea to record Carinna's glorious all-encompassing laughter. It occurred to me that I could lay it over the video soundtrack, so I played it again and the part that made her laugh even more than the crocheting suggestion when the Chair declared, with equal indignation to other councillors pulling her up on her poor chairing of the meeting, "I'm not here to absorb abuse and I'm not going to be standing for it, or sitting for it!" I just about managed to capture it all but my sides were hurting so much with laughing I could barely hold onto the laptop I'd got aimed at Carinna to record her laughter. We both had tears running down our faces.

Editing became neigh impossible after that. In between the tears and laughter seizures, I begged her, "Please stop laughing, I don't think my pelvic floor is strong enough for this!" Which of course, made her laugh even more...

We eventually calmed down enough for me to get the video done and I uploaded it on the Sunday morning before we headed for our morning sauna. I was pleased to have got it done and uploaded and I could completely relax now that I didn't have that hanging over me to finish. On our way to the sauna one of people camping nearby came up to us and said, "Which one of you has that laugh?" I immediately pointed to Carinna.

He said, "Please don't stop, you light up the whole campsite with that laugh!" He wasn't wrong, Carinna has the most contagious laughter. Any time away with her usually means aching rib and diaphragm muscles for days afterwards.

We were halfway to the sauna when Carinna realised she hadn't got any water and also wanted to take her glasses off. She said she wouldn't be long and to go on ahead. When I got into the sauna there were two naked men sitting there displaying all and sundry. There's always someone starkers in a sauna, which is a bit off-putting. I don't particularly want to see anyone naked in a sauna, regardless of what sex they are. At least Carinna would be along any moment to even up the numbers.

I did inwardly chuckle that I'd literally only just uploaded a video about women not wanting to be exposed to naked men and here I was entering a room with two naked men. I wondered if it would register with Carinna when she came in. Speak of the devil, I could hear the external door, which opened into the shower cubicle section, thank goodness.

When the internal sauna door opened, it wasn't Carinna it was another naked man. I was getting quite a collection. What on earth. Was it international nudist day or something? I'd not seen any signs on the door. Another few minutes passed, still no sign of Carinna.

The door opened again. It was another naked man. This one walked in and immediately said, "Hello, Rachel, I'm a big fan of your Council Watch!" I managed to stop myself saying, "Yes, I can see that!" Instead, we started chatting about councils.

Where the bloody hell was Carinna? I knew she wasn't great with her time awareness skills, but this was getting ridiculous. I'm good at faffing, but Carinna is master level. She's also a master at chit-chatting to random strangers for extended periods of time. A skill I don't possess. Two or three sentences of small talk is usually about my limit.

Finally, the door opened once more...

Unbelievably, it still wasn't Carinna. Yes, you've guessed it, I kid you not, another naked bloke. Everyone had to shuffle up to accommodate his large frame. So, there I was, completely surrounded by naked men having only just uploaded a video on women not wanting to see penises in leisure centre changing rooms. In every single direction there they were. Five of them to be precise, in a room the size of a broom cupboard. Oh the irony.

The difference of course, is that I had chosen this, well, kinda. I knew I was going into a mixed facility where there was a likelihood someone would be starkers. Especially as a lot of people aren't expecting there to be a sauna at an event like this and don't have swimwear, so rather than get their pants sweaty, they opt to go starkers. It wasn't quite as mixed as I had anticipated, partly due to the AWOL

Carinna, but I had made the decision to put myself in an environment where there was the possibility of male nakedness.

It's a very different scenario to women and girls getting changed after a swim, in what should be a female-only space, to be confronted by some bloke pretending to be a woman because of a fetish, and getting his rocks off because of the intimidation and distress his presence causes. The councillors' argument is that predatory men can easily walk into a female-only space, so therefore it makes no difference having a mixed gender facility, as long as there are cubicles for privacy. However, The Times newspaper researched Town Council sports centres and swimming pools, and found that ninety percent of the issues reported were in unisex changing rooms.

Exposing themselves is not something any of the transgender people I have known would do. They didn't have anything to do it with for a start, but even so, it wasn't in their nature in the first place. I'm talking about those men who pretend they are transgender purely to gain access to women and girls.

I get a lot of abuse from people who say there is no such thing as transgender and I do understand where they are coming from. But equally, I've had long conversations with those whose lived experience and belief is that they have been born in the wrong body. Just because I have compassion for the torment that belief brings people, doesn't mean to say I agree with the surgery. I don't. A decade ago, I had a medical professional tell me just how many health problems happen as a result of taking the hormones which go with gender reassignment surgery. But if someone has already had the surgery, I accept them as they are. It's not my place to judge them over their life choices, even if I have concerns over the health aspects.

The online abuse I've received because I have expressed compassion for those who believe they have been born in the wrong body and that I can see a difference between them and the opportunistic fetishists, is off the charts. I'm also very aware that sometimes the reason for the surgery is because of sexual abuse as a child. The day I cannot feel compassion for a small boy or girl who was raped, and then as an adult choses to have gender reassignment surgery because they want to disassociate from the body which was abused, when no amount of surgery is going to truly fix that level of trauma, will be a very dark day. It also doesn't mean I don't understand why women don't want any biological men, no matter how they identify, in their women-only spaces. I do see it from all sides, but first and foremost, women's rights cannot be taken away to accommodate men, however they may identify.

But anyway, back to the crammed naked bloke sauna... the problem with naked people of any gender, regardless of how they identify, especially in a small sauna is where to rest one's eyes. With shelved seating you can't look up, and you can't look down. When the sauna is as full as it was now, there simply isn't anywhere you can look, so you end up having to maintain eye contact with whoever you are talking to for way longer than is comfortable simply because you daren't look anywhere else.

Still no sign of, Carinna!

The door opened again, surely this must be her... No. For crying out loud! It was another man but at least he had his underpants on. He took one look at the packed naked bloke sauna with me primly sitting bolt upright in the middle, in my bikini and he about-turned and muttered that he'd try again later.

By the time Carinna did eventually bless us with her presence, it was beyond comical. She opened the door to see me sitting there tightly squished into a room full of naked men. What were the odds of a naked full house? I had inadvertently won the naked men lottery. I knew it would take a moment for Carinna's eyes to adjust to the low light levels, especially without her glasses. It was just a matter of time till the penny dropped.

One of the naked blokes took Carinna's arrival as his cue to leave and I could see realisation beginning to dawn on her face as he squished past her in the cramped space, now her low light adjusted eyes took in the scene. I shot her a look that conveyed 'what took you so long?', combined with a tilt of the head and raising of eyebrows indicating there's a lot of naked men in here!

Had I thought of it, I should have got up and insisted she have my seat so that she too could enjoy the delights of being sandwiched in a room packed with naked men. My kindness holds no bounds for situations such as these. It's what friends are for, sharing life experiences. But alas, I didn't think of it until afterwards.

I decided to avert my 'I'm not impressed with how long it took you to get here' gaze away from her because I knew it wouldn't take much to make her get the giggles and then we'd both be in fits at the situation we now found ourselves in. It's doubtful the naked men would have appreciated us being unable to stop laughing at their nakedness.

It always amazes me just how many people of both sexes go naked in saunas. I have no issue with naked bodies, other than very few people have one you'd want to see. I'm not entirely sure what the etiquette is. Do they want people to look at them or do they not care either way? Is it rude not looking when someone brazenly presents their naked form in front of you? I've no idea. I do know I'm very selective over who I want to see naked. So, for future reference, if I've not specifically requested to see you naked, it's a very safe bet, I don't want to.

When the numbers reduced, Carinna whispered to me, "Well that was unexpected!" I shot her another look.

"Yes, as was the time it took you to get in here!"

"Oh, I decided to go and clean my teeth and then got chatting to someone going back to the tent."

My first book had an unwanted-naked-people-encounter at the end of it and here we were again. Thank goodness this one didn't involve the breaking-the-sound-barrier loud farts from the delightful man on the beach.

## Dire Finances

I completed recording my Misadventures audiobook not long after we'd got back from Gloucester and released it on my own website, as well as via the Spotify platform, who delivered it everywhere including on Audible. Whilst it sold well on my own website, it didn't do anything on the other platforms. I hadn't realised what a big chunk Amazon would take. They are good on Kindle books, but on Audible you don't get much at all. Unless you have a runaway best-seller, it's not going to be a backup earner.

I'd enjoyed the experience of recording it, but finances were getting quite serious. I couldn't continue with Council Watch for any longer, plus with the 5G videos still going, it was becoming draining. A sure sign I needed to quit. So, I did. I told everyone I'd had enough and that was it, I was going to call it a day at the end of October.

That was certainly the intention, right up until I received a direct message on Twitter from one of the councillors asking me to please phone him.

# 28

# Implausible Emergency

I knew it was going to mean more work before I'd even picked up the phone. Scrutiny Chairman, Darius Laws, informed me that on 12th November the Panel were going to be scrutinising the Council's Climate Emergency. Darius suggested I bring along four speakers as he wanted us to finally get the airtime we'd been asking for over the previous eighteen months. He said he didn't know about climate, but was genuinely curious to hear more. He'd taken the liberty of booking us four speaking slots out of the maximum of eight which was allowed.

Whilst I knew there and then that it was going to be a complete waste of time, I appreciated his efforts and being true to his pre-election promises, not something many manage, so I agreed. At least it wouldn't be me speaking this time. I'd only got two experts lined up, but with the climate class group I'd joined, I knew who to ask to get more and I had a bold idea on precisely who I wanted.

I'd had the wobbles about joining the weekly advanced climate classes. I'd really wanted to learn more, but I knew I'd likely be very out of my depth.

The tutor, David Siegel, said participants should have a Masters degree level of education. I didn't. I have trained myself over the years not to talk down to myself, but before I could stop it, reading the climate class signup page, the old unwelcome voice piped up, "this ain't for you darling!".

Being dyslexic has always made learning difficult. Information goes in and then falls off a cliff in my head. It may or may not surface again sometime later. My mother puts it down to my impatience. I never crawled as a child, I just grabbed hold of the sofa one day, hoofed myself up and off I walked. To be fair to young me, no one else was on their hands and knees crawling around the floor, so why would I?

Apparently crawling is a very vital stage of wiring the hemispheres in neuro-development. By today's standards, most people wouldn't notice my dyslexia because I grew out of the worst of it. I'm probably the only one who notices the residual difficulties. My editor is probably muttering at this point, as grammar is tricky when you're not a 'words' person.

By the time the climate class came along, TNT had announced they were shutting down. I hadn't wanted to do a whole hour on discussing climate without knowing what I was talking about and had postponed the interview with Lembit. It had been one of my main drivers for joining the class. Without the TNT interview looming, I didn't need to do the class. Curious Me, the one who wants to know how everything works, was still quite insistent that even if

I never had to speak about climate ever again, she wanted to know.

Financially it was crazy to sign up to a class I could ill-afford, but yet, Curious Me would not be silenced, she wanted to know and that's all there was to it. Like an itch that needed to be scratched once and for all. I reluctantly signed up, thinking this was insane, that I wouldn't understand most of what was said but reasoned, even if I can only grasp ten percent, it will be ten percent more than I knew then.

As it turns out, I haven't been anywhere near as out of my depth as I'd envisaged. Yes, there are some of the science bits which go over my head, but on the whole, I've been OK. David has since taken the Masters degree part off the sales page as I told him I very nearly didn't sign up because of it.

Each week, David would line up expert guest speakers to give the group a talk on a specific aspect of how the climate is considered to work. No one truly understands all the drivers, but some aspects have very obvious cycles. It can get a little complicated when various cycles coincide, but nonetheless a lot is known. I learned more in the first two weeks of David's classes than I had in a whole year on my own. It became very obvious, very quickly, that $CO_2$ is not the primary driver for temperature.

The week prior to the phone call from Darius, I'd attended a lecture with one of my favourite climate experts, Greg Wrightestone - CEO of the $CO_2$ Coalition, a non-profit science-based, educational organisation, who discuss climate issues and the beneficial aspects of $CO_2$. Greg had worked for the IPCC reviewing the climate papers. He'd written the book 'Inconvenient Facts', which we'd held up and referenced in our council meetings. He was a really lovely man, so I felt that because we'd already mentioned him to the Council, it would be incredible if we could get him to address them. David gave me his email address and I asked if he'd be one of our four speakers.

He agreed and asked if I needed anyone else. I did indeed. Other than who'd I'd already lined up, Paul Burgess, Ralph Ellis and now Greg, the person I'd want most in the world would be physicist, Dr William Happer of Princeton University. Dr Happer is a genius, and should be as famous as Stephen Hawkins. He probably would be had so much of his work not been classified.

Dr Happer has directly served under two US Presidents and been an advisor to two more. He's also the man who got Reagan's Star Wars Programme up to work when no one else could figure out how to get the laser beam effectively through the atmospheric distortions. To my immense surprise and thrill, that is exactly who Greg asked!

Remarkably, Dr Happer also agreed to speak at Colchester Council. The email from him came through just as Carinna and I left to go to Bristol to the UK Column Live event. This was nothing short of incredible. To have this calibre of experts willing to speak to the councillors. Even the Council would struggle to not accept a man as brilliant as Dr Happer, who had helped five US Presidents. People often tried to discredit him by saying he was funded by big oil, which wasn't true.

The Council wanted to know the bios of who would be speaking. I duly provided them, but when they realised they'd be speaking via Zoom, Councillor Laws was informed this wasn't possible for 'Have Your Say' speakers to do this. A new rule apparently from when they'd made changes earlier in the year. I did point out that the distance the speakers would have to travel to get here would be a lot of air miles and did they really want people to fly and drive long distances when they believed there was a climate emergency?

Of course, that got me absolutely nowhere, but I can never resist pointing out hypocrisy whenever I get the opportunity. I then had the idea to see if they could come in as guest expert speakers and not as speakers to 'Have Your Say'. The Council have expert speakers all the time via Zoom. Councillor Laws pushed hard for this, and the Council did eventually agree, as long as the members of the Scrutiny Panel didn't object. The Scrutiny Panel comprised of opposition councillors to the Lib Dems, so was an awkward mix of blue and red team councillors. By this point it was late Friday night, which meant we wouldn't find out until Monday, which didn't leave our experts much time to prepare.

We'd also need precise times. Dr Happer's schedule is very busy, as is Greg's, so it was going to be quite a logistical miracle providing a time slot away from the 'Have Your Say' part of the meeting. Councillor Laws informed me that the Council had now added the green bin collection issues at the beginning of the agenda, and who knows how long that was going to take. It was proving to be an impossible situation.

Greg got in touch with me on Sunday asking if it was going ahead. He said that he and Dr Happer were at a convention in California and when they'd told the scientists over dinner that they were planning on speaking to Colchester Council in England, two of them turned round and said what big fans they were of mine!! Well that just blew me away, and them too, I think.

I knew in my heart it wasn't going to happen long before it was confirmed. They hadn't been able to get in touch with everyone to authorise the expert speakers. So, guess who was going to have to go in and speak. And I had to provide my full speech by midday.

It's probably the quickest speech I've ever written, and I got it to them at ten minutes to twelve. They confirmed that they had received it, and informed me I could speak the following evening.

Here's what I wrote. Read it in the tone of voice of someone who doesn't want to be there when they should be speaking to highly qualified scientists...

*"Good evening.*

*To properly scrutinise the Council's climate emergency, you must evidence what the reduction in global temperatures will be, as a result of spending millions of tax payers' money to reach your Net Zero goals.*

*You must also define the exact parameters of the climate emergency, or how will anyone know when it's over?*

*Considering neither the IPCC, nor the UK Government has formally declared a climate emergency, why have you? Who here is qualified to make that judgement?*

*The IPCC Policy Maker's report is listed in the Council's references. It is written by politicians who vote on each sentence, which makes it very different from the full report that's written by scientists. Paul Burgess shows this in a video he created for you with the latest AR6 report, which shows there isn't a signature of anthropogenic emissions in extreme weather events. So, where is the claimed emergency?*

*Your update report states the Council voted unanimously to declare a climate emergency in 2019, but what about now, with only 20 of those councillors remaining?*

*Those that voted were not given any evidence, they were left to do their own research. How many did? Or like most people, did they rely on the misleading mainstream media?*

*Do any of you know $CO_2$'s ability to cause warming is inversely logarithmic? Or what an emission height is?*

*Or how much of the infrared spectrum can be absorbed and emitted by $CO_2$, compared to water vapour? Because if you don't understand these basics, how can you possibly make informed decisions? It's a shame the highly qualified experts we had lined up to talk to you tonight weren't allowed. Rather ironic that Council insist $CO_2$ experts travel long distances, instead of using Zoom!*

*The offer is still there for you to speak directly with experts who've worked for the IPCC & written peer-reviewed climate papers -because you do need expert advice that hasn't been funded by those who profit from the 4 billion dollar-a-day*

*Net Zero industry, or unelected and unaccountable organisations like the UN, with agendas that don't serve us.*

*We do need to make decisions that protect the planet and not create worse pollution & destruction, mining rare earth minerals for EVs & renewables, creating millions of tonnes of waste that is too expensive or hard to recycle.*

*The Government's NESO report shows Net Zero will cost every household in the UK thousands per annum in increased bills. Whilst your climate emergency may have the best of intentions, the road to hell is paved with those, so you really do need to scrutinise this properly, or we will all be paying a very high price. We'll lose our valuable farmland, our beautiful countryside, our self-sufficiency, and our freedom, all because of listening to fear mongering instead of facts."*

The Scrutiny Chairman told me, "I have noted what you've said. I'm sure we're going to tackle some of this during the course of this evening at the latter part. I am wide open to this discussion and I also note that in the desire to provide us with apparent green energy the Government is crashing ahead with producing pylons made in Germany and China, and copper not made in this country, to put pylons all over East Anglia blighting the countryside, ripping up hedgerows, killing birds, frankly crushing the rural tourist economy in East Anglia in the event to do it.

So, I am with you with some of these concerns. I'm not an expert either, though you did kindly offer to provide some experts, it was a practicality challenge - we have to consult with every member around here in order to bring external guests in. I have to have a majority in favour of doing that. I wasn't able to get that simply because time ran away from us. It wasn't an attempt by anyone to not allow experts to come here and it may be the case that as a consequence of tonight a subsequent meeting happens in this forum in which we do have a bit more time to process who could come in and speak. I'm very open to hearing them, so there's no attempt to quash conversations from my end."

He asked me if I'd like to respond.

I replied regarding their recent council office refurbishment which was mentioned in the meeting agenda. "You've spent 1.6 million on LED lights and ventilation and an air source heat pump for one building. This Council is heading towards bankruptcy and when you think you don't even have enough money to keep the toilets open in Castle Park (£5,500) so you must get your officers to put in real terms what the difference in temperature is because on that building you've got To Be Confirmed so you don't even know (how much $CO_2$ you'll save, let alone the difference to temperature it will make). You've spent £1.6 million, and yes £528,000 was a Government grant, but where did that money come from? It's still taxpayer money and you have no idea what you are doing, so what difference that is going to make.

You need evidence-based decisions, or this is misappropriation of public funds, so you really do need to scrutinise this properly because it is utterly ridiculous!"

When I got up from my chair, an environmental

campaigner said rather loudly to me, in his broad Northern accent "You're speaking out your backside!" Little did he know the number of months of research that had gone into this. He was also completely blind to the fact that I was trying to help the environment by not having every last part of the earth dug up, destroyed and polluted by mining for rare earth minerals, which in turn would cause millions of tonnes of hard-to-recycle waste at the end of their short life.

We all got up and left them to it and went for dinner. There was no point in sitting through hours of pointless waffle. While I was at dinner, my phone started pinging. One of the Council Watchers, Martin from Richmond Council Watch, had the fortitude to carry on watching after we'd left and had some surprising things to report.

Councillor Willets had told the panel, "I sit here perplexed this evening. I thought we had an emergency and this was our decision. It wasn't anything to do with national politics, it was our decision that the Council would be carbon neutral by 2030. I looked up the definition of an emergency earlier, the UN definition - 'an emergency is an urgent unexpected and usually dangerous situation that poses immediate risk to health, life, property, environment and requires immediate action.'

I don't think what we're talking about this evening is an emergency at all. I think we were just carried away and it may have been okay at the time, but perhaps we need to reconsider whether we're talking about emergencies, or whether we're talking about sensible management action, and it may be disappointing for the Scrutiny Panel to suggest that to Cabinet, because I'm sure there are one or two activists who really believe we should have the superglue out, but I think for most of us, we've been convinced by two presentations this evening that setting the target of 2030 is perhaps not the best way.

A climate change policy, rather than an emergency, because I don't believe we've got an emergency. I don't believe we want one either."

The Chairman then said, "I think you know we all want in this room for there to be clean air. We all want clean water and we all want to be able to celebrate the beautiful landscape and countryside that we live in. I find the word solar farm a slight oxymoron. It's not a farm, and I'm not convinced about where solar equipment is made, how it's made, and the impact on the environment etc., but I'll leave that.

Scrutiny notes that the definition of the word emergency dictates that Council is missing its own self-imposed objective, and their significant Capital budgets are identified to assist with the carbon reduction schemes. If Cabinet is unable to achieve this, it should consider reconsulting with Full Council to ascertain if the will of Council is to consider this an emergency, as opposed to managing opportunities to reduce carbon and improve our environment and public realm within existing budgetary framework and business plans sure.

So that was my formal recommendation, do I see all those in favour? I see four. Okay, I see all those against and I see abstentions. Okay thank you. Four in favour, two abstentions. So that motion is carried."

What a surprise, I didn't think that would happen. Now I don't doubt for one minute the real reason they are questioning the emergency has only a tiny amount to do with us and more to do with the reality of the situation that they are nowhere near their targets and they're spending a fortune getting nowhere. Basically, reality has hit, and they can see this isn't possible.

I knew not to get my hopes up because the Lib Dem Cabinet would be the ones the following week to decide if they were going to put their beloved climate emergency back to full Council to vote on, or not.

The following day, Councillor Laws messaged me to suggest I go along and speak to the Cabinet two weeks later. I told him that was a bad idea. Let's just say we know a few Council insiders. Several have reported back that those in charge hate us and hold us in the highest levels of contempt. As much as I felt it was a waste of time, I thought that if none of the usual faces were there, it would be less antagonistic and they would be more likely to back down, if that slim possibility was at all likely. I didn't want it turning into a battle of egos. Let's make it as easy as possible for them to reconsider their position. I called on two people the Council hadn't seen before, and we worked on their speeches.

In the meantime, the next big event was the farmers' protest in London over the inheritance tax issue. It was a drizzly day, but several of us went along to support from Colchester. We'd also arranged to meet up with lots of people we knew, but it was so packed and mobile phone signal was almost non-existent, that it became almost impossible. Carinna and I missed the first train, but managed to find Cheryl at least and a couple of others.

Jeremy Clarkson struggled on stage with his bad back, and gave a great speech right up until the end, when he begged the Government to be better. From then it went further downhill, with various insincere sounding politicians taking to the stage. Despite the drizzle, between forty to sixty thousand people turned out, though the mainstream media tried to play it down by saying it was ten to twenty thousand. The photographs painted a truer picture. I did a video reporting our experiences and put it on the Council Watch YouTube channel.

The other interesting event was a petition, which took off like wildfire, to call for another general election. We all knew the petition was a waste of time, but it was still fun to see it take off at such a pace, as well as uniting people. The new Labour government under Kier Starmer was not proving to be popular. Not surprising having gone back on so many election promises so quickly. At least the other parties have the good grace to wait a while before they shaft the population when in power. Labour wasted no time in showing their true colours, with taking away the pensioners' winter fuel allowance, accepting more freebies in the first few weeks than the last few Labour governments put together, and of course penalising the farmers with IHT, to name but a few.

Cartoonist Bob Moran, who Carinna and I met and got an autographed book from at the UK Column Live Event in Bristol, had drawn the perfect image. The cartoon showed a JCB with a wrecking ball with Rishi Sunak getting out of it and throwing the keys over to, 'Starmer the Farmer Harmer' as he was now known. Like many of us, Bob sees through the left-right charade and all the rest. He lost his job at the Telegraph because he had the courage and bravery to challenge the mainstream narrative. His book is an illustrated testament to all the crazy.

The following week it was time for the Cabinet meeting to see if they would take the advice of the Scrutiny Panel, and put their self-declared climate emergency back to full Council to vote on again. It was touch and go whether either of the two speakers I'd lined up were going to make it as Steven had a bad accident slipping on glass and his wrist required surgery. Our other speaker, David, had not long come out of hospital and was going in the day before for a check-up for heart surgery. He hoped they wouldn't keep him in like the last time he'd gone in. Thankfully both our speakers were OK on the day.

David was the first to speak. We tied his medical condition into his speech.

*"As a pensioner, I'm deeply concerned about the future and how we're supposed to be able to afford to pay our bills. The cost of electricity is ever-increasing, largely because of the push for renewables, as well as carbon tax. Out of £114*

electricity from gas power stations costs, £60 is carbon tax, which is more than the gas itself!

As pointed out in the latest NESO report, there is no viable long-term storage for renewables, so gas power stations are essential as backup. We have to pay for these stations to run all the time, as well as the cost of renewable energy. We also have to pay for wind power, even when we're not able to use it, or store it. And even then, the report says we're going to have energy rationing and blackouts.

So, if we need to keep the gas on, it's impossible to ever reach Net Zero! And what real difference will it make anyway? Technically, we are still in an ice-age and it's the coldest period for over 10,000 years. Warming is not unexpected! Climate is always changing! I'm yet to be convinced this time it's down to us. It seems like a big money-spinner and a crazy one at that.

Canada, for example, exports coal to China, which they burn in their coal power stations to produce the electricity needed to make solar panels, which then get shipped back to Canada! How is this saving the planet? And what's going to happen to all these panels at their end of life? It costs more to recycle them than to make them - who foots that bill?

I've had a heart condition since I was a child. I was what's known as a 'blue baby'. I've had multiple surgeries growing up, and I'm due for more soon to replace 3 valves. It's a struggle for me to stay warm at the best of times. Without the winter fuel allowance, it's even harder. How are we supposed to afford all this?

I'd like to know how much more taxpayers' money this Council intends to spend reaching its Net Zero goals? Has anyone here worked out if your climate emergency measures are making any difference at all to global temperatures? If you can't prove they are making a difference, then you need to stop wasting money. We've families who are homeless, a cost-of-living crisis, and no one can afford council tax increases."

Next up was Steven. I watched from home, hoping the strong painkillers he was on for his wrist surgery didn't interfere with his reading abilities.

*"I'd like to start by thanking the Council for reviewing the climate emergency declaration.*

*In 2012, the Government estimated reaching Net Zero would cost the UK around 1.25 trillion pounds (£44k per household). A more realistic current figure is 4 trillion which is £140k per household. That is a lot of money to spend on a theory with very little evidence to support it.*

*Net Zero also comes with huge environmental costs. Rare earth mineral mining would have to increase by 2000%, leading to irreparable damage to associated habitats and ecosystems, not to mention the estimated 200 million metric tons of hard-to-recycle toxic solar panels and turbine blade waste, every 15 to 30 years.*

*And what will Net Zero in the UK achieve? The IPCC's own figures state that the UK's Net Zero target will make a difference of less than one thousandth of a degree centigrade to global temperatures. We can't measure that, so how will we know if spending 4 trillion pounds has worked?*

*Has a cost benefit analysis been done on the Council's Net Zero initiatives?*

*It is important to know how much will it cost Colchester residents to reach Net Zero. And will it definitely save the planet when countries like China will not interrupt their own economic growth by limiting $CO_2$?*

*And what are the risks to Colchester residents if global temps do rise by 1.5 degrees?*

*The Holocene Maximum was up to 7 degrees warmer than it is now, yet polar regions were fine. Where is the emergency?*

*Climate is judged on a minimum of 30 years, though usually hundreds and thousands of years of weather patterns. We need to stop believing that every extreme weather event is proof of climate change. It isn't.*

*Finally, I want to correct something read out in the recent Scrutiny Panel meeting - that reducing every little bit of $CO_2$ helps. It doesn't! $CO_2$ does the bulk of its warming between 50 to 150 ppm. We wouldn't want $CO_2$ levels to be that low, as all plant, and therefore animal life, would cease!*

*As someone who values maths, science and truth, I think it's important to evaluate the evidence with cold logic and icy rationality. However well intended this Council was in declaring a climate emergency, the race to Net Zero is going to bankrupt us all, and for what? Less than one-thousandth of a degree is the best case scenario. If the Council is convinced that climate change is an imminent threat, perhaps mitigation would be a more cost effective response?*

*The Government may refuse to acknowledge the flaws of Net Zero, but we must take a sensible approach at local level. We can't afford not to.*

*Thank you."*

They both got a very polite brush off from the Council Leader. For all the qualities I dislike in the man, he is always well-mannered, unlike many other councillors across the country we've seen in our time on Council Watch. He then passed it over to another councillor to deal with. She came out with a mind-melting amount of word salad.

Steven pushed them on why they had declared an emergency, but weren't behaving as if there is one. And he asked what the costs and benefits were of the measures they were taking.

Surprisingly, both Councillors Laws and Willets were there to drive home that there wasn't an emergency. Hilariously, the Council Leader responded by saying it was the spirit of the climate emergency he felt was important and he didn't think they needed to change the wording. Shame he wasn't equally into the spirit of making evidence-based decisions. He then thanked them for their thoughtfulness for taking the time and trouble to come in and put their points of view across. He said they would look at the naming in 12-18 month's time when the next review would come up.

I knew ahead of the meeting that they weren't going to discuss it. The meeting agenda said there was nothing to consider from the Scrutiny Panel. Their minds had been made up before they'd even stepped foot into the meeting. It's doubtful it will ever be discussed. By then Devolution is likely to have happened and the smaller councils amalgamated into one giant dysfunctional council, with a mayor more than likely calling all of the shots, like lots of Sadiq Kahns up and down the country. Something to look forward to.

I'd done all I could and seen it through to completion. We'd had a few mini-victories along the way but nothing to really write home about. Council Watch had a life of its own. My original hopes of reaching the councillors had proved naive and fruitless. Yes, we reached some, but not enough, and certainly not those who were calling the shots.

Never having been interested in politics, I hadn't experience of how tribal it is. Councillors don't think freely enough. They are guided by whatever colour team they are in. Few are willing to turn against that, especially when the other teams constantly oppose them. It's a very lonely place for independent thinkers, and rarely attracts them. They are ensconced in a system which swallows them whole and woe betide anyone who goes against it. Councillors aren't really the ones running things anyway. They are for the most part figureheads, with very little power and control. It's those behind the scenes, the ones we don't vote for, and can't get shot of, that appear to be pulling the strings.

The value of Council Watch has been showcasing just how bad things are. Jaw-droppingly bad. It's woken the public up. Many people have come up to me saying how they've shared our videos with family and friends, and it's been the catalyst to make them question the narrative more.

Council Watch videos have certainly got the conversation about EVs and the Green agenda talked about on social media in a way it wasn't before. For that I am grateful. It hasn't been a complete waste of time, even though it's often felt like it. It's also been good for us as individuals. Like me, so many people up and down the country have gone into their councils and found a voice they didn't know they had. Yes, it's frustrating not getting anywhere, but standing up for what is right, fortifies the soul in ways I'm unable to adequately express in words.

People in the parish of Fairlight started filming their council meetings to raise awareness of the goings-on, and before long the entire council quit and was replaced. This is what we need to happen everywhere. People taking charge and running things themselves. What's been particularly frustrating for us in Colchester is that we have a number of good councillors, but despite them being well-meaning and trying their best, they blindly follow the dictates of their political parties and the Government. If we can't reach good people who've given up their time to do something few people are willing to do, what hope is there in the bad councils?

As frustrating as Council Watch has been, I'm grateful for all the wonderful people doing it has enabled me to meet. That has by far been the best part. I'm glad I've finally been able to step back, and Sharon, one of our top-notch researchers and main council meeting viewer, is continuing with the videos. Carinna and Cheryl also intend to do occasional videos, and I have a couple of interviews I'd promised to do. We've got a lot of people all playing their part behind the scenes, alongside Sharon, like Sue, Tracy and others who enable Council Watch to be what it is, with watching council meetings and doing research, as do the donations we get from our viewers, which will go towards a video editor and leaflets. So, a huge thank you to everyone who has helped and contributed.

The pressure does need to be kept up, and more people need to be aware of just how bad these councils are. We need the best people running them, not the worst. When the time comes, I hope the legacy of Council Watch will be good people deciding to run as independent councillors. We had two brave souls lined up for the Essex County elections, but they've been cancelled for the foreseeable because of Devolution, which will most likely be the beginning of the end.

With Devolution, the plan is to merge local authorities into giant unitary councils, which will cost millions and then have them run by Sadiq Kahn type mayors, who are likely to be part of the Global Covenant of Mayors for Climate & Energy, and C40 Cities who are supported by ICLEI - a global network of cities and local governments working to advance sustainable development, including climate action. These mayors will have an enormous amount of power, and it's how Agenda 2030 and Net Zero targets will be forced upon us all. It's billed as giving local people more power and control, but of course it won't be in reality. Sandi Adams has researched it thoroughly, and views it as a Trojan Horse, as <u>Carinna told full Council on the 17th March 2025</u>, to which the Council Leader replied, that he couldn't see that. Carinna retorted with, "neither could the Trojans!"

The only way this gets better is if we all make it better. If people keep voting for who we've always had, we will get what we've always got. I think the people of Colchester deserve better than having councillors who blindly follow political parties, and certainly we could do without the councillor with a cocaine habit, or ones who've made a pass at a colleague and then become vile upon being rejected. For all their Diversity, Equality and Inclusion training, what goes on behind closed doors is shocking, according to council insiders we've spoken with. Awful things have been said, and good councillors have left as a result. Walls have ears, councillors, and so do Council Watch.

And that's just one of the political parties. In the others, we've been told about who likes to dress up in their wife's clothes, which one has a gaming addiction, and many more qualities and affiliations with secretive societies we'd prefer councillors not to have.

People in the video comments always suggest I should run the Council. Having spent two years watching hundreds of hours of council meetings, I can honestly say, I couldn't do it. The meetings are mind-numbing and can go on for over four hours. At least at home I can speed them up or pause and come back. I couldn't cope with all the rules and regulations. If I'm going to run something, I get in and do it. I'm not the personality type to be having endless hours of conflab getting nowhere. I'd want a role where I can sack people. Councillors can't do that.

So no, councils in their current form are not for me. I've given Council Watch everything I've got for two years solid, and at Christmas I announced that I was done. Well, more or less, extracting myself hasn't been easy! I ended up doing an interview with the wonderful women from Teignbridge with Father Ted writer, Graham Linehan. He wanted to showcase the jaw-dropping battles the ladies had been having with their council over protecting women and girls' right to have women-only spaces at the leisure centre.

Graham lost his career over campaigning for women's rights. Because of his gender-critical views, Father Ted the Musical was cancelled. He's a true hero, and it cost him his marriage, his income, everything. It was an honour to be included in that interview. I just make the videos and do a bit of commentary, it's Jenny, Jane, Cathy and Gilli who do all the incredible battling. Though I must admit, I was rather chuffed when ex-tennis player, Martina Navratilova commented and retweeted one of the videos I'd made of them. http://bit.ly/4niYece

I've still got a couple of interviews I'd promised folks I'd do, so I'm not quite as done as I would like, but I'm getting there. With what I was doing prior to Council Watch, it's been a five-year tour of duty. I need time out, my elderly parents are needing a lot more help these days so, I'm unashamedly taking it. I've done as much as I could, when I could. Other than being a testimony to a very weird time in history, this book is in part to pass the baton over. Others need to take over now.

We get a lot of 'you should' people in the comments on the Council Watch videos. They tell us we should file legal challenges against the Council and a whole host of other 'shoulds'. Council Watch has stretched us all to the limit with the time and effort it takes just to do what we've done. There aren't enough hours in the day, expertise or financial backing to consider legal action or any of the other 'shoulds' people have suggested.

If those that suggest the 'shoulds' want to organise and do them, please be our guests. There is such a predisposition to have others do things that we need to change that to everyone doing. It's not down to any one individual to save the day. This, in my opinion, is a group test. We will pass, or fail this, together.

There's also something that's been niggling away for a while. I can't help but wonder if we're all being played...

"Finding ways to be happy and joyful when the world does everything to make you miserable is the ultimate act of defiance!"
- Rachel Mathews

# 29

# What Does the Future Hold?

It's hard to make sense of why the world's most powerful people, who already have more money than they could ever spend in a lifetime, want more money, power and control. For those of us who aren't psychopaths, it's also hard to imagine the depths of awful those pulling the strings are willing to inflict on us. Too many of us make the mistake of judging people by our own standards, and because we would never set out to cause harm to people, we have trouble believing others would. I've heard many theories about what's happening...

My religious friends tell me this is the ultimate battle of good vs evil and that we are living through the End of Days, and this is the Book of Revelation, the Final Judgement. If this is true, I can't imagine a better way of destroying The Creation than corrupting humanity so we lose our minds, morals and connection to all that is good and destroy it ourselves, all the while convinced we are being noble and righteous in the process. Replacing this perfect, incredible natural world with an artificial one, which will enslave what's left of humanity, is nothing short of evil genius.

Others tell me they believe the good guys are in charge now and we're seeing all the crazy playing out, so it wakes everyone up. It's a 5D chess game. Ascension is imminent. I certainly hope so, but I'm not convinced. In 2020 my friend in Otivar, Spain, told me about the book The Art of War. She said people don't fight as hard when they believe someone is coming to save them. Telling people the good guys are in charge is the oldest trick in the book.

I'm a great believer in hoping for the best, but planning for the worst. If it isn't the good guys running the show, and everyone stands by thinking everything will get taken care of, then it will be a case of 'when good people do nothing, evil prevails'.

My main reason for concern is that I don't think it will do us any good as a society if someone else comes in and clears up this mess. It's like mummy and daddy coming home after a party has got out of control. The children only learn when they take responsibility for their mistakes and clean up their own mess.

Collectively, we let this mess happen by not having taken an interest sooner in how things are run.

None of us want to be involved, but we should. It's the one thing Council Watch has categorically proven, that the people running the show, really shouldn't be.

We will have learned nothing as a society if we don't step up and sort it out ourselves. It will be a never-ending cycle of good guys, bad guys, worse guys, even worse than the worse guys. I think we can do better than that, which I'll cover shortly.

So regardless of whether people believe we are going to be saved by the 'White Hats' or 'Beings of Light', that's no excuse not to get up off our backsides and make sure we participate in creating the world we want to live in, rather than continually leaving things to others.

My current view ties in with my Earth School theory. I view it as we've collectively not been paying attention in class, larking around and enjoying ourselves, allowing the bad kids to lead us astray.

My suspicion is that the real battle is internal, with ourselves. Every one of us needs to find courage to speak truth and act upon it. The more people who speak the truth, the more who will hear it.

We must not allow ourselves to be further enslaved by a corrupted system, which, when you really dive into it, is the embodiment of evil. Whatever happens on this physical plane, the personal growth which occurs when we take a stand and do what is right, not what is easy, is ours to keep. Every advancement we make as individuals enhances the collective. Evil will always destroy itself, it's the nature of the beast, but we don't have to let it take us with it.

It's easy to fall into the trap of thinking we are too small and cannot possibly do anything to affect change. I saw a video of a speech given by Professor Dolores Cahill in 2020 in London. She was amazing, such a powerhouse of a person. I remember thinking the world needed more people like her and how I could never be like that. She seemed to shine forth like a lighthouse. In comparison I felt like a meek little tea light. But then it occurred to me, a tea light can illuminate a room and millions of tea lights, the world. We can all come together as a tea light army, casting out the darkness, which is trying to devour us.

Those who are orchestrating the evil acts are clever, very clever. The people who they have doing their bidding may not be, but those pulling the strings most definitely are. Which does make me wonder if we're being played more than is obvious.

## Cynical

My gut tells me something is amiss. Cynical Me, also feels, fool me once, shame on you, and I'll be darned if I'm going to allow myself to be fooled again. Looking back over everything I've been involved in over the past five years, I can't help but wonder if we've been fighting the wrong battle. Is this a case of bait and switch?

The climate stuff, when you look into it, is so preposterous, it defies belief it ever got this far. Everything about Net Zero is so clearly flawed it hasn't a hope in hell's chance of succeeding. Renewables can't provide enough energy. Just watch any of the videos Paul Burgess and others have produced and you'll see it's the impossible dream.

There aren't enough accessible rare earth minerals to make the electric vehicles required, the whole thing is doomed to failure. It simply can't succeed. That fact will become apparent to even those who believe in it passionately. They've certainly needed Net Zero, but as soon as the Digital IDs and currencies are in place, I wonder if it will still be pushed, was it ever meant to succeed, or was it just a vehicle by which to get us to this point?

Look at all the time and energy many of us have put into calling this farce out. It's interesting how now it looks like the Green agenda may be switched over to the War agenda. Has it slowed down because there's been too much push back, or has part of its purpose been to keep us embroiled in nonsense? Everything happening in the world keeps everyone pitted against one another. People are so deeply engrossed fighting one another that they don't see those that are really responsible are pulling the strings.

Throwing everything at us at once to break us, perhaps? How much crazy can we take? Could you have imagined prior to 2020 that people in key positions in government would be unable to define what a woman is? Did you envisage people would be sacked, sued or arrested for stating basic biology? The world has gone mad. By design.

We're all so busy fighting one another and getting caught up in the drama, are we missing the bigger picture? Of course, divided we fall, that's undoubtedly part of it, but my hunch is that we're also being kept busy by the magicians. Our attention diverted.

The so-called saviours that many people champion because they are getting rid of some of the nonsense, if you look closely, are still rolling ahead with a lot of technology telling us how great it is. Are they the ruling equivalent of a parking fine? When you open the dreaded letter informing you of your parking infraction, it says the fine is £70, but if you pay within fourteen days its only £35. It's such a relief it's only £35 that most people pay it without even acknowledging they shouldn't be fined at all! Is that what is happening here? We're all so relieved when someone deals with some of the 'wokery' that whatever is rolled out next will be acceptable in comparison?

## The Game We Shouldn't Play

I can't help but feel we're all caught in a game of 'pull me, push me'. The whole world pulled to the 'far-left'. Is the obvious backlash pushing us to the 'far-right' incoming? I'm watching closely the seemingly few good people rousing the public with calls of restoring our national identity and removing all the illegal immigrants, and I don't disagree with their viewpoint.

When I outstayed my welcome in Spain, I knew I'd broken their rules and I was willing to accept the consequences of deportation, if caught. And I was at least paying my own way and putting money into the Spanish economy. So, I have no issue with evicting those who are here illegally and didn't seek sanctuary through official channels. What we need to watch closely, however, is what proposals are brought in and what changes to the law are made to tackle the mass illegal immigration, when we get a change of government.

We've seen this particular game played out before. Hitler was incredibly popular, until of course, he wasn't... He came in during economic turmoil when people were desperate, and promised them that the only way to avoid Communism was his totalitarian regime, though he sold it with a bit more aplomb than I just have! The Nazi Party promised to protect the farmers, small businesses and ease the economic distress of the people. Who wouldn't buy into that, especially in times of desperation and extreme hardship?

Whilst we may not have a UK Hitler as yet, the parallels are there, the powder keg fuse has been lit. Many have assumed Starmer and Co. are going to be the worst villains, but I wonder? I have a dreadful feeling that the worst will be whoever is set up to be our saviour, if history is indeed set to repeat itself. Only this time it will be much more sophisticated and fatal for our freedom.

It was interesting that the Council Watch channel was going great guns gaining viewers and subscribers, despite what we said about the climate. We'd get the UN warnings under the YouTube videos, but never a ban or strike. As soon as we covered 5G, the channel became shadowbanned. Viewing figures fell off the cliff overnight. People were being unsubscribed, likes not allowed, comments from viewers were reported to us to have been deleted by YouTube.

Then there was all the insanity with the Council refusing to acknowledge something so obvious a child could see it, regarding using the names of dissolved companies on the safety declarations. They fought us tooth and nail on it. Why? If anything, we were doing them a favour, they could have been liable for not getting the documentation right, something councils are usually meticulous about.

I contacted all the opposition parties and gave them enough ammunition to call for a vote of no-confidence on a council leader that we're told, few like. Whilst initially two of the three replied saying they'd discuss it with their group and get back to me, they never did. I chased them up by email and publicly on social media. Complete silence. Who silenced them? They never normally miss an opportunity for political point scoring. Curious.

The technology advancements are coming at an alarming pace. The Internet of Things is just the beginning. Research the Internet of Bodies. Yes, it is as macabre as it sounds. The trans-humanism which is being brought in is the stuff nightmares are made of. The systems which have already been developed will enslave us all and at a speed so fast people will not know what's hit them. The pieces are all being lined up and rolled out. If we're all so busy arguing over nonsense, it will be so much easier to collapse everything and offer the ready-made digital solutions. I think our collective eyes are off the ball.

Digital ID's are now being inserted into everyday activities, with suggestions from the Government that all under 25's should have a Digital ID in order to drink in a pub. Get them young, get them used to it.

The Government are suggesting a Digital ID will take the stress out of house purchasing, making it cheaper and easier. I suspect there will be many more reasons for people to get a Digital ID. Food shortages will be an obvious one, a sensible way to ration when things become difficult. And on the list will go. It will be sold as highly advantageous, lots of carrots for those who comply. Those who refuse, will be given the stick. Will it become impossible to get online or have a bank account without a Digital ID? They will always give you a choice, they have to, we live in a consent-based system. But you can bet modern life will be made virtually impossible without one. They've already built the Digital ID infrastructure with GovUK One Login which controls everything from DVLA to benefits. Clare Wills Harrison has written much about it on her Substack, Conscientious Currency.

My suspicion is that they will push things so far into chaos that the population will beg the Government for Digital IDs. Especially if there is a war and all our soldiers are overseas. They would be sold as the perfect way to control the chaos and to know who should be in the country legitimately or not. Though it would not surprise me if they offer an amnesty to all those here illegally. The more our cultural identity and values become watered down, the easier the Stakeholder takeover will be.

I fear our supposed saviours will be the ones to snare us in the digital prison. For our own safety, of course. The level of control and restrictions this digital dystopia will bring, will make Hitler look like an amateur. If we do not learn from history, then we are, most definitely, destined to repeat it, with bells on. And what could be more delicious for the evil ones, than having us believe we're being saved whilst they are double-crossing and destroying us, and all the while with us cheering them on. As someone wrote in the comments of a Council Watch video recently, "The ignorant will always participate in their own demise".

Once you realise how bad things are and the direction of travel, it's only natural to want to do something about it. I still believe it is important we stand up and speak out, but having tried to do something about this mess, I wonder if that is part of the snare.

## The Opposite Tack

Having come out the other side of trying to change things, what feels better to me, instead of reacting all the time to whatever 'they', whoever 'they' may be, are doing, would be to realise that to serve ourselves better we need to focus on what we want to create both individually and collectively. Otherwise, we are forever in a reactionary position. That isn't where the power is. Thoughts are powerful. If we keep focusing on all the bad stuff that's potentially coming our way, we become co-creators and we will help make it manifest. You get what you focus on, after all!

I think the power lies in our humanity, spirituality, creativity and community. Something which is being stripped away from us, especially with AI coming more and more to the forefront. We're surely at the tipping point now. Societal values are being systematically broken down, we're losing ourselves. To make matters worse, we spend so much time and energy fighting amongst ourselves.

I see so many people who are supposedly on the same side falling out, often over one thing they cannot see eye-to-eye on. I rarely agree one hundred percent of the time with those I've worked with on projects. Many hold views I disagree with, but as long as we have enough common ground, and are both heading in the same overall direction, then as far as I'm concerned, we can work together. I focus on the things we agree on, and I don't make an issue of those we don't.

If every single one of us did that, it would be like a giant chain of humanity. In one hand, we have an opinion that agrees with the person who's hand we are holding. In our other hand, we may have an opinion that person doesn't share, but someone else does and they take our hand and so the chain grows. Everyone linked together by some overlapping beliefs which unite them. This is how we unite people and groups with different points of view. We each act as a bridge between differing viewpoints when we can.

Humanity coming together doesn't mean we all have to live together. If anything, the past few years has shown us it's better when birds of a feather flock together. I'm not talking about superficial things like gender, skin colour, sexuality etc, I'm talking about a meeting of minds, and core values.

For instance, there are some people who love rules and regulations, others hate them. The one-size-fits-all, doesn't fit, not by a long shot. I wonder if societies of the future will be made up of groups of like-minded people. There could be technologically advanced cities for those who wish to live that way and others with minimal technology. There might be communities who want to live with no tech and as in touch with nature as possible. People would then move to the areas with the lifestyle and values which attract them. Forcing any set of ideals onto others doesn't bring unity. Giving people options of how their towns and cities run and function could be the way forward.

All those billionaires who have sunk their money into developing Digital IDs, expiring and fully-controlled digital currencies, facial recognition, autonomous vehicles, AI running everything, lab-grown meat, facilities to create drinking water from recycled sewage, it would be a shame to have all that time, effort and money go to waste, so I think we should create a special place where they can all live together with anyone who wants to join them and enjoy all those lovely things they've had created. Have a glass of freshly squeezed sewage water whenever they fancy to go with a 3D printed burger. Enjoy the fruits of their labour directly.

This is why I think it's important for us to take control ourselves, so we can create the world we want to live in rather than have it dictated to us. The corporate takeover isn't serving us. We do need to put people and the planet before profit and politics, just not in the way the predator class have lined up for us, their way is one of enslavement and imprisonment.

If you think about it, we have a world abundant in resources. Everything you could ever need is right here, provided by this amazing planet. Then there's us. A world teeming with incredibly creative people. Surely we can create a better system than we have now? The few have all the wealth and resources. Whenever people are sold a lie of equal distribution, it becomes Communism. There must be a way of creating something good which is neither of those.

If we take away the food source from those who prey on us, we could create an amazing world. Poverty and war exist because they create it. Debt exists because they create it. The entire system is enslavement. It's time it changed. If we got rid of the big corporations, easy enough if you stop spending money with them and ditched political parties and just started running things ourselves with the best outcomes for people, we'd have control.

There's enough food and resources on this planet for us all. The poorest countries are kept poor by those who have too much. Our wealth relies on exploiting their cheap labour and raw materials. Our debt-based economy keeps us all enslaved. Our entire world is inverted from health to wealth, and everything in between. And we all go along with it.

It's about time we stopped looking outside of ourselves. Stopped waiting for someone to come and save us. Someone to lead us and instead, self-organised. I've seen it happen naturally in the Colchester Stand in the Park group. They don't have a leader, it's more of a collective. People take it in turn to voice suggestions or organise something, and then whoever likes the idea helps out. It's really simple and effective.

It does require people to drop their egos and function from a place of power and get along with one another. Some people organise and speak up more than others, as you'd expect, but everyone knows they can, and they do, when they feel the desire to. There's no pressure and it's not reliant on any one person. Strong people with no leader creates strength because anyone can step up when needed. When people are aligned with the same core values, it's very powerful, that's what leads them.

I know capable people who are waiting and wanting a leader, someone to follow, not realising their own potential and capability. Stop looking for answers outside of yourself and trust in your own abilities. The only person who can save you is the one who looks back at you in the mirror. Come together with other likeminded people and form small grassroots communities which can work alongside other groups when the need arises. Lots of little decentralised groups working together will be very hard to stop.

## Visionscaping the Future

I've asked a lot of people the question about what world they would like to create if they could create anything. Most people can't answer. We simply can't imagine anything vastly different to what we have now.

That's a problem.

I'll have a stab at it for the purposes of idea exploration, and with a bit of luck you'll come up with better ideas.

# 30

# My Ideal World

I'd like to live in a world with as few rules and regulations as possible, where people truly are free. That would take an advanced society to achieve. People would need to get along and take full responsibility for their own lives and actions. In this world, there wouldn't be poverty or unnecessary suffering, everyone would have what they need. People would be custodians of the natural world, rather than exploiters of it. Our value system wouldn't be largely based around money and material possessions but contribution, community and creation.

Nothing particularly earth-shattering there. I'm more of a creative problem solver than visionary. I hope others will come up with something much more imaginative, but for now we'll work with this example to outline the design and construction process. Though with the current state of society, even the above sounds improbable! But anyway, let's take a crack at it.

Now that we have a desired outcome, which can be honed and polished as we progress, what would we need to do to get there? The first step is what I'm doing now, sharing it with others, to refine and improve the vision. Ideas need to be shared to reach a critical mass of people wanting the same.

Our current political system is failing us. The people are not the masters it serves, and we need to be. It has been hijacked and perverted to serve the world's richest and faux-powerful. Real power doesn't force, manipulate or coerce. Which unfortunately means we'll have to do what few want to do, and start running everything ourselves.

I'm not sure the UK will last many more years with this current government. They are more than ready for the masses to rise up with physical violence, sometimes it looks like they are purposefully trying to goad us into it. Clive de Carle floated the idea at his event that rather than protesting, if everyone in the country planted food instead, it would be more empowering than protesting.

Taking Clive's idea further, if everyone also stocked up with food and stayed at home, it would shut the entire country down. We could collectively demand the resignation of the current lot and a new General Election be held. Which we could fill with independent MPs. It's not like they could come and arrest us for staying at home! You can see why they love us fighting amongst ourselves, anything but unity.

In my UK Column talk, I told the story of a hypothetical nation where the people had integrity and didn't tolerate tyranny and they collectively refused to serve any politician who backed policies which harmed them. After all, why would people serve politicians who don't serve them? Imagine if these political wrongdoers couldn't get a parcel delivered, no trades person would come to their homes, they couldn't get served in shops or restaurants and any businesses that did cave and serve them would be boycotted by the public and would lose all their customers.

So yes, we must run things ourselves. Once in positions of power, that's where the fun and games really start. The system is set up to protect itself and it won't relinquish power easily. The politicians aren't really running the show, they are merely figureheads, doing as instructed. It's the people behind closed doors that run everything. We'd probably need to sack the majority and start again.

The system was never meant to be political with a left-right divide, it was just meant to have local representatives thrashing out the concerns of those they represented in Parliament. Our system has been taken over by nonsense. If MPs are serving the needs of those they represent, whether they lean to the so-called left or right is irrelevant. It's the will of those they serve which should take precedence, not the will of a political party.

To create a new society, we need the best people running things, not the worst, which is what we have now. We all need to look around us and nominate those individuals we think would be good, honest and fair. Then we need to persuade those people to step up and serve their communities. If it was done this way around, we hopefully wouldn't end up with the small-minded, clueless, weak, power-crazed individuals which governments at all levels seem to attract.

That said, I do want to acknowledge the excellent councillors there are who try their best. We see you, and appreciate all that you try to do. It's amazing anyone would put themselves through being a councillor with everything they have to contend with. Sadly, the good councillors are rarely the ones running the show, and they are very much in the minority. This is something we must fix, the good ones need backup. There's a council in Devon which has eight independent councillors who are doing their utmost to serve their constituents, and holding the council to account, but they are being blocked and silenced at every turn.

We need to get more good people in place taking over all the local councils first, then replace the Government at the first opportunity. The councils are critical because they are the boots on the ground carrying out the orders from Government. We need people in place who won't follow destructive orders, and who will do what is right.

Then it is vital we get to the children. Completely change our education system to one which really educates, rather than programmes the next generation into the slavery system. Children should be taught how to look at both sides on an argument and encouraged to think critically. A tall order, when so few adults can do it. But it can be, and must be, taught. They should also be taught practical real-world skills. The most I had at school was home economics. I'd have loved to have learned how to make things, but back then, only boys got to do woodwork.

Children must learn about the English Constitution, so they know and understand their rights. Understanding money, interest payments, another important skill. How to run a business, would be another useful one for young adults. How to grow food, and I'm sure you can think of a million other things you wish you'd been taught in school, but weren't.

School could be such a fun place to be and learn skills. Emotional intelligence should also be taught. Just imagine what the world would be like if it was full of people who took responsibility for their own state of mind. Teaching something as simple as EFT, would transform children's lives and the world in a single generation. It would give them the ability to process trauma in the moment, or quickly afterwards, so it doesn't take root. Imagine living in a world full of emotionally healthy adults. So much of what is wrong in the world today comes from emotionally damaged adults lashing out. Emotionally balanced, happy people don't need to control or manipulate others. Nor do they feel it necessary to be cruel, destructive or greedy.

**Work Life Balance**

Something which made me sit up and think when I first read Tim Ferriss' 'Four Hour Work Week' book, was when he asked, who decided that everyone in the world should work from nine to five or longer?

Why are we spending so much of our lives working? The best of us is going, usually, into someone else's business. Even if you're an entrepreneur, with your own business, chances are you're working far too many hours in it.

It was reading that book that changed my life, and how I ended up becoming a Digital Nomad for ten years. As I discussed in my first book, Tim showed me it was not only stupid to spend my life working, but also unnecessary. Work smarter, not harder. When you think of all the people around the world needlessly spending the majority of their lives working, some in awful conditions in sweat shops making a load of crap no one really wants or needs, how did we ever get sucked into this insanity?

I look at the Amish community, where they haven't been sucked into a modern world, and whilst they undoubtedly work hard, and live a strict way of life, there's a lot to be learned from them. When someone in their community needs a barn built, the whole community turns up to help and it's done in a day.

What if we only built things we really needed and we all helped one another? I've witnessed it happen with our Colchester group. In fact, I think it was Carinna who started it. When I first met her, she was offering everyone swapsies. She'd do physio if they would help her with things. Before long, we'd all lost score of who owed who what and then people in our group would just turn up and do stuff for one another, knowing that when we needed help, we'd have an army of people willing to help us.

It set up such goodwill and community spirit and I know if I ever need help with anything, people will be there. To begin with, I was a bit reticent because I assumed I'd end up designing gardens for everyone, something which is time-consuming. But what ended up happening was that people would ask me for things I hadn't considered of value, like, researching what should go in a natural first-aid kit (which took weeks), they wanted me to tell them what I'd got and where from.

Carinna knew I'd looked into healthy cookware, so I spent a morning going through her kitchen cupboards tut-tutting every time I saw something made of aluminium, or covered in Teflon. Then Cheryl and I took her shopping to get replacements. And that's how our little community in Colchester is, everyone just does stuff for everyone else without expecting anything in return. We are there for each other. It's made us a tight group. We know who we can rely on when the 'shit hits the fan'. And you can't tax helpfulness, it's not bartering, it's community.

When Cheryl moved her salon, there we all were loading our cars and driving all her natural hair and skin products to their new location. I found it quite amusing that I was now in the removals business. Like so much of the last few years, another thing I never pictured myself doing. We've all realised that we have life skills beyond what we formally do for a living. We've all got to know each other a lot better as a result of helping one another. Imagine if the whole world functioned like this.

The image of the 'Parable of the Long Spoons', comes to mind. This parable depicts heaven and hell with a banquet of delicious food piled sky high in both. In hell, they are starving because the cutlery is too long and people can't feed themselves with it no matter how hard they try. In Heaven, everyone is well fed because they use the long cutlery to feed each other. As a child, I was always puzzled why no one thought to just pick the food up with their hands, therefore bypassing the need for the over long cutlery altogether! Now, I understand the image, it's not about just feeding ourselves that's important.

So why is it most of us work for corporations or governments, when we're all capable of just sorting things out between us? Imagine a small town or village where local people kept the place tidy and maintained. They repair the roads and plant flowers and sort out the village hall etc. They'd take pride in their village, everything would get done on time, no waiting for the council. The community would all chip in, and those who sort things out could be paid for their time and effort. It would build a strong community.

People's contributions would go on things the community needed rather than councillor vanity projects, and nonsense the Government has been persuaded to push forward. The money wouldn't be siphoned off to go to other councils or Government, it would stay in the community. This type of system would require proper grown-upping, something few want to do, but we are all more than capable, when push comes to shove.

There would be some form of structure needed for the community to come together, especially for the larger places, and a team would be needed to oversee things, but for the simple day-to-day stuff, we could do it ourselves either physically or hire someone if everyone chipped in for it.

How much do we really need? A roof over our heads, food, clothes, ability to travel. If we didn't have big bills and debts, and were only making things of real value the world needs, how much time working would we really need? So much of what is done and created is nonsense. Thousands of people involved in making 'brands' and junk that no one really needs. Then all the effort persuading people they want and need the pile of junk these companies have made, meaning everyone is chained to the work treadmill to pay for it. Whole industries exist to flog crap to the masses.

## Traditional Crafts

I'm really drawn to making things. I'd love to start with furniture. Perhaps a coffee table and work my way up to the dining room table and chairs. Something unique and stylish. I've no skills to do this, but I'd learn. It would be so nice to get rid of the horrible Ikea stuff I purchased because it was cheap when I got my first house. How satisfying it must be to make something beautiful that could last several generations. It would take me weeks, perhaps months, but it would be a much nicer use of my time away from a computer, doing something real, rather than making videos about dysfunctional councils and the people running them.

I envisage a world where we do a minimal amount of work to cover our essentials, and the rest of our time is spent doing things we enjoy, as well as contributing to our community. I'd be more than happy to have school kids come and join me on the allotment and I'd teach them how to grow vegetables. Or spend an afternoon a week teaching young people how to make their own furniture, once I'd learned myself, of course! Skilled people passing on their knowledge to future generations.

If we all put our time and energy into our own lives and our community instead of continually on the treadmill corporations and governments have created for us, I think we'd all be a lot happier. We're nearly all caught in the debt trap. But if we went back to something like the Bradbury Pound, a fiscal mechanism which was used at the start of the First World War to stop the banks from collapsing, we could do away with that as well. True Sovereign money, backed by the country's assets and GDP, instead of the valueless Ponzi scheme we're currently using. I interviewed a lovely man called Justin Walker on this subject, I've added the video to the Resources page on my website.

There are billions more of us than those few who control the world's money supply and the corporations and governments that control us. So, my interest is not trying to iron out our current problems back to a more tolerable level of enslavement, I want us to re-design the system so it can't be so easily corrupted. Taking the best of how the system should work, with the rule of law alongside, creating well-educated, emotionally intelligent humans to go with it. The more higher minded and emotionally intelligent the humans, the fewer rules and regulations required.

What system could we create that isn't based on cronyism, Communism or corporate greed? But instead, contribution, conservation and care for one another. Could it be a matter of creating a society with a higher-minded moral code, as well a high price to pay for corruption and exploitation? Is corruption really as inevitable as it seems?

How many people would be willing to get involved in human-trafficking if the punishment was ALL their assets seized and given to the victims, with life imprisonment? No getting out early. Life imprisonment for any involvement, from the driver to the customers. I am not for the death penalty. Life is sacred and no government should ever have the authority to kill the population, it will be mis-used, of that you can be sure. Real, long-lasting punishment for heinous crimes, I do support.

I don't remember which county it was now, but I know there was one, many moons ago who trialled paying their government officials so well it helped deter them from corruption because they had too much to lose. There certainly needs to be a means of true accountability. We need to create a system that works, even if someone who isn't ideal gets into a position of authority.

An open ledger of accounts so we can see how those who are supposed to be serving us are spending our money. This is something where AI could be very useful - to flag up when there is unnecessary spending, or when firms have been chosen to work because of a connection to the decision maker, rather than on merit. Too many decisions are made behind closed doors, there needs to be more public involvement and accountability.

Though my preference would be to create a society with such high values that people don't rip each other off to line their own pockets. But we're a way off that likelihood at the moment. It will take several generations to undo the damage that's been done through the mainstream, degrading education, society and values at every opportunity. We need an ideal to aim for, something so worthwhile people will be willing to put the work into achieving. We need good people in place to oversee future generations get a good start in life, then they can take over and do even better.

We need to collectively create a better world. We need ideas and to start to create them now. There are millions of people beginning to realise just how bad things are. Not enough realise it's by design, it's not just ineffective people in charge, they are very effective, and their strings are being pulled by those who do not have our best interests at heart. There needs to be somewhere for these people to go, a new vision they can grasp hold of. It's like someone leaving an abusive relationship, they have to have somewhere to go to find shelter, and I feel it's the job of those of us, who've been round the block a few times, to provide it. If we've already started to create a better system, it won't take much persuading to get people to join it.

I also think that if we all focus our efforts on creating that better world, rather than constantly battling with those who seek to take everything, we'll turn things around much quicker. There's so many more of us than them. All it will take, I say tongue in cheek, is a unified population. To do that, we need a unified vision. Something so compelling and inspiring that we will do whatever it takes to collectively, and peacefully, achieve it.

I suspect each and every one of us hold a piece or two of that future jigsaw puzzle. We need to start putting those pieces on the table, moving them around, forming enough of the picture so that others come along and add their pieces, and together we create a new world that actually does what it says on the tin. A society built on respect, honesty and integrity, and care for our fellow humans.

If we can extricate ourselves from this tangled web of deception, the days of top-down rulers are over. False promises have well and truly reached their expiration date, so too has the left-right circus, and corporate greed and exploitation. Enough. We just need good people, making good decisions, that serve the needs of their communities. We should celebrate our differences, not try to push everyone into the same round hole of conformity to things they don't wish to conform to. One size does not fit all.

We need to set the wheels in motion creating the world we want to live in. If we don't, a world we don't want will be forced upon us. It really is that simple. Make a positive change, or endure a dreadful one.

The end of the old corrupt world doesn't mean there won't be opportunities, far from it, there may be more. Let's use 'healthcare' as an example. There's an inverted system if ever there was one. If you took your car to the garage because you could hear a concerning clunking noise coming from the engine, would you accept the mechanic telling you to turn your radio up so you couldn't hear the noise any longer? No, of course you wouldn't. Why then do millions of people readily accept medications that mask their symptoms rather than fix the root cause?

The masking of symptoms then has a whole host of side-effects where, of course, more 'medications' are required to mask those symptoms. How about if the focus was on wellness instead of sickness? Imagine if we had wellness centres everywhere that people could pop in, for free on the National Health Service whenever they were feeling run down. There could be all sorts of natural treatments and detox protocols. People could book themselves in for a week, or perhaps a day a month, and talk with physicians on how they could be as healthy as possible.

There would be plenty of money in keeping people well. Big Pharma (the P is silent) would have to get a lot smaller as fewer drugs would be required, but there could still be a lot of other things to profit from. Those that are wedded to pharmaceutical drug taking can still do so if they wish, but wouldn't it be nice to have a choice? Painkillers, anesthetics, antibiotics etc do have their place and can be life-saving. There are a lot of plusses to modern medicine, especially surgical advancements, but it would be nice to combine the best of both worlds and have the focus on wellness ahead of pharmaceutical drug taking and surgery.

Intravenous vitamin C can work miracles in some illnesses. As can sodium bicarbonate. In his book Sodium Bicarbonate Nature's Unique First Aid Remedy, Dr Mark Sircus discusses how it can be used as a natural form of chemotherapy. It's already used before, during and after chemotherapy because it helps to protect the kidneys from the chemo poisons, and without it, people would die. Many cancers require an acidic environment to thrive. Sodium bicarbonate is an alkalising agent which, when combined with other anti-cancer protocols, has shown to be very effective, without the horrible side-effects of regular chemo.

Sodium bicarbonate is already used in emergency room intensive care medicine, but it has many less-widely known applications. It is a vasodilator, increases blood fluidity, it helps get more oxygen into the cells, is anti-inflammatory and helps with the detoxification and neutralisation of toxic substances. It has many applications which Dr Sircus discusses in his book. Pharmaceuticals have their place, but not above some of the simple, cheap, effective, natural protocols like this, which could be used as preventative medicine in wellness centres.

Entrepreneurs Mark Attwood and Gary Kealy have already set up something similar with a wellness clinic in Boyle, Ireland. They do it on a donation basis, offering hyperbaric oxygen chambers, Brown's Gas and all sorts of other treatments. Wellness centres would be a huge industry, creating lots of jobs and product requirements. And likewise, the food industry could also be transformed.

## Nutrition

Imagine if food was valued for its nutrient density instead of how large it was. That one difference would have huge impact on health, and how farming is done. Regenerative agriculture methods and good soil management would be required, artificial fertilisers wouldn't be so prevalent.

Replacing table salt with mineral salt would be another easy health enhancing option. The amount of food which uses harmful sodium chloride because it's cheap, instead of using nutrient dense, healthful, mineral salt.

People could still buy junk food if they wanted, but there would be a 'Crap Tax' on it. The poorer quality the food, the more it costs, especially if it's high sugar, artificial sweeteners and seed oils. The tax would then go to subsidise the nutrient dense healthy food.

'Crap Tax' could extend to products. Anything poor quality that doesn't last long could be highly taxed because it's going to end up in a landfill much sooner than quality, long lasting products, not to mention use up precious earth resources. Handmade goods from the UK should be free from VAT. Obviously, in an ideal world there wouldn't be any tax at all, so these are just for the interim.

These are just a few ideas off the top of my head. If we all put our minds on the world we want to live in and then set about creating it, we would create an amazing world together. We have everything we need. We are ALL part of the solution. Those who choose to do nothing are part of the problem. We could create heaven-on-earth, but it's been hijacked by the wrong-uns. Time we sorted that out. In order to unite it is essential we do our 'Shadow Work' so that we come from a place of calm centeredness, rather than the angry, wounded, child. Then we can achieve great things together.

## The Vital First Step We Can Do Now

While taking over the governments of the world is a long and drawn-out process that would undoubtedly be met with incredible obstacles and resistance from the powers that shouldn't be, there is something simple we can and must do right now:

## Save The Children

Children are being exposed to ideologies and information that are incredibly harmful. I know of a seven-year-old boy who was traumatised and suffered years of nightmares after his teacher told him he could be a girl. Two friends of mine had their teenage children convinced at school that they were a different gender; it took both families two years and a lot of stress to help their children overcome these beliefs.

The parents I know who have chosen to homeschool have found the process incredibly challenging. Their incomes and careers have suffered tremendously, not to mention the effects of isolation on their children. Few people are able to pull their children out of school and homeschool, even if they desperately want to. That's where we come in…

## Helping The Homeschoolers

You've probably heard the phrase, "It takes a village to raise a child." Yes it does, and we are that village. Each of us has skills and knowledge that could benefit younger generations. Some of us have land or facilities where groups of homeschoolers could gather once or more a week to teach their children together, sharing the workload and reducing the stress of going it alone.

There is also an army of good, 'old school' retired teachers and skilled individuals with vast knowledge who can help educate the next generation.

In the mornings, children could be taught the curriculum that parents are legally required to cover. Afternoons could then be dedicated to 'Life Lessons' with everything from arts, crafts, music, carpentry, building, growing food, herbalism, The English

Constitution, EFT, critical thinking, and whatever else the children are interested in.

Volunteer "travelling teachers" from all walks of life could visit various groups in their local area. Obviously, these people would need to be thoroughly vetted, and parents could take turns being present to ensure what is being taught is appropriate.

If we can work together to help as many children as possible escape the school indoctrination camps and instead equip them with knowledge, life skills, and emotional intelligence, we will be building an army of intelligent, sovereign beings for the future, people who can truly turn things around. We've collectively dropped the ball and allowed the world to become so corrupted; the very least we can do now is play our part in equipping future generations to do better. And we need to act now. Once our generation is gone, there won't be the people with the skills and good moral compass to turn things around.

I've created a page on my website ([www.rachelmathews.uk/help](www.rachelmathews.uk/help)) with a list of homeschooling hubs. Hopefully one day we'll have a database to connect people and resources to support homeschoolers everywhere. Please spread this idea far and wide. The children need us to be that village, right now.

The End
(and the beginning of the new)

Dear Reader,

I know many of the topics I've raised in this book are challenging. If you've not researched them thoroughly, it may be tempting to dismiss what you've read, but I urge you not to. The time for sticking our collective heads in the sand is well and truly over, if not for ourselves, then for future generations.

The burden of knowledge can be overwhelming at times, but I also urge you not to lose hope or faith, no matter how bad things look. There may be little we can do individually, but collectively, we are unstoppable. Never forget that. The catch of course, is that it has to start with us individually…

Speak up and spread awareness. You'll become empowered in the process. Becoming empowered in this world which has gone mad, will not only help you, but everyone around you, too.

Wishing you all the very best for the future and what we can create together.

With Love
Rachel (and the dog, of course!)

## More Misadventures!

What have been your key takeaways from reading this book? And what is your ideal vision for the future? Let me know in the comments on Amazon or on my website: https://www.rachelmathews.uk/books

## About The Author

Rachel has been an international garden designer for over 30 years. These days, when not writing books, her main passion is teaching a worldwide audience online. Her garden design courses and free web classes are available at www.successfulgardendesigner.com.

Photograph: www.inbalphotographer.com